THE TOWN ON
BEAVER CREEK

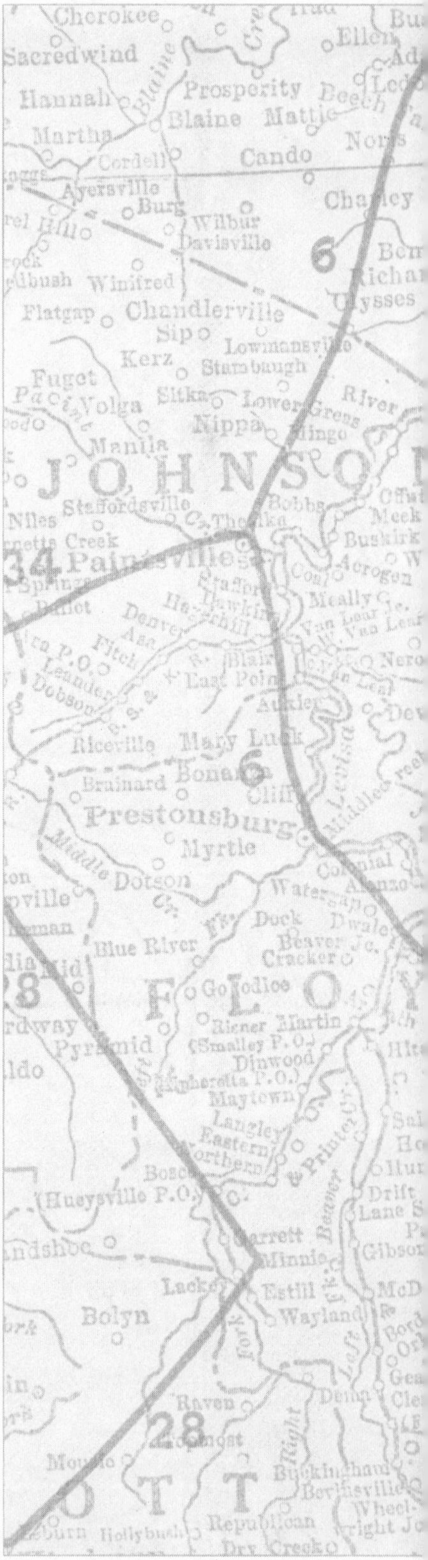

RANDOM HOUSE | NEW YORK

THE TOWN ON BEAVER CREEK

THE STORY OF A LOST KENTUCKY COMMUNITY

MICHELLE SLATALLA

Published in the United States by Random House,
an imprint of The Random House Publishing Group,
a division of Random House, Inc., New York.

RANDOM HOUSE and colophon are registered
trademarks of Random House, Inc.

Unless otherwise credited, the photographs
in this book are from the author's collection.

LIBRARY OF CONGRESS CATALOGING-IN-PUBLICATION DATA

Slatalla, Michelle.
The town on Beaver Creek: the story of a lost Kentucky community /
Michelle Slatalla.
p. cm.
ISBN 0-375-50905-4
1. Martin (Floyd County, Ky.)—History—20th century.
2. Slatalla, Michelle—Family.   3. Martin (Floyd County, Ky.)—
Biography.   4. Martin (Floyd County, Ky.)—Social life and customs—
20th century.   5. City and town life—Kentucky—Martin
(Floyd County)—History—20th century.   I. Title.
F459.M37S55 2006
976.9'22—dc22   2005051922

Printed in the United States of America on acid-free paper
www.atrandom.com
2 4 6 8 9 7 5 3 1
FIRST EDITION
Book design by Barbara M. Bachman

For Mary's girls,
Margaret, Judy, and Jo

After my mother moved north and married, she missed her hometown in eastern Kentucky so much that my father decided to reconstruct it in our basement. In the 1960s, he built a scale model of the town of Martin, surrounded by mountains fashioned from chicken wire and plaster. The results looked like a movie set created for a heartwarming Frank Capra film. In a valley sat a little town, its Main Street dotted with replicas of the places my mother had loved most: the Hob Nob Café, Grigsby's Five-and-Dime, and Mr. Keathley's motion picture theater. All the houses had vegetable gardens and yards with laundry lines and snowball bushes. At the depot, tiny figurines of old men sat on a bench in the sun, listening for a distant train whistle to signal noon. My father built a trapdoor in the middle, and my brother and I liked to climb up to sit in the creek bed. We turned off the ceiling lights and crouched like giants, imagining a world of tiny winking streetlights.

That town is long gone. Martin's brief and improbable heyday, which it enjoyed when the eastern Kentucky coalfields and the railroad employed thousands of men, ended decades ago. Now a four-lane highway cuts through the Cumberlands, and twenty-two-wheel trucks hauling coal roar past the outskirts of a virtual ghost town. My mother's Martin has been supplanted by a sadder version, with a boarded-up movie theater and a dime store where the shelves are nearly empty of inventory. Both the high school gym and the railroad depot burned years ago.

The town never should have existed in the first place. Built on the banks of a cantankerous creek, Martin flooded often, forcing families like mine to stack their furniture to the ceiling before they fled for higher ground. The water swept away livestock, outhouses, and pets. Buildings became waterlogged. Linoleum buckled. Wood rotted. Eventually, most people left. Those who stayed got old and wistful for better days.

A town that was always doomed in theory now also is doomed in fact. An ambitious ten-year federal flood-relief project is under way to demolish the decrepit remains of Martin and to move residents to a brand-new version of the town on higher ground. The first buildings to go were two dilapidated houses that Dick Osborn, one of the town's first residents, built nearly a hundred years ago. Under the $100 million project, which calls for razing about two hundred houses and stores and churches, Martin's residents will move to a modern planned community that will boast luxuries that earlier generations never imagined: a town square with a fountain, a bike path, zoning guidelines. For the Army Corps of Engineers, the exercise of tearing down and rebuilding an entire town is a creative approach to solving a stubborn problem in a place where traditional floodproofing remedies like levees and floodwalls will not work. Some think it's a colossal waste to spend so much money on a town where the entire assessed tax value of properties is a puny $10 million. Others say that razing the town is the only way to save it. "It's our only chance for a future," Mayor Thomasine Robinson said when I visited her soon after the flood of 2003. That year, water was five feet deep in the middle of Main Street, forcing the mayor to commandeer a big old army truck so the fire department could evacuate residents. Those problems will disappear in the new town.

But so will the past. Under the plan, not one memento of my family's life in Martin will survive, not a pew from the Church of Christ, where my mother sat in the back row and swung her legs in time to hymns; not a brick from the high school my uncle Red helped build in 1938; not a scratchy mohair seat from the Martin Theatre, where my grandmother sat through Saturday matinees. Instead, the last residents of Martin will move to an unfamiliar landscape that offers "a variety of compatible and complementary architectural styles in order to provide visual interest."

Sometimes a town is past saving. But its history shouldn't be. I wish

I could say that along with its clock tower and its complementary architectural styles, the new Martin-on-the-hill will have a museum full of early deeds and vintage photographs and public records to describe the rise and fall of an unusual American town during an astonishing century. But there will be no museum. There are few artifacts to display; over the years, the floods got most of the paper.

Some things are lost forever. My father eventually dismantled his model town to make space for floor hockey. And after my grandparents left Martin in the 1950s, my grandmother pined for the hills of Kentucky all the rest of her life. But some things can be found again. What I discovered there were memories. I collected and assembled them, as truthfully as possible. In cases where recollections differed, I chose the version that the most people agreed on. I put quotes around statements that people remember hearing.

I never lived in Martin. But like one of the locals who sees the water rising and runs into the house to retrieve the things that are most dear, I grabbed as many of the old stories as I could carry. I put them in this book to save my family's past from progress.

THE TOWN ON
BEAVER CREEK

CHAPTER 1

When he was seven, my uncle Jack saw a man dying of rabies on the county courthouse lawn. The man wore bib overalls, and as he convulsed and choked, his boot heels flung divots into the air. He begged for water. Someone brought a dipper cool from the pump, but he could not swallow. After an ambulance took the farmer away and Hesta reappeared on the concrete steps in a rush to catch the next Sparks Bros. bus, Jack tried to forget the strange scene. But as he leaned against his mother on the vinyl seat and the bus hurtled past steep, rocky hillsides on every hairpin turn, he could not help feeling parched.

Not long after, Jack was playing with a stick in the vacant lot across from his house. It was a hot summer in Martin that year, but not unusual. Eastern Kentucky tends to turn miserable by August, and in the 1930s an icy RC Cola was the only sure cure. But cold pop was a rich kid's pleasure. There was none at home, where Hesta had no ice and no plans to part with fifty cents for a fifty-pound block, not with seven mouths to feed on Fred's railroad wages. For Jack, who spent most days playing in the miserly shade of a single tree in the lot, the only possibility of relief was the hardware store, where Gardez Dingus ran an electric fan for the convenience of shoppers and idlers. He started across Main Street as a shimmer of heat rose. The wooden sidewalk burned like a branding iron on bare feet.

Something caught his eye over at the Pure Oil. J. C. Stephens's yellow bulldog, paws powdered gray, wandered in the dust near the gas pumps. The dog lived around the corner and was rarely seen on Main Street. His job was to lie in the yard and wag a greeting when J.C.

emerged from his billiards hall across the street from his house. The poolroom had a reputation for fair play and level tables; customers who exited tipped hats at the dog. Too lazy to bark, the dog was never seen chasing his tail. Except now. Jack hoped for the tail's sake that he didn't catch it; the dog had a powerful jaw.

The bulldog was walking funny. He ambled lopsided past wooden buildings that sported movie-set false fronts in a vain attempt to appear taller than a single story. The dog favored his right side as if he had a thorn in a paw. Model A Fords crawled past him, competing with farm wagons for parking spots at the hitching posts. Two centuries were clashing on Main Street. In front of Dermont's grocery, a farmer's wife in a flowered bonnet and button-up shoes wore an ankle-length skirt and chose potatoes from the same burlap sack as a young woman with hair bobbed like a flapper's. A blacksmith's shop was next door to the service station, where an auto mechanic worked six days a week. Downtown Main Street had as many houses as stores. Front yards were small, reserved for the show of a prize climber or a magnolia, but backyards were big enough to put fruit trees—apple, cherry, and mulberry—to work for jelly.

Jack knew he should stay away from the dog. But a strange fascination lured him on. The dog took a few tentative steps toward the barbershop. Jack followed at a respectful distance. It stopped. Jack stopped. The dog peered into the dust as if looking for answers. Jack kept his eyes on the dog. The dog growled at nothing.

Jack wanted to call his mother to come take a look. He turned toward the house, then stopped. Take a look at what? At a dog acting peculiar? Plenty of Martin's citizens survived the humidity by snarling through the entire month of August. Hesta, in her current frame of mind, would ask a lot of unwelcome questions about why he had left the vacant lot without permission. She didn't want Jack wandering around Martin, an uncivilized dirt-poor dirt-road town that in her opinion the family had had no business moving to a few months back. She compared Martin to the high standards of what she'd left behind a hundred miles west in Mount Sterling, a town that had boasted a business square, fancy Victorian porches and cupolas, and a fire department. Martin, with sidewalk boards laid across railroad ties, could not measure up. Here kerosene or gas lamps still reigned and indoor plumbing was a rumor. The creek flooded in the spring and in the summer developed dangerous sinkholes that could suck a child to the bottom. Coal miners poured into saloons on Friday nights, to spend their pay on taxed whiskey when they could afford it and on moonshine when they couldn't. The county deserved the nickname Bloody Floyd. Most men— as well as some women—carried pistols and nearly every day there was a senseless murder in the jurisdiction; at the current rate, within ten years 90 percent of the county's forty thousand residents would be dead. As Hesta could have pointed out to Fred, if she were the sort of wife to nag, she had barely had time to unpack before two men died in a gunfight over a school trustee election a few miles away. The unfortunate vacancy's effect on the curriculum was unclear, but it had an immediate impact on the mood of her household. The violence proved Hesta's point that Floyd County was not a safe place to raise a family. Decades might have passed since the Hatfields and the McCoys had made eastern Kentucky notorious for fools' feuds, but on nearby Middle Creek farmers were still hoeing one another to death over a disputed acre.

The dog snarled again. At any other time of year in Martin, where unconventional behavior was not a condition that automatically required intervention, the dog could have wandered forever without attracting attention. Laws against eccentricity would have gotten a lot of humans thrown into jail ahead of a canine. Next door to the Mynhiers lived a girl whose foibles had prompted her nickname, Emmy Who Takes Off Her Underwear. Her nearsighted mother stepped to her porch rail several times a day, squinted toward the vacant lot, and bawled, "Emmy, you put your ba-l-o-o-o-o-mers back on, right now!" Humans got away with acting strange for years. But an oddly behaved dog faced tougher scrutiny during rabies season.

The dog wandered past the barbershop, foaming at the mouth.

Mad dog!

One of Jobie Click's customers, with a shave in progress, was staring out the window.

Rabid dog! Get inside! Shouts came from every direction at once.

The dog spun around, angry at the noise, ready to attack the source.

Jack hid behind an oak with a convenient low branch. From there, he could see a thick white lather around the dog's muzzle.

The dog confronted a suddenly deserted street. Downtown looked as empty as dawn on New Year's Day. Shop doors were shut, windows were closed, people who minutes before had been conducting business had disappeared. Judge Bush and his honey wagon were nowhere to be seen. Nor was Granny Crisp, who moments earlier had sailed by in one of the fashionable hats she bought in Prestonsburg to avoid trading with Farl Ratliff, whom she considered a foreigner. For once, even Jack's older brother Walter wasn't playing penny poker with pals in the alley behind Kiser's.

It was rare to feel lonely on Main Street. Dick Osborn, who had once owned most of the land on which the town now stood, usually could be counted on to wander around his dominion absentmindedly carrying on a conversation with himself. (Dick said he liked to hear a smart man talk.) If there was a report of someone walking down Main Street in a bathrobe, carrying a pot of steaming turnip greens, that person could only be Dick. At the depot, he spent hours searching the platform for the reading glasses he'd lost; he always found them inside the crown of his fedora. But today he was restocking the shelves at S. D. Osborn Farm Supplies, around the corner and out of harm's path.

Also missing was Doc Walk Stumbo. Although Beaver Valley Hospital was at the southern end of town, Doc Walk spent as much time stalking around Main Street in riding pants and boots, checking the collection status of the slot machines he rented to merchants, as he did examining sore throats at his walk-in clinic. The town's most revered citizen by virtue of being the only person capable of saving everyone else's life as well as the only doctor in the county with a moonshine still in the cellar beneath his office, Doc Walk rode his horse where he damn well pleased. This included the sidewalk and in the aisles of stores. He bought tobacco without dismounting. Today not being tonsillectomy day at the hospital, Doc Walk was caught up in a poker game in his office.

A man on a horse appeared from a side street. The dog spun, moved instinctively toward the horse, growling, snarling, ready to attack. The horse spooked and ran in the opposite direction with his rider whipping his flanks.

The dog hesitated. He shivered, the only creature in the state of Kentucky that felt cold at that moment. He paused at an intersection, unsure of which way to turn. The dog's house lay down a side street. If he continued north along Main Street, he would reach the Elams' restaurant. There the dog might encounter Bess, who had been running the place alone since Orville got shot to death at a honky-tonk "tourist camp" near Pikeville, as she swept out the doorway. In that direction was Pone Branham's house, with little Magdalene playing in the front yard. Beyond lay the schoolyard, full even in summertime of kids intent on Red Rover.

Getting attacked by a rabid dog would be an unpleasant fate, but not a surprise to any of them. So many sick dogs were staggering around the county that, years later, everybody would remember a different case of rabies. There was that time when a big dog with slobber just streaming out holed up under the clothing store and had to be dispatched with a shotgun from a distance of twenty-five feet. There was that dog that bit the seventeen-year-old boy from Weeksbury. One bad year, the health commissioner imposed a dog quarantine after forty people, mostly children, were assaulted. A rabid dog was a reminder to a town that was trying its best to appear modern and enlightened that sophistication was still an illusion in eastern Kentucky. Dick Osborn owned a newfangled Model T Ford and Doc Walk was offering radiation therapy to cancer patients. Ratliff's was stocking the latest dress styles alongside the usual galluses for overalls. Lula Slade brought an Italian cook from Ashland to make spaghetti at her restaurant, and the Canary Cottage had the prettiest booths anyone ever saw, flamingo-colored and each with its own lamp. Clotheslines and outhouses were out of sight, relegated to backyards. But civilization meant nothing to an unlucky dog, bitten by a feral raccoon and looking for a place to lie down where the sun wouldn't hurt his eyes, willing to attack anybody who stood between him and a place to die.

The dog took a few steps toward the school. He stopped. He turned. He stumbled past Kiser's and then lurched toward Skeans' Restaurant, where a thirty-five-cent hot-plate special (dessert and drink included) awaited the lunch crowd, past the service station across from the drugstore.

The dog turned the corner. He was headed home.

Through windows, dozens of people saw the dog pass. They saw him hesitate at the edge of Stephens's yard. Then, as if pulled by an invisible string, he walked straight across the grass toward the dark, cool crawl space in the back.

The dog vanished beneath the house. With the immediate danger over, the curious emerged. Jack crept up to join a crowd that was gathering at the edge of Stephens's property, wondering what to do. Neither J.C. nor his wife, Lori, was anywhere to be seen. The house looked closed up and the curtains drawn, which was too bad because Lori knew how to handle any situation. After her first husband, a pharmacist named Oscar Preston, had been killed in an unfortunate shoot-out at a dance, she'd gone ahead with plans to open Preston Drug Co. in a little wooden shack that sat on cinder blocks. The drugstore had made enough profit for her to pay Dick Osborn for a prime lot on which she'd built this house, one of the town's earliest.

Although the crowd outside her house would have been happy to cede the decision-making to Lori, in her absence nobody got hysterical. Stoicism was required to live in a town that had rickety swinging bridges, rattlesnake season, and floods that swept away livestock. So was patience. People were used to waiting for the last reel of the Saturday night western to arrive by horseback from another town where the same movie had started playing an hour earlier. They waited for the mail to arrive over the mountains. They waited for the creek to go down so they could go home to throw away the water-bloated furniture.

A large man appeared like a bad omen at the end of the block. He was in no hurry as he walked toward the Stephens house. He weighed well over two hundred pounds, looked taller than he was, and despite the heat wore a suit coat to hide the fifteen-pound bulletproof vest beneath. It was a metal vest, and it looked like armor except for lacing under his arms like a ladies' corset. Police Officer Tavis Flannery had ordered it from a catalog.

"Where is he?" Flannery asked. Flannery was the full extent of the law in Martin and nobody liked to summon him on purpose. Even with a rabid dog terrorizing the town, there was a legitimate question about which was preferable to have on the street. Tavis was cordial to everyone but loyal to nobody. When merchants greeted him heartily, Tavis lifted a hand to acknowledge the homage. He didn't stop to chat because he liked everyone to keep moving. If there was trouble, Tavis could pick up a man by the collar and hold him off the ground for as long as necessary. In addition to a pistol, Flannery carried a blackjack, but that was a visual aid. He rarely needed to use it to arrest a troublemaker. Usually it was enough for him to say, deadpan, "Let's go." He only said it once. Those who cared to live did not resist.

Tavis walked around the house, assessing the state of affairs. He shone a flashlight toward the crawl space. He couldn't see anything under there. But he wasn't afraid. Tavis had been taking care of himself since the summer before his fourteenth birthday, when his father had died in a gunfight with a neighbor and ended up beneath a headstone that said, "Killed in a shootout with Abbott Barnett." A large part of Tavis's childhood had been spent on target practice; his aim was equally true with pistols and rifles and shotguns.

A low, menacing growl came from beneath the house. Not having observed the dog himself, Tavis couldn't say for certain it was rabid, and without knowing, he hated to shoot J.C.'s dog. He and Stephens got along well, as J.C. never allowed overt liquor in the poolroom. Killing a man's dog could lead to grudges, and grudges meant enemies, and Tavis had enough of those already.

"Keep back," Tavis said.

Tavis pulled on a pair of leather gloves. He took off his suit coat and laid it across the fence. His dressy high tops—he always wore black ones, because black looked more official—he could not protect from the dust. He pulled his .38, got down on his stomach, and, with the torch in his other hand, inched his way into the crawl space. The last glimpse of him was of his boots. Scuff marks were the only evidence his bulletproof bulk existed.

Quiet fell over the crowd. A minute passed. It felt like forever.

Beneath the house, the crawl space was less than three feet high. It smelled like death under there, like rotted mice and old leaves and rusted tin and cool clay that never dried out. Even with a flashlight Tavis couldn't see more than a foot or two in front of him.

A rasping, grating sound seemed to come from every dark corner.

The dog was breathing heavily. Tavis moved the beam slowly in the dark, sweeping the perimeter.

On the street, Jack hopped from foot to foot. He wondered if anyone at home was looking for him. He hoped not. Jack tried to look as invisible as a small boy in patched denim dungarees—short pants were too sissified—could look. He scanned the faces in the crowd, searching for anyone who might report him to his mother. He stood as still as he could. When he couldn't take it anymore, he started hopping again from the tension. Where was Tavis? Hop hop. What if Tavis never came out of there? Hop. What if the dog did?

A shot rang out. It was the loudest sound Jack had ever heard. Then came another. And another. Jack counted six, fired in quick succession, before another silence.

Nobody moved.

Nothing growled.

Nothing snarled.

Noises came from the crawl space, noises that sounded like something big and heavy dragged across rocky ground.

A dusty black boot appeared. Officer Tavis Flannery backed out, filthy with cobwebs. He dragged the dead dog by a haunch. Even its fur looked lifeless already, dusty and blood-matted.

Tavis heaved the dog into the sunny backyard and prodded it with his boot. "Don't anybody touch it," he warned.

The crowd surged forward to hear what had happened after the light from Tavis's torch had hit the dog's eyes. The dog had attacked, seventy pounds of rage and pain lurching to its feet to lunge. That's when Tavis started shooting.

He inspected the dog. He counted bullet holes—six in all, including one through the chest. "The last one got him," Tavis said. He wiped his boots.

Everyone congratulated Tavis heartily but respectfully. Nobody clapped him on the back because nobody wanted to touch him.

The crowd dispersed quickly. It was too hot to be outside. Jack walked back to the vacant lot. Nobody noticed Jack had been missing. He picked up the stick he'd been playing with earlier. His throat was parched.

CHAPTER 2

*My father used to speak of his trip to Sandy as his first
attempt to find Kentucky and said that it was a failure. . . .
The country around the Big Sandy was forbidding . . . and
my father and the others became discouraged. When spring
came, they returned home.*

—DANIEL BOONE'S SON NATHAN,
IN AN INTERVIEW

I n the beginning, there was bad weather. Then came the early
settlers, who endured it. Then came a town, built by the hardy. By the
time my family arrived in eastern Kentucky at the height of a hot summer in 1932, the citizenry had something to boast about: surviving the
cold, the heat, the dry spells, and the floods.

MARTIN
POP. 860

The greeting was succinct. Identical signs sat alongside the highway, one at each end of town. Neither sign said "Welcome to," because
a third line of print was an unnecessary expense. Duplicate signs were
luxury enough, a folly that dated back to the early 1920s, when Dick
Osborn had a vision of a town built on his family's land.

In those days, plenty of property had been available. Dick's father,
who had the gristmill, had owned hundreds of acres, and his mother
was one of the original Dinguses. Dick unfortunately did not own any

Osborn land, a detail that might have deterred a less determined founder. Deemed too sickly to farm, Dick had lost his birthright on account of a nervous stomach. Instead of land, he inherited the family's general store (which stocked digestive tonics). Dick made a good profit and used the money to buy his five siblings' inheritances. From his brother Tilden, Dick amassed sufficient acreage to divide into lots. Next he built a low swinging bridge across Beaver Creek so prospective buyers could walk from Cracker Bottom to inspect the property.

Dick had many talents. He was an ordained minister, had been admitted to the law in 1910, wrote poetry, was on the verge of finishing a novel, and expected to serve a stint as police judge despite being the most outspoken Republican in a county of Democrats. But Dick was no engineer. The day after his real estate auction, the weight of the crowd tipped the footbridge, which dumped dozens of buyers into water as unforgiving as the town's future. Beaver Creek was low at that time of year, just deep enough to flail in until Kelly Conley arrived with his rowboat to rescue everyone. In a different place at a different time, the plunge might have been considered a warning. But not here. The unexpected baptism only whetted enthusiasm. Dick's lots sold for $200 apiece. Dick, who left the household accounts to Myrt, somehow managed not to get rich off this. In the flush of excitement inspired by the auction (or maybe by the subsequent dunking), merchants established an entire business district, consisting of a saloon, a shoe repair, a barbershop, a general store, and Dick's farm-equipment emporium. Civic-minded citizens raised $5,000 to buy twenty-five building lots downtown, and then donated them to build a school. The town christened a Front Street and a Back Street as well as a Main Street. With three dirt roads, the future had seemed limitless—or at least promising enough to justify two signs at the outskirts. A head count of 860 was optimistic and raised questions about whether the total included cows and chickens, as well as their owners. But the population estimate turned out to have been an act of foresight. The mines and the railroad attracted newcomers during the Depression. With the arrival of my family in 1932, the signs technically should have been changed to "Pop. 869." But who would have paid for it?

Not my family, certainly. My great-grandfather had worked steadily for the Chesapeake & Ohio Railway since October 1917, but the $170 a month he earned was barely enough to cover expenses. Rent alone cost $20 a month. Even if Fred Mynhier had been the wealthiest man in town, his wife still wouldn't have authorized frivolous expenses. When it came to purchases, my great-grandmother Hesta had priorities. Jewelry, good. Sir Walter Raleigh pipe tobacco, tolerated. Anything the kids asked for, probably unnecessary.

Hesta's first view of Martin was through the smoke-smeared window of a train. She had a baby on her lap, a toddler asleep against her shoulder, and five other children who were complaining bitterly about the scratchy mohair seats. It had taken nearly fifteen hours and two train changes to complete the hundred-mile trip. Hesta had resented every minute, even the luxurious first leg of the journey aboard the Fast Flying Virginian. Like the rest of the C&O's name trains—including the Sportsman, the George Washington, and the Kentuckian—the plush Fast Flying Virginian invoked awe. Its engine was the fastest made, and its speed limit was at the engineer's discretion. Barely an instant after the FFV left a station, the train's speed would climb magically to eighty miles per hour. Nothing else on land went that fast. Passengers in the plush, air-conditioned club cars could order drinks and sip them while enjoying the view as they hurtled through rolling bluegrass and fertile river valleys.

The Mynhiers, entitled to free passes because Fred worked for the C&O, had departed Mount Sterling at 9:33 the previous evening. The FFV's seats were wider and softer than other trains', but the children's excitement had defeated any hopes Hesta had of their falling asleep during the trip. The train had stopped first at Preston at 9:52 P.M. and, as uniformed porters came through the cars offering drinks, snacks, and candy, had reached Salt Lick (10:05 P.M.), and Morehead (10:25), Olive Hill (10:57), Grahn (11:09), and Hitchins (11:25). Upon arrival in Ashland at 12:10 A.M., they had faced a seven-hour layover before boarding the Big Sandy Division's No. 36 passenger train. The Ashland station had a waiting room with an all-night lunch counter, where Hesta had bought ready-made sandwiches and coffee. For the kids, magazines from the twenty-four-hour newsstand had been an adventure. For Hesta, the stopover had meant a stiff neck from stretching out on a wooden bench to nap. At 7:15 A.M., they resigned themselves to the basic accommodations of a local train headed east to Catlettsburg (7:29 A.M.), although the children pointedly mourned the glamorous FFV. Twenty miles south, old pastures and gentle dips started to give way to earnest foothills that they would subsequently refer to as "footstools." After a stop in Louisa (8:24), the train reached the edge of the Cumberlands and the valley narrowed. Here the children learned the definition of "mountain." There was barely any sky to see and sheer, steep rock on either side of the train as it made its way to White House (9:21), to Paintsville (9:46), to Van Lear Junction (9:52). Prestonsburg (10:21) was a reprieve; at 641 feet above sea level, the county seat sat at the lowest elevation in Floyd. The climb resumed, on to Beaver Junction, near the town of Allen (10:50). At Allen, the Mynhiers had changed trains again, boarding the Beaver Valley branch's No. 58 at 11:12 A.M. They had traveled the final five miles alongside Beaver Creek, as Hesta watched the brown, muddy water churn on the rocks the way her breakfast churned in her stomach. She dreaded the move to Bloody Floyd.

As the train pulled into Martin at 11:20 A.M., she saw a weak excuse for a town. Things had changed considerably since the early European settlers had arrived to find some of the most remarkably luxuriant land that has ever existed in the United States. The magnificence that had spread before them at the turn of the nineteenth century, green and velvety and as rich with possibility as a bolt of fine, rippling fabric, had been replaced by a few white frame buildings—Zott Dingus's liquor store, Cline's grocery—that fronted a lackadaisically graveled street. The soil of the lush valley no longer smelled like a strong, irresistible cup of coffee by the time Hesta saw, through a bug-spattered window at the tired age of thirty-six, her first glimpse of the only town she ever would consider home. It was not love at first sight.

"You all sit down," Hesta snapped at the children as the train slowed. "Mary, take the baby."

Hesta came to conquer. That day she stepped from the train into the heart of eastern Kentucky, a region so mountainous and isolated that, more than a thousand years after peaceful, buffalo-hunting Native American Mound Builders had built a civilization that buried its dead

Fred Mynhier in
the army, circa 1910

Hesta Kelly
Mynhier soon
after her marriage
to Fred, circa 1915

in big piles, those same grass-covered heaps still dotted the countryside, undisturbed. Hesta was ready, like the Iroquois and the Cherokees and the Shawnees before her, to flourish in the wilderness. Floyd County was no stranger to the effects of foreigners; Hesta arrived more than two centuries after a renegade raiding party kidnapped pioneer Jenny Wiley and scalped her children, nearly a hundred years after steamboats began to transport loads of coal and timber up the Big Sandy River, and nearly three decades after the first passenger train lines cut tunnels through the mountains to reach the county. Those disruptions were nothing compared to what Hesta was capable of.

On the platform, Hesta wrinkled her nose at the heat, steered a strand of auburn hair back into her bun, and issued a string of orders about which trunks belonged to her, where they should be stacked, and how they should be loaded into the waiting wagon.

"Careful, or you'll break something," Hesta said.

She spoke from experience. In nearly seventeen years of marriage, Hesta had lived in eight different towns in two states. Given that she had seven children, a house full of furniture, and a heavy-framed, five-foot-long scenic painting that depicted an apple tree in full flower in the front yard of a picturesque cottage, she might well have stayed put after leaving that train platform. Upon finally reaching Martin, another person might have nailed the furniture to the floor. But not Hesta. She was a serial mover.

In earlier years, this predilection went unnoticed. Before Martin, most moves were preordained by Fred's job as he worked his way up from brakeman to conductor, to better hours, to higher wages, to more prestigious routes. It was not her fault that after they married in West Virginia, they moved in quick succession from one nondescript little town to another, from New River to Quincy by the time Red was born, to Hugheston and eventually to Riverside (where my grandmother Mary was born in 1918), and finally, by the time Pauline was born two years later, to Kentucky.

It already sounds exhausting, especially factoring in three children under the age of four. Census records confirm that there she was in the downtown district of Paintsville, Kentucky, by the spring of 1920, living within walking distance of the train station with neighbors who included another brakeman, a miner, and (fortunately downwind) a fellow who worked in a livery stable. After Walter was born in 1924, Fred and Hesta moved to Henclip, a fancy name for a remote hillside with a cluster of shotgun-style houses. The Mynhiers' house backed right into a cliff. To reach Henclip from town required navigating a footbridge, a berry patch, and a steep flight of wooden stairs. The obstacles proved as effective as a moat. Visitors were infrequent.

Hesta remembered her residences by the action that had unfolded in each. In Ashland, Jack was born a few days before Christmas in 1927. In Salt Lick, the house burned down. In Mount Sterling, Hesta realized her children would one day have lives of their own. She watched Mary skate down the steep slope of High Street toward a town square fronted by brick buildings, hurtling along for the first time with the sensation of how it felt to be headed somewhere. Walter learned to read. And Jack, barely out of diapers but already embarking on a thorough investigation of available dangers, shut his finger in the door of a Model A Ford in a neighbor's garage.

In Martin, Hesta would keep moving. There was no need to leave town; the C&O's depot was a major hub where Fred would work for the rest of his life. Instead, she left houses. She would move so frequently over the next two decades that friends wouldn't be able to keep track of which house was hers.

She moved fast, too, not bothering with trunks or suitcases. She crammed whatever she could into a big old washtub—and Hesta could shove as much into a washtub as other, less motivated packers could squeeze into a moving truck—and she'd say to whichever son was handy, "You take this to the other house now."

It was not unusual for her children to eat breakfast in one house, wait for her to wash the dishes, and carry the stack to another house in time to set the table for supper. She occupied each new house like a conquering army. Her rosewood console table went there, family photos there and there—and when in the late 1930s she finally would obtain a big Kelvinator refrigerator with a round motor on top, the appliance had to be placed just so in the kitchen to show it off to its best advantage. It was the tastiest color, light blue with pale cream trim, and no one could look at it without thinking of ice cream. Her treadle sewing machine went to the parlor, along with Fred's easy chair and pipe rack. Her cedar trunk, in which she jealously stored private papers, sat at the foot of her bed.

What drove her? She had a good reason, a secret she'd keep from her family for decades. Most people, though, assumed that Hesta simply wanted *more*. No matter how much she cautioned her children against getting uppity, she still sought upgrades. She moved to get more rooms. She moved for cheaper rent. For a better floor plan. For a parlor with a wall long enough to anchor the sofa. For gaslights (she saw them glow from every window in a house the family would later occupy briefly on Main Street).

She lived like someone on the lam. No one could imagine what she was running from. But Hesta was always peeking out from behind the curtains, inspecting passersby. To call her suspicious was an understatement of mammoth proportions. She behaved more like a fugitive felon than like a fine, upstanding wife and mother. She turned away strangers. She approached her post office box with trepidation, peering at unfamiliar return addresses with loathing. She lied to census takers, routinely misleading them even when they inquired about such innocuous categories as "Your Birthplace."

Kentucky, she lied in 1920.

Children's birthplaces?

Kentucky, she lied in 1920.

Ten years later, she owned up to her own home state. I was born in West Virginia, she admitted in 1930. But, she still insisted, all the children were born right here in Kentucky.

Fred, a mild man, viewed her machinations with aplomb. He came home from work, examined his surroundings, and congratulated himself: "Well, I found where I live today. Who knows about tomorrow?"

Equanimity came easily to Fred. He had a job to escape to. He was not under her constant observation. Or at least that's what he sincerely hoped.

One year and three houses after she moved to Martin, Hesta caught a glimpse through the front window of a coming invasion. She watched her husband as he walked home from Dermont's with a sack of barley over his shoulder. To other people, the scene might have looked unassuming. There was nothing overtly threatening on a summer evening about the sight of a neatly dressed man in dark pants and a pressed shirt, a mild tinge of gray at his temples, returning after a long day at work. But Hesta saw trouble.

Hesta was always on the lookout. She watched Fred walk into the back room off her kitchen, sling the sack onto the floor, and sink into a chair to remove his shoes. He said hello, as if she were born yesterday. As nonchalantly as air, he moved through the room. He assembled the ammunition he needed to occupy the mudroom—her mudroom! He had a fairly short list of equipment: corn, sugar, malt, hops, the barley, and water. He had a butter churn—Hesta's butter churn—that could hold ten gallons.

"Home brew?" she asked.

"I thought I'd give it a try," he said.

She simmered. How could this insurgency against her sovereignty have been launched without warning?

Her next move would have been easier if Fred had been planning to drink moonshine, a far more potent brew whose manufacture had remained against the law even after the end of Prohibition in 1931. Against moonshine she would have stood on firm ground. But home brew? The alcohol content was so low that revenue agents weren't interested. A weak brown batch of home brew was considered so innocuous that even the C&O's official *Book of Rules*—which stringently forbade many other pleasures that an employee might consider (on duty or off)—didn't mention it.

Fred followed the rulebook religiously. Most railroad employees did. A violation could lead to termination. Employees were expected to carry the leatherette volume in their pockets and to pull it out whenever a dispute arose on the job. A lot of the rules were arcane and silly, but that didn't prevent old-timers at the yard from trying to enforce them. There was the "superiority of trains" section, for instance, which explained right-of-way issues in excruciating detail. One rule advised: "In the event that two trains with equal priority arrive at a junction simultaneously, both shall stop and neither shall proceed until the other has passed." Fred never could understand that one. But when it came to the rules, he liked to err on the side of caution. On the topic of employees' personal lives, the book had this to say: No narcotics. No playing cards, no use of tobacco while on duty—and no wrinkled clothes, either. Although nobody had ever been fired for failing to press his pants, let alone opium eating, Fred and most of his colleagues played it safe. Where else would they find steady work during the Depression? Rule G said, "The use of intoxicants by employees while on duty is prohibited. Their use, or the frequenting of places where they are sold, is sufficient cause for dismissal." Railroad employees stayed out of bars and away from the roadside shacks where bootleggers sold moonshine in pint fruit jars. Railroad men who followed the rules bought their own liquor, took it home, and drank in private.

Hesta was not a drinker. It was rare to see respectable women of her generation take even a sip. The first record of her imbibing was one Christmas when her sons secretly spiked the eggnog. She became very cheerful and never suspected why, just assumed a holiday libation was supposed to have that effect. Had Fred suggested making eggnog that day, he might have gotten a more positive reaction.

Fred was not a heavy drinker, either. If he had been, home brew would not have been his medicine. It tasted like slightly flat, watered-down beer. It had a bitter aftertaste. And cough syrup would have gotten him drunk just as fast.

If he'd been making moonshine, it would have been easier to understand what drove such an argument-averse, even-tempered man to risk Hesta's disapproval. Moonshine tastes like power. It's clear and quick and can slip past lips as easily as water. Slow sips minimize the hot, burning sensation and the smarting eyes. The real trouble starts after moonshine takes possession of the stomach and threatens to kick other vital organs out of the way to prove who's boss.

The local economy depended on moonshine. Farmers had learned during Prohibition that their corn crops were worth far more as whiskey. The most talented moonshiners had cult followings. One resident of Ice Plant Hollow sold such high-quality white lightning that he earned the respectful nickname "The Vintner" in an homage to Omar Khayyám's *Rubáiyát,* a book one of his customers found on a library shelf at Martin High School: "I often wonder what the vintner buys one half so precious as the stuff he sells." It was a good bet the vintner didn't spend his profits on home brew.

Fred's humble demeanor belied his love of adventure. These days his subversive cravings could be satisfied by lifting a lid to see if his mash was bubbling yet. But not so many years before the incident with the butter churn, he'd been a wild fourteen-year-old boy who ached to see the world. He'd run away from home to join the army in 1910, and subsequently sent home a postcard dated August 7 to explain his exotic new life. A photo on the front showed a vast city of tents at the base of a craggy peak. A scrawled explanation on the back said, "Dear Parents, This is the picture of the 11th Infantry camp at Pole Mountain, Wyoming." After conquering the Wild West, Fred had gone south to witness history, first while posted at Fort Hood during the Mexican uprising (where he saw Pancho Villa arrive at the border to negotiate a treaty), and later at Fort Leavenworth, where he was among those assigned to escort the first federal convicts to a faraway prison called Alcatraz. He'd seen the Pacific Ocean. A lot of people in Martin barely believed in the Pacific Ocean.

Fred's adventures these days were tamer. Sometimes he found a garter snake in his vegetable garden while hoeing at twilight. Most nights he smoked a pipe in his favorite chair, thumbing through the newspapers and reading about other people's exploits. In a town where a double feature constituted a novelty, making home brew was a daring escapade.

He knew the basics of brewing. Any Kentucky boy would. Fred was a descendant of the early German settlers who brought their family recipes for whiskey from the old world. His ancestors had been tinkering with moonshine blends ever since they encountered corn flourishing in the nitrogen-rich soil of Kentucky. Fred had grown up in Bath County, a hundred miles west of Martin, with plenty of opportunity to watch his uncles and cousins perfect the techniques. He knew brewers faced danger. If he'd been making moonshine, Fred would have worried about an explosion under high pressure. With home brew, the detonation was more likely to come from Hesta.

"How long will it be in the house?" she asked, in a tone that wasn't wholly friendly. She was not a large woman, but with eyes as sharp as a bird's and her arms folded over her apron, she wasn't someone he wanted to set off.

"A few days, that's all," Fred said. So much of marriage was an effort to buy time.

Hesta frowned. Normally she considered it a mistake to cede, even temporarily, control over any part of her territory. Hesta's father had died in a coal mine accident when she was a girl, leaving her mother to collect just enough insurance money to build a boardinghouse, which had in turn left Hesta with a vivid memory of what it was like not to have one corner to claim as her own. Now, in a house overrun by seven children (with at least one of them, Walter, being an above-average lock picker), Hesta kept close watch over every inch of her terrain. And she was happy to annex more. After she swept her front porch every day, she swept the yard and the street in front of the house as well. The stove was her command center. The scent of her crisp-fried bacon issued directives—*set the table, wash up now, cut that up for the baby*—that her subjects found irresistible. In the morning she ruled by sausage gravy, and at supper through fried chicken, if she felt magnanimous. Slow-simmering beans, fried potatoes, a pie: she knew her strengths. Some evenings, Fred pulled a chair up to the table to keep her company while he read the newspaper. Usually this pleased her. But if she happened to be feeling unappreciated or overworked or was in a mood to quarrel, she would pick up a coffee cup and throw it hard, not at anybody in particular, but just to hear it hit the wall. Fred would lower the newspaper, look over the top of his spectacles, and say, mildly, "I wish you wouldn't do that, Heck." The nickname he meant fondly. But when he raised the newspaper and went on reading, it made her madder than ever.

Hesta hoarded her privacy. She kept her valuables in a battered metal box. She never let anyone examine her treasures, which included Fred's ring from the Masons, locks of hair from various babies, and top-secret official papers she hid from even the people to whom they pertained. Hesta's cache was rumored to include Fred's discharge papers, as well as proof of her marriage, death certificates of the two infants she had lost to bronchial pneumonia, a photo of her placing flowers at their graves, and confidential documents relating to her oldest son, Red, who did not resemble his siblings. Hesta never discussed any of this. The key to the metal box she hid separately.

Condoning home brew would have been a fatal concession in a larger battle she was fighting against Bloody Floyd. With her children already exposed to frequent gunfights, to drunks passed out in the street, and to Tavis Flannery, did they also need a step-by-step lesson in how to manufacture alcoholic beverages? She had lost too much ground already. She had married an orderly, punctual man who kept his shoes so shiny that she could check her rouge by looking at his feet. Fred belonged in a civilized world and, by extension, Hesta had expected to inhabit it with him. She wasn't asking for Paris. But she would have enjoyed paved roads, electricity, and indoor plumbing. Instead, she was giving up her butter churn.

Fred measured his ingredients carefully. If he'd been making moonshine, the recipe would have called for a hundred gallons of water in an airtight still, to which he would have added a sack of meal, ten pounds of yeast, and a hundred pounds of sugar. For home brew, he used similar proportions on a smaller scale. After it fermented, he would bottle it. Moonshine required more steps. Moonshiners had to boil their fermented mash and trap the rising vapor in a long, twisted coil called a worm, which was grounded in a "thumping keg" of cool water. The condensation was the moonshine. The goal was one hundred proof. Making moonshine was a long week's work to earn eight dollars a gallon. All Fred had to worry about was how long it would take for his mash to ferment before he could bottle it. A few days. Maybe longer. It was a very sensitive process.

He instituted a daily ritual. After work, he would lift off the lid to peek into the churn for signs of progress. Was the color right (brownish)? Was it bubbling enough? Was it bubbling too much? He didn't mention to Hesta that soon the kitchen would develop a sour odor of malt.

The battle over Bloody Floyd raged on in the Mynhier household. Not that an outsider could have detected dissension. Night after night, Fred sat in his chair, and from there he regularly brought Hesta's attention to the positive aspects of local life, as chronicled in the newspaper. Ladies' silk dresses (in pastel shades) were on sale for $2.95 at the Midland Stores Co. (This might have impressed her more if she bought dresses, instead of making most of her own on the heavy sewing machine she'd carted across the state.) Come Saturday, the Unique Theater in Prestonsburg was showing *The Nevada Buckaroo*, starring Bob Steele. (This might have impressed her more if she liked westerns. A Victorian romance was more to her taste.) And here was cause for celebration: following a picnic lunch, the Beaver Valley golf team members had putted well in their most recent match last week. What could be more civilized than putting?

Talk of golf could not fool Hesta. "What's that smell?" she asked.

Fred wished he had a book of rules for dealing with spouses. At work, he could communicate effectively with hand and lamp signals. At home, he wished he could hold out a lantern at arm's length to persuade Hesta to stop barreling down the track at him. He knew that she knew that moving to Martin had made sense. There was no other place where he could have been promoted to yard conductor during the Depression. He'd explained the facts to Hesta so many times that he could recite them, without deviation, from memory: Martin serviced the biggest mine on the C&O system, the Inland Steel Company's mine in Wheelwright, a mine that produced enough coal to fill 115 cars a day. To route those cars—along with various other boxcars, flatcars, and tank cars—the C&O needed experienced men. Some days, when the length of the trains stretched for two miles, switch lists numbered nearly seven hundred cars. Fred kept track of all of them, as well as rescuing the "astrays" that should have gone elsewhere. If only Hesta would stop acting like she was an astray.

One day Walter, who at age eleven was old enough to know better, sneaked into the mudroom and lifted the lid to peek. If he also planned to take a taste, he never mentioned it. He released into the air an odor that was difficult to ignore.

"What do you think you're doing?" Hesta asked. She was the only one quick enough to sneak up on Walter. Now she looked unmovable, with her arms crossed over her chest and ice in her blue eyes.

"Nothing, Mom," Walter said. He had some experience with delicate situations. He found himself entangled in them fairly often. Over time he had developed a theory that it was best to stick to a standard, simple answer when conversing with any adult he viewed as a potential adversary (parent, teacher, preacher, an uncle whose son's finger Walter had nearly chopped off accidentally; the list went on).

She didn't move. She didn't say a word. This was her strategy for dealing with obviously guilty boys.

"I just wanted to see what's in here," Walter said. It wasn't really an elaboration, since anybody could see that was what he was doing. She shooed him out with the air of someone who had been dealt three of a kind.

When Fred came home from the yard, she was waiting. "Get rid of it," she said as he came through the door. "That one"—and here she gestured to Walter, who had slunk into the next room, where he had believed he could listen unobserved from the doorway—"that one, he had his nose down in the churn just a minute ago."

As Fred saw it, he had two choices. Either he could agree to her demands and risk spoiling his home brew, or he could endeavor to discipline Walter. It might have seemed an obvious choice. But Hesta had her favorites.

In every generation—among her cousins, her children, and eventually her grandchildren—she anointed one or two who could do no wrong. While the rest of the rank and file cooked and cleaned and fetched heavy buckets of water for laundry, the chosen lived a more rarefied existence. So Walter had plenty of time to play poker with his buddies in the alley behind Kiser's poolroom. And he always had a penny for candy. By virtue of his brash self-confidence, Walter would likely have been her favorite even if the sons born before and after him, John Paul and Joe, had survived infancy. But every time she looked at Walter, Hesta remembered John Paul toddling along stiff-legged in his miniature overcoat and matching wool cap. She looked at Walter and saw John Paul, pulling a red wagon everywhere he went. John Paul got the measles and pneumonia; he died not long after he learned to say "mama." Walter lived, and for that she would always be grateful to him.

"It just needs a few days," Fred said. "It's still working."

Hesta was not amenable. A chicken blinked more often.

"Three days?" he suggested.

"I want something done with it now."

"All right, Heck," he said in a tone that indicated a nickname wasn't always a pet name.

He found a funnel, some bottles, and a capper to ensure each would be airtight. He lifted the lid of the churn. The batch was still bubbling, clearly not ready. But Fred was a thrifty man and the idea of wasting ten gallons of perfectly good home brew was more than he could bear. From generations of farmers, he had inherited the belief that with hard work it was possible to produce with honest labor everything necessary for survival: eggs, feed corn, a smoked ham on Thanksgiving. Fred bottled every drop in the churn. It was four o'clock in the afternoon when he started, and by the time he finished, it was dark and still hot. Fred cursed as he worked, but under his breath so she couldn't hear. He pressed a cap on each bottle and stood them up like soldiers on the counter.

That was the end of the discussion, at least until two A.M. The whole family lay in their beds, still hot but sleeping, when all of a sudden a shot rang out. It sounded as if a gun were firing in the house. One after another, the explosions went off, at irregular intervals, loud enough to wake the landlord in the next county.

Hesta shot up in bed. Walter sat up. Mary, Pauline, Jack, and Red ran from their rooms, instinctively drawn to the racket. Betty, who was barely more than a baby, and Billy, who was even younger, started to cry. Everybody headed to the kitchen, where the noise seemed loudest, to investigate its origin. Everyone but Fred. He already knew.

He pulled the covers over his head.

Here is what Hesta saw. In the back room, every one of those bottles had blown its cap. The room smelled like a combination of rotten eggs and stale beer. Gallons of home brew streamed down the walls and dripped off the ceiling. Hours of mopping lay ahead.

The next day Fred sat so pitiful in his favorite chair. Hesta didn't say a word. The butter churn she scrubbed without complaint.

—

Hesta eventually won the Battle of Bloody Floyd, but not the way she would have liked.

Early one Saturday morning in the winter of 1935, Officer Tavis Flannery got a report of rowdiness at Bessie's Beer Garden on Main Street. There was nothing unusual about the complaint. Even a town where most citizens meant well, worked hard, and were just trying to get by suffered lapses. Occasionally a preacher got apprehended on his way to a revival meeting with a cage full of writhing copperheads. Or someone stole a plow. When it came to violent crime, drunken stabbings were frequent occurrences. So when Mrs. Elam told Flannery she needed help to quiet two rabble-rousers named Step-'n'-a-Half and Tootsie, the situation sounded positively mundane.

Flannery wore his gun belt anyway. If he was awake he wore it. No one could remember seeing him unarmed in public since a notorious gunfight at the depot ten years earlier, long before he became a police officer. The depot, the closest thing to a town square in Martin, was crowded even on the chilly winter day when a ticket agent started the trouble by making an ungallant remark to someone else's wife. It would have been impossible to prevent the comment from reaching the husband's ears several towns away. When the husband arrived by train a few days later to avenge his wife's honor, the ticket agent was expecting him. The agent pulled a gun and, within seconds, was dead. Pistols cracked, passengers leapt for cover, and an unlucky deputy sheriff who rushed onto the platform to investigate got murdered, too. In the mayhem, Tavis Flannery—who had been the sort of youth who could be found reliably at the center of any trouble—took a bullet in the buttocks.

Doc Walk Stumbo was waiting with orderlies and a stretcher as the Right Beaver train carrying the wounded came around the curve. Although Doc Walk was used to making house calls on a horse, an emergency whistlestop appointment turned him even testier than usual. He had an unusually forceful bedside manner under the best of circumstances, cursing at patients who ignored his advice, and was even rumored to have performed, during an occasional appendectomy, a simultaneous hysterectomy on an unwitting patient who had enough children already. Having determined it was faster and more efficient to remove tonsils under local anesthesia without the aid of ether, he was not well liked among the local children, either. Examining the wounded gunslingers, Doc Walk delivered a single diagnosis: "Damn fools."

Grumpily, he gave one man a shot, bandaged another's hand, applied salve to a third, and advised the orderlies not to waste a stretcher on a fourth, who was obviously breathing his last. Before Doc Walk could pass judgment on Tavis, Flannery raised himself on one elbow and said, "I'm not about to die, so you'd damn well better get this bullet out of my ass if you want to say the same, Doc." Years later, Tavis still received preferential treatment at the walk-in clinic.

By the time Tavis sauntered into Bessie's Beer Garden, the two women were gone, but he knew where to find them. Walter Kiser, who owned a saloon across the street, was sweet on Step-'n'-a-Half, whose nickname referred to the limp she'd gotten from polio. Despite the infirmity, she still was pretty enough to attract any man's attention. Although she had a reputation for ducking her bar bills, Step-'n'-a-Half could count on Kiser for sympathy.

Kiser was otherwise mean. He was massive; among his betting customers, the best guess was that he weighed three hundred. He wanted to fight all the time. Since moving to town a few years earlier, Kiser had bought several pieces of property, including the house in which the Mynhiers currently lived. He did not tolerate late rent payments. He'd had trouble before with Tavis Flannery, with Tavis taking drunks out of his saloon while Kiser was still making money off them.

Tavis came through the saloon's double doors in his bulletproof vest and said to the women, "I'm taking you under arrest." He knew from experience that Step-'n'-a-Half carried a knife. From a safe distance, he gestured toward her pocketbook. She shrugged, then pushed it away, out of her reach. Tavis grunted his approval. He took each woman by an arm and walked out the door and down the steps.

The trio had barely gone three steps down Main Street when they heard a loud voice call Tavis's name.

He turned and saw Kiser in front of the saloon.

"What are you going to do to them?" Kiser said.

"I'm taking them to jail."

"You're not going to take any damn one to jail."

Tavis looked flabbergasted that anyone would challenge his authority, especially a foreigner from West Virginia. Tavis, who had grown up on Bucks Branch in a hollow where his family had lived for nearly a hundred years, traced his lineage back to one of the county's first Flannerys, a farmer named Isaac who had married one of the valley's Halberts in 1836. He was royalty. Nobody in town even knew who Kiser's parents were.

Kiser reached for his gun. Three sharp cracks broke the silence. Kiser fell to the ground. By the time Tavis walked over and prodded him with a boot, a crowd had gathered in front of Bessie's Beer Garden across the street. Walter Coleman, who worked for the railroad with Fred, was there. So was Pone Branham, who lived on Main Street. So was my uncle Jack, who had heard the shots from the vacant lot where he'd been playing, and his brother Walter, who upon hearing gunshots had sprinted without a second thought toward the excitement. Short enough to worm their way at elbow level through warm-smelling wool and worn denim, the boys saw Bessie Elam wringing her hands. They saw Tootsie and Step-'n'-a-Half in handcuffs, and they saw for the first time what death looked like, a fat man with stubble on his chin in the middle of the road, fifty-seven years old and never going to see fifty-eight, with blood soaking his shirt and pooling, dark, in the dirt.

Flannery holstered his gun. A pickup truck pulled up and four men loaded Kiser into the back. His body was limp as laundry; transporting him to the hospital was a courtesy so Doc Walk could avoid having to come out in the cold to inspect the obvious before he wrote on the death certificate, "Killed instantly by gunshot wound through heart."

"Nothing more to see," Flannery said. He turned to the women. They didn't need to be told. They resumed their march toward the lockup in Brawley's Camp.

Even though he was a lawman, Tavis had to be officially arraigned. Local business owners posted a $10,000 bond on his behalf. Later, he testified that he had fired in self-defense. A jury heard that three bullets entered Kiser's chest and side at close range. Then they voted to acquit.

Not long after, the Mynhiers moved out of town, or at least out of downtown, to a neighborhood called New Addition. It was a half mile down the highway, over a rise. It was a world apart. There, Hesta got a mudroom that didn't smell like rotten eggs and a neighborhood devoid of saloons and liquor stores and the other bad influences of Bloody Floyd. If it wasn't the way she would have chosen to win the battle, at least she won.

CHAPTER 3

My *grandmother went to work for Doc Walk Stumbo when* she was still in high school. The prospect of another capricious boss didn't cow Mary after sixteen years of living with Hesta, and everything else about the job appealed to her. High ceilings, slate floors, and the whisper of fans overhead lent the hospital an air of hushed gentility that was missing from the rest of the town. On all the patients' bedside tables were brass bells—just like the ones on the reception desks at the best hotels—to instantly summon a nurse. My grandmother had a kind streak and was happy to plump pillows, refill water glasses, and chitchat with patients all day, if that was what it took to cure them. Doc Walk's wife, Annie, who hired her, told Mary that if she worked her way up at Beaver Valley, in no time she could become a licensed practical nurse and earn as much as fifty dollars a month.

Annie Stumbo was an inspiration. She ran the pecuniary side of her husband's operation. She was as sweet-natured as her husband was obnoxious, so no one begrudged her scrupulous oversight of the bookkeepers. Her only child, born in 1918, had lived for barely a day before dying of what his father described on the infant's death certificate as a "non-developed heart." Ever since, Annie had devoted herself to protecting her husband's interests. She kept close track of the receipt books in which was tallied how much the county owed the hospital for indigent care (at the rate of four dollars per patient per day in a hospital that had a hundred beds, the bill totaled tens of thousands of dollars a year). Everyone in Annie's family had a good head for business. Her father kept a parrot in his store in Martin, and made a good living selling bologna and work clothes not because the profit margin was high on such items, but because the bird's keen eye kept shoplifting losses to a minimum. "Pa, Pa, that boy over there is stealing overalls," the bird would bawl on occasion, prompting John Wesley Elliott to hold out a hand for the merchandise: "Boy, you'll have to give them back." Annie's baby sister Lula ran about a hundred businesses on Main Street; she and her husband, Edgar Slade, had a restaurant, a gas station, and one of the only wreckers in the county powerful enough to pull any vehicle from a ditch. They built and managed an apartment building as well, and even had a scheme to own property out west. Six months of the year, Lula homesteaded six hundred acres in Wyoming. Nothing scared the Elliotts, not snakes, not prairie dogs, not Doc Walk. At the hospital, Annie jingled reassuringly because she carried the keys to the drugs and every other room in the building on her waist, and the medical ward could hear her approach long before she appeared to say "Good night, sugar, feel better tomorrow" to each patient. If requested, she knelt with them to say a bedside prayer.

The first assignment Annie Stumbo gave Mary was reception, where the main objective was to keep people from pestering Doc Walk if he wasn't in a mood to be bothered. Mary sat at a desk on the ground floor and listened to walk-in clinic patients describe symptoms they feared incurable. Sympathetically she made notes ("Been coughing since Easter, particularly bad at night") and herded them to a wooden bench to wait. She told them Doc Walk was making house calls. She never said he was upstairs in his office, counting coins collected from the slot machines he rented to merchants. She never said he was in the basement tending his still. She never said he was at a Democratic Party meeting, arguing about a proposed boundary line change for the Rough and Tough voting district. She said Doc Walk would see them as soon as possible, and patients believed her because they could tell she was rooting for them. Seven decades later, what people remember about her is that she was a beautiful girl, which was true enough. I have old photos tacked to the wall above my desk to remind me of how her eyes started to laugh a second before she delivered a punch line. In one snapshot, she stands barefoot at the base of a waterfall, sure of herself on the rocks, with her shoulders thrown back, her pants rolled up, and a gaze that dares the photographer to join her in the shallows. She was pretty, but no prettier than her sisters. The Mynhiers were striking. They looked elegant draped across furniture. Among the sturdy farmers who had populated the valley for generations, the Mynhiers stuck out like willows in an apple orchard. Even the pronunciation of their Scottish surname, which rhymed with "tin ear," sounded strange to Floyd County's Salisburys and Mayos. What people really meant when they said Mary was beautiful was that she had a vivacity that was rare among the junior staff. Most of the girls who lived in the hollows up around Stephens Branch were pale as cave fish. They spooked easily, and skittered fearfully if a patient's bell beckoned. Mary was self-confident, and when Doc Walk stalked past the waiting room as if it were empty, she called out, "Good morning."

He usually ignored her. He took the stairs two at a time to reach his office, where as often as not he rejuvenated himself with a swig from a jug before emerging to face the sick. Then, on an average day, he saw five dozen patients from all corners of the county and performed two or three operations.

"Who's first?" he would bark.

A little boy named Lowell Martin had a sore throat. To see Doc Walk, his mother brought him all the way from Hueysville. Their home was on the right fork of Beaver Creek, past Maytown, way up near Eastern, in a tiny community that a stranger might not even notice. Passing through, it was nothing but a few pastures and a farmhouse or two. But to anybody who grew up nearby, the name Hueysville evoked a rich landscape of extended family, of cousins and uncles and brothers who were related closely to almost all the nearby neighbors and distantly to everyone else in the county. Lowell Martin's grandmother, for instance, was an Allen, and her brother was Dr. J. H. Allen, a popular physician from Maytown who had graduated from medical school at the University of Louisville a couple of years behind Doc Walk. Allen was one of the few serious competitors Stumbo had in Floyd County. Dr. Allen's patients were so loyal that they made house calls to *him;* a prospective patient who knocked on his door on a Sunday morning could expect to be treated on the dining room table. Dr. Allen had not endeared himself to Doc Walk by being a Republican, and certainly not by working at a brand-new rival hospital that Dr. Orris Gearheart built in downtown Martin.

As Doc Walk strode into the examining room to see J. H. Allen's great-nephew, it was as if God had chosen to wear riding pants and boots to work that day.

Lowell looked scared sitting on the edge of the table, so by way of greeting Doc Walk said, "You be quiet."

He turned to the boy's mother.

"Well, what's wrong with him?" he barked.

Lowell's mother said a sore throat.

Doc Walk grunted.

"Open your mouth," he said. He painted the back of the boy's throat with something bitter. It tasted horrible.

He delivered an instantaneous diagnosis.

"Strep."

Lowell's mother was terrified. Strep could lead to rheumatic fever and rheumatic fever could kill a child. It happened all the time.

"He'll be fine," Doc Walk said. And he was.

Doc Walk was a frugal man. Mary learned to use the sterilizer in his office to boil used syringes, surgical instruments, glass slides, test tubes, and rubber gloves. After drying, gloves got powdered. Doc Walk hated waste of all kinds, especially the waste of his time. If he went to the trouble to deliver a baby, he expected the mother to subsequently keep it alive. Postpartum, he made surprise inspections. One Sunday morning he trotted up to an isolated shack to find a newborn left alone, mewling in a cradle. He snatched up the child, blankets and all, and rode half a mile back toward a church from which he could hear the faithful singing, "On a hill far away . . . stood an old rugged cross. . . ." Arms full of baby and reins, he kicked the door open and rode down the center aisle.

Singing trailed off. The aisle hadn't been built to accommodate horses. The walkway was barely wide enough for a nervous, swishing tail. The church ceiling was low because, again, the carpenters had humans in mind. The horse rolled its eyes, skittish, prompting those seated within the kick zone to edge away. Children cowered; some of the youngest noted without surprise that God had turned out to be a vengeful fat man.

Doc Walk spied the errant mother, raised his crop, and pointed it at her, ready to call down lightning bolts. He bellowed to her to get back home and take care of that baby. He handed the infant to a nearby parishioner and rode off to his next patient.

It irked Doc Walk not to control the world. But it was some comfort to control county politics (Democratic voters outnumbered Republicans 9,500 to 6,500, and as party chairman, he controlled the Democrats). He recently had been elected county judge as well, a position that gave him the power to hear civil cases, perform marriages, and sit on the Floyd Fiscal Court, which managed the county's finances. There he voted to authorize payments to himself for treating the county's poor. His jobs would have kept most people busy. But Doc Walk craved even more power and influence, and so when the federal government set up a local Emergency Relief Committee to disburse thousands of dollars to pay for food and clothing for the county's poorest residents, Doc Walk got himself appointed to that, too. Soon after, he managed to persuade the governor of Kentucky to increase the relief committee's membership from six to nine, enabling him to add three political cronies to the group. The mayor of Prestonsburg and the deputy county clerk were on the committee, too, but when it came to big decisions—like how much to reimburse the merchants who supplied the food and clothing, and which merchants were eligible to participate—Doc Walk made them all.

Unfortunately, political shenanigans couldn't keep his mind off other annoyances, such as the new hospital in town. Before, Doc Walk's main rivals had been granny women, mountain healers who dosed patients with herbs and folk remedies such as black gum potions (a general restorative), squaw weed (to stop hemorrhaging), dried rattlesnake (for fever), or even boiled sheep dung (to cure measles). It hadn't been difficult to persuade patients to place their faith instead in a physician with a degree conferred by the University of Louisville, the finest medical school in the state. But a new hospital wasn't so easy to dismiss, especially after Gearheart christened it Martin General to make it sound like the hometown choice.

Annie Stumbo told everyone at the next Ladies' Aid meeting that she saw no reason to worry. After all, Beaver Valley was bigger (it was the only four-story hospital in the county) and better equipped, by virtue of having a modern laboratory, an X-ray machine, and the most up-to-date treatments. Hadn't her husband spent $35,000 on an itty-bitty piece of radium to cure cancer? True, a foolish employee had accidentally thrown away the metal, but a mail-order Geiger counter had saved the day. Now that Doc Walk had found the radium in the garbage dump, disease was again on the run.

After totaling the hospital's monthly receipts, however, Annie realized that a lot of Beaver Valley's patients were switching to Martin General. So she told Walk she agreed with him that Martin might prove too small to support two hospitals. She told her husband he was right to think about selling Beaver Valley and building a new hospital on the edge of the county, where there was less competition.

In response, Doc Walk started to wonder if Martin was too small to support two hospitals and, if so, should he sell Beaver Valley and build a new hospital somewhere else?

This was not the first time Annie had pointed out to her husband how smart he was. Back in 1929, after his older brother Edward had died suddenly from falling off a horse while making a house call, Annie had told Walk she agreed that it was a good idea to buy out his remaining business partners—his mother and Edward's widow—for $5,000 apiece so he could own the hospital free and clear. She'd been right that time too, because he'd been collecting more than $30,000 a year in indigent payments ever since.

Annie said she agreed with Walk that it was a good idea to accept an offer from a group of six doctors from Pikeville who wanted to buy the hospital for $40,000. She agreed that it sounded like a nice profit.

Soon after, the hospital's sale was front-page news. The article didn't mention that Doc Walk's contract with the buyers precluded him from building another competing hospital anywhere in the county. Nor did it mention his plans to start construction, almost immediately, on Stumbo Memorial Hospital in Lackey, which was about three feet over the line into the next county. "Dr. Stumbo plans, it was said this week, to return to private practice," the newspaper reported.

Other staff defections followed. Not everybody was comfortable working for out-of-towners. Many of Beaver Valley's employees got jobs at Martin General, and eventually my grandmother found herself working at Gearheart's hospital, as well.

There she learned how to take care of the dead. In those days, if patients died at a hospital, the staff washed and dressed the corpses before sending them home in an ambulance to be waked in their parlors. It didn't matter how the previously live patient had been dressed upon arrival at the hospital. Preparing for eternity required shined shoes, combed hair, and straight seams on stockings.

One day an old lady died at the hospital. The supervising nurse told Mary to wash and dress her, told her which clothes to put on her—including a pair of white stockings—and then said, not unkindly, "You go ahead. I'll be back in a little while."

After the nurse left, Mary looked at the body and felt a little funny about it, just her and a dead woman in a room. She'd seen plenty of dead people before, of course, including her grandparents, but this was the first time she had to interact with one of them in any way other than as a mourner. She remembered her two baby brothers who died of pneumonia and how Hesta had taken care of them. She screwed up her courage and went to work.

She got the dress on first. Then she picked up the stockings. On one, a small hole had been darned near the toe. She pulled it over a foot and an ankle and up a leg—tricky work—and paused to admire the result. Then she started on the second one. She bent the woman's knee, gently, so she could get the rolled-up stocking around her toes.

All of a sudden, the woman's leg stiffened up and shot straight out into the air. Her foot almost hit Mary in the face.

Mary was so shocked that she dropped the stocking. She backed away from the bed. She was shaking. She tried to catch her breath, but then she gave that up and turned to rush out of the room.

In the doorway stood a young man in a white coat. He looked too young to be a doctor. But she recognized him as Dr. J. H. Allen's son Claude. In high school, Claude had played guard for the Maytown basketball team, spoiling many a Martin victory. Claude had inherited an unhurried bedside manner. His father did not rush even if a knock on his door on a Sunday morning meant a man with a fishhook in his neck would soon be bleeding all over the parlor floor. In a case like that, J. H. Allen folded his newspaper crisply before reaching for his doctor's bag. "I've never hurried a day in my life, and I'm not about to start now," he told his family.

Claude took his time, too. He peered around the doorjamb.

"Who called for help?" he asked. Everything he said sounded like a joke he wanted to share.

"She kicked me!" Mary said.

"That happens," said Claude, who was home on break from medical school in Louisville, where he had learned the symptoms of rigor mortis.

"She nearly gave me a black eye," Mary said.

"That would have been a shame," he said. "Do you want to take a break?"

"I can finish," Mary said.

"Holler if you need help," he said as he turned to leave. "I'm pretty good at buttons."

After he left, she finished dressing the body. And after that, not much bothered her at the hospital.

CHAPTER 4

Freezing rain began to fall on the Midwest soon after New Year's in 1937. The storm from Canada rushed south, over the Great Lakes, to pound Ohio. Day after day, the rain stubbornly refused to turn to snow. A week later, as high waters swirled through creeks and streams nearly three hundred miles away from Martin, a bridge collapsed in Shelbyville, Indiana, and effortlessly tossed both Mrs. William Fisher and the car she was driving into the Big Blue River. Things got worse. Police boats began to evacuate Indianapolis. In Kentucky, the Licking River swelled. The Illinois Central's railway tracks disappeared beneath seven feet of water at Makanda. The National Guard rescued one hundred families in Missouri. By January 20, as President Roosevelt began his second term by taking the oath of office in a downpour, water from the Ohio River covered 150,000 acres in Indiana and northern Kentucky. The Great Flood of 1937 was officially under way.

By the time it was over, the worst flood in American history would render hundreds of thousands of people in eight states homeless. Seventy-five percent of Louisville would be underwater. Cincinnati's chief of police would issue a command to shoot looters on sight. Damage estimates would top $200 million. As the entire city of Paducah—all thirty thousand residents—was being moved by boat to higher ground, influenza would break out among the evacuees and cause a panic.

After flying over the devastated Midwest in an airplane to view the damage, *New York Times* reporter Meyer Berger would write, "Louisville looked like a new Atlantis with from three-fourths to four-fifths of its total area almost eave deep in dark brown water. Cincinnati, except for a few high spots, seemed planted in a chocolate sea."

In Martin, Beaver Creek emptied into the Big Sandy, which flowed into the Ohio River at Catlettsburg. So in late January, when word reached town that Catlettsburg's business district was underwater, my family suspected it was time to start stacking the furniture to the ceiling.

The creek rose slowly enough to give everyone plenty of time to dread the outcome. Jack watched from the bridge, a sturdier steel version that had replaced Dick Osborn's wooden footbridge, as water as milky brown as spilled coffee swirled by. Jack was ten, not old enough to have permission to be out alone in a crisis but big enough to know how not to attract the unwanted attention of anyone likely to report him to Hesta. He listened quietly as the old-timers congregated at the rails to diagnose the situation.

Bulldog Hayes (whose house was on low ground): "It's coming up fast."

Floyd Skaggs (who also lived within a block of the creek): "Might be a bad one."

No one would know from the flat, affectless way they spoke that the water posed a personal threat. Hayes was a jowly railroad engineer who could get grouchy over little things (he didn't like kids to play in his yard or to disturb the litters of puppies he was raising to sell), but he wasn't the sort of man who believed in public displays of emotion. His body language said he'd lived through worse. When things looked dire—as they did now—he pulled on his boots and went up to the bridge to investigate. He had an unpleasant report to carry back to his neighborhood: the water was rising a foot an hour. Although urgent news like that couldn't wait long, Hayes figured he could afford to give the weather another five minutes or so to come to its senses. He'd rather report a miracle.

Skaggs, who was well liked in town, was just as reluctant to admit defeat. On his face Jack could read worry about his wife and his son Billy, both of whom probably were at home stacking the chairs on top of the kitchen table.

A cold and steady rain pelted the men, each raindrop icy enough to burn their skin. It should have been snowing. It was the middle of January, for God's sake, and there was no reason on earth for the heavens to dump so many unwanted, unseasonable inches of water onto the unsuspecting town of Martin. No reason, except that the weather in Floyd County was always contrary—and often just this side of unbelievable. Year-round, the climate served up surprises. The local newspaper regularly reported irregularities. "Hailstones as large as hens' eggs fell Tuesday night, damaging the roofs of houses and cars and killing chickens roosting in the open" was the story one recent May. Another time in March, Beaver Creek got so swampy that it became the unlikely habitat for an alligator: "Proof that an alligator was removed from the stream now hangs from a post at the Clear Creek railway station."

Now the gray sky promised further punishment.

Hayes: "Weather looks bad."

Skaggs: "Bad."

As they slouched against the rail, the sharp report of a .22-caliber pistol punctuated their conversation every few seconds. They did not react. Along the bridge and the shore, a dozen other men took aim at big brown water rats scurrying up from the creek, as the rodents evacuated their holes for drier ground. They were vicious-looking creatures, but a hollow-point bullet could blow one apart. There were too many dead rats to count. The muddy churn swept the bodies away.

The current also carried a crazy collection of wreckage: broken branches, lumber, tin cans, milk bottles, dead hogs, caskets (Hayes: "Funeral parlor up Left Beaver must have flooded out." Skaggs: "Yep."), privvies bobbing along on their sides, and an assortment of furniture. Chairs and mattresses and somebody's yowling cat stranded atop a trunk. Even sofas could float.

At first, the men on the bridge had hoped for a run-of-the-mill-it-must-be-nearly-spring sort of a flood. But as bad news from around Kentucky trickled in—the state prison in Frankfort looked like an island surrounded by a moat, rowboats were navigating the streets of downtown Louisville—they realized they might be in for a record-setting, life-threatening, terrifying flood that could erase the whole town of Martin. The problems started up north, at the Ohio River. Word of the Ohio's rampages had reached the C&O yard office via direct company phone lines from the depot in Russell. In Catlettsburg, where the Big Sandy flowed into the Ohio, the water was so high in the business district that rowboats were the only way to navigate the streets. In Ashland, the Union bus terminal was underwater and the WCMI radio station was practically afloat. The Big Sandy was backing up. In Martin, it was time to brace for the worst.

Jack knew he should go home. Both upstream and downstream, neighbors' yards were already underwater. A curious trick of geography had turned the town of Martin into an island with a colossal moat of hot chocolate frothing around the perimeter. But Jack couldn't take his eyes off the pole.

The pole was a two-by-four that somebody had driven into the ground a day or so earlier to measure how fast the water was rising. On the pole, three lines were marked at different heights. The bottom line indicated a safe level for the water. If the creek crested below that line, the town would stay dry. But the bottom line on the pole was gone. The creek was inching up to the second line: flood stage. It would reach that level in an hour, or less, at this rate. At flood stage, water would start to seep into the streets of Martin. At first the puddles would look deceptively low and placid at the edges of people's yards and filling low spots in the road near storm drains. An inexperienced eye might overlook the dangers. A boy might be tempted to stomp in them. But nobody who had lived through a Martin flood would make that mistake twice. Once the water started to creep into town, it moved fast. A careless boy could get stranded on a high spot within minutes.

The third and highest line on the pole meant simply: underwater. The whole town might as well glide away at that point. Nobody ever stayed on the bridge long enough to see the creek get that high.

"Everybody off the bridge," Bulldog Hayes said. "Go home."

Some of the men turned abruptly and ran. Jack headed in another direction, toward the storm drains at the south end of town. Jack stopped running when he got to the Ashland Oil service station. The nearby drains were located at the lowest point of Main Street. He was a few blocks south of the center of town on the road to Beaver Valley Hospital. As he skidded on the slick wooden sidewalk, he saw water start to bubble up from a manhole, a sickening brown stew that oozed out of the ground and . . . just sat there. It looked like a puddle at first, then a bigger puddle. Within five minutes, the puddle was a small pond and Jack could see the shore of it as it edged inexorably down the street in his direction.

He considered heading home. But as he turned, he saw the creek to his left, a hundred feet away, rise and crest its bank. For a second, it was just a trickle, then it was a stream, and then a wave of water headed toward the Pure Oil. It flowed determinedly into a culvert near the manhole, and when it reached the puddle—boom!—it was a vast glassy lake covering that end of town. Walter, who had seen it happen just this way the last time there was a flood, had claimed you could hear a big bang, an explosion of sound when the two distinct streams of water met each other. The noise, Walter said, was the result of the cold creek water smacking into the warmer ooze from the storm drain. Jack didn't hear anything. But that didn't necessarily mean Walter was lying. Walter heard things other people didn't.

Jack raced north now, trying to reach home before all the puddles in town connected, running barely ahead of the water as it claimed new territory and began to expunge the known world.

Over time, a town that floods nearly every year will develop certain traits that other towns don't have. There's a telltale odor, for instance, a musty, wet-wood smell that lingers in the air long after the water has receded and the world has dried out. Houses sag around their foundations where the creek has found a way in again and again and again. After a while, wood siding surrenders. I'm bloated and I'm always going to be bloated, it says. After a few floods, wood never really dries; it rots instead. If there's a breeze, passersby can catch a whiff of the decay and see the ghosts of high-water marks on the walls. No amount of scrubbing can completely remove those faint black lines. But the odor is worse. It smells like dried mud. It smells like ruin, like poverty, like defeat.

A town that floods every year starts to look tired after a while. People get fed up and quit painting their houses. They get a little slower about replacing the buckled linoleum in the kitchen, because why spend money on something that will get ruined again come spring? Garbage in the treetops is another giveaway. Driving along the winding old road to Martin, in even the driest weather, it's possible to see souvenirs of the last flood caught in high branches of low-lying trees. Toilet paper, plastic bags, sometimes even a mattress stranded too high to reach.

In China, dynasties rose and fell because of earthquakes. In Pompeii, a volcano wiped out civilization in an afternoon. In Martin, the floods came nearly every year. But although the water moved inexorably through town, leaving behind a trail of mud and muck and ruin, the residents stayed.

A town like Martin was a special case. Destruction was routine, ruin and damage a constant threat. People who lived there could predict with surprising accuracy when the next flood would come: next year. And the one after that: the following year. The cycle of natural disaster—evacuate, clean up, brace for the next one—was so common that it became a seasonal routine almost as familiar as the annual Easter pageant.

Why stay in a place like that? It wasn't always so bad. When the first settlers found themselves becoming irrevocably attached to the land and the mountains, floods didn't affect them personally. In 1860, the population was so sparse—fewer than 6,400 people lived in all of Floyd County—that there was plenty of high ground on which to build houses. The fertile lowlands were planted with crops. The highest water ever recorded was in February 1862, when the Big Sandy crested at a height of 49.8 feet. Although the river was four stories high, few homes were damaged. Topsoil washed away. The fields got rocky. But the log cabins were safe on dry land.

By the 1930s, when narrow Beaver Valley got crowded, families who had lived on the same land for generations didn't want to leave. And newcomers stayed for the jobs that had lured them in the first place; the same trick of geography that made the valley so vulnerable to flooding also created an ideal central location for the C&O to expand to transport coal out of dozens of local mines. Miners and railroad workers had steady paychecks that would have been nearly impossible to replace during the Depression. Some people stayed because they had never lived anywhere else, and never wanted to. It didn't matter if other places were easier to inhabit, or if there existed towns—not so far away—where the land and the weather didn't conspire against the occupants at every turn. The Crisps and the Flannerys and the Flanerys (the spelling was fluid, as well, among different branches of a single family) and the Osborns and the Osbornes and the Halberts stayed for family, dead and alive. They lived on the same land as their parents and grandparents, ancestors who now were buried up on the hillside above the town. If they moved away, who would go up to the town cemetery to put flowers on the headstones on Memorial Day?

By the time Jack reached New Addition, which was still dry, the creek had triumphed over downtown Martin. First it invaded the backyard vegetable gardens of Front Street, making itself comfortable as inch by inch it covered the furrows and the bales of mulch. From there, it was a short trip up the back steps and into the kitchens of the Allen house (Tom Allen ran a hardware store) and the Dingus house (Perk Dingus was a railroader). From their back windows, they could see the cold, dark water creep across the lawn. Across the road, the Skaggses and the Griffiths were hurriedly packing. They knew they were next.

From Front Street, the water rounded the corner toward J. C. Stephens's house, ready to breach the fence and obliterate the yard where the rabid dog had staggered home in search of a dark place to die. But a funny thing happened. The water lapped at the edge of the Stephenses' property, along all four sides of the lot's perimeter, but never came closer. The house, built on a little knoll, was just high enough to stay dry on its own little island. J.C.'s wife, Lori, who had bought the property from Dick Osborn at his long-ago real estate auction, hadn't realized at the time that she was purchasing a particularly fortunate piece of land. But over the next twenty years, with each subsequent flood, the luck had held. While neighbors waded out of their front doors to brave icy water, carrying meager bundles of clothes wrapped in sheets, the Stephenses stayed dry.

Farther south on Main Street, at the Slades' house, the water crept in through the door. Lula Slade told her youngest girls, Sis and Bud, to sit quiet on the three-quarter bed in the sunporch. The twins held hands as they watched the water seep across the floor toward the fireplace, and into the grate, where it got the coal wet. When the icy water reached a depth of a foot or more in the house, Sis started to worry that the current might get strong enough to carry the whole lot of them, house and all, down the road to Allen, but her mother said, "Stay on the bed." They kept dry there.

By late afternoon, Main Street looked unfamiliar. One particularly low house was floating like an unmoored pleasure craft on the waves of a strange new sea. At the house where the home brew had exploded, the mudroom was three feet deep in icy muck; the yeasty smell of Fred's exploded hopes would soon be replaced by the odor of soggy, mildewed wallboard. On Main Street, the hard-packed dirt where Walter Kiser fell bleeding in front of his saloon was washed away. In the basement of Beaver Valley Hospital, Doc Walk Stumbo's empty moonshine still bobbed merrily, tethered by a long copper pipe.

The Mynhiers were on high ground. Hesta's latest move had saved her metal box from becoming so waterlogged that the papers would have disintegrated into mush. The family was in no immediate danger greater than the threat of uppity rodents, yet they couldn't help but feel vulnerable. What if they still lived uptown? They would have lost everything—Hesta's treadle sewing machine, the oil painting of the apple tree, the rosewood console table, Fred's favorite chair, photos of babies long dead.

The next day, my grandmother stood on the front porch to survey the new world. Across the road, where only yesterday there were acres and acres of cornfields, she could see nothing more than a lake. Water had surged through barns and fields, fatally surprising cows and horses. Dead livestock drifted on a surface that was eerily still. There was no current anymore, because all the pent-up water had finally found enough space to spread out. No one could stop a flood. How could anyone even fight back?

From the Mynhiers' porch, rooftops were visible above the water line. But front yards were submerged, along with sheds, outhouses, and snowball bushes. Some neighbors—the Turners, the Smiths, the Keys, and the Caudills—had awakened at daylight to learn they lived in isolated havens, cut off from dry land and from one another by a deep pond that hadn't existed when they'd gone to sleep. Some were waiting, in attics, for rowboats to rescue them.

It was a disaster. But to the children, it was magic. Even a blizzard

that dumped two feet of snow onto the town wouldn't have transformed
it into such utterly foreign territory. The Mynhier boys walked along
the highway, over the rise to town, where the road was still dry. Past the
street where the Stapletons lived they got a glimpse of the fate they'd
narrowly escaped: the highway ended abruptly at the shore of a new
lake. In the distance, where a business district had bustled as recently as
yesterday, the familiar buildings—the five-and-dime, the theater, the
poolroom, Mrs. Hunter's restaurant—were vacant and marooned. The
upper stories were still above water, a tableau not unlike Atlantis surprised in the act of submerging. What if the world stayed underwater?
If you dove down in the middle of that water (in some places, it was
nine feet deep), would you see a museum exhibit of how life used to be?
A big hydrangea bush, branches swaying in the deep? Someone's work
boot dangling at eye level, like a chunk of fruit in pudding? Would you
have to do the breaststroke to the theater if you wanted to see *King
Kong*? Walter rolled up his pants and let the mud squish through his
toes. He could see an argument for life staying this way: everyone could
live in a boat. No more baths, just a swim.

Rowboats took over Main Street. They were the only form of transportation that could traverse the new terrain. The sick were rowed to
the hospital, where Doc Walk stood in a second-floor window ready to
help them over the sill. Walter floated down Main Street in a rowboat,
marveling at the new height from which he could address the universe.
With the tip of his paddle, he could touch the very top of the new Main
Street stoplight as the boat passed.

A few days later, the water was gone. All the roads and houses were
slicked in mud. Fences and street signs and sidewalks had to be hosed
down. Some of the men climbed up into trees to try to dislodge the
swollen mattresses that dangled in high branches. The town fathers
took an official head count only to discover that people were missing,
swept away in the night. A blind woman named Cora Collins Turvie
had disappeared walking along the edge of the road the night the backwater had come up; later she was found drowned. Other bodies never
reappeared. Fires broke out in houses where the water came up over the

thermostats of floor furnaces and caused electrical malfunctions. All the stores in town flooded, all the inventory was waterlogged and ruined. At George Cline's clothing store, tons of soggy shirts and overalls had to be thrown away. The roads were obstacle courses, strewn with uprooted trees and branches, with garbage, with personal papers, with life stories.

The county Department of Health sent a truckload of cleaning supplies and nurses to give typhoid shots. The truck parked in a vacant lot of Main Street. The head of each household went down to sign for a case of strong-smelling cleaner, four gallons to a case, one case per household. The stuff came in a square tin can with a handle and a cap you had to unscrew and a seal beneath that you had to break. It made your eyes water.

Martin's residents were stoics. Their walls were warped, their roofs were shifted, and their foundations were cracked. Plywood was peeling. Mattresses were moldy. Silt filled their stoves. So they doused everything with bleach and moved on with their lives.

Two weeks later, the Martin PTA went ahead with plans to stage a play called *Henpeck Holler Gossip*. The performance was well attended. Soon after, the annual Fat-Lean Man's Ball Game (also sponsored by the PTA) ended in a tie. Extra innings were played. The Fats won.

The month of March arrived. The town was ready for spring. Then it snowed.

CHAPTER 5

NEWS OF THE COUNTY: MARTIN
March 19, 1937

The Home Economics class surprised Mrs. Earl Lynch (née Miss Helen Jarrell) with a linen shower Friday afternoon. The bride was the recipient of many lovely gifts. Minted chocolate chips, ice cream and angel food cake were made and served by the class.

— *The Floyd County Times*

M*ary missed the linen shower because of the snow. All things* considered, she wasn't sorry to have skipped the festivities. She felt like a phony at these parties. For her it was pretend. She endorsed the idea of new linens. But when it came to embroidering them, she lost interest. Her own experience in Mrs. Wurm Allen's home ec class hadn't been an unqualified success. The only homemaking skill she had mastered was making peanut butter fudge. She wouldn't have enjoyed returning to the home ec classroom—not even for ice cream—to be reminded of how much hadn't changed in the two years since she'd been a senior. Without attending Helen's shower, Mary could have predicted the conversation, which revolved mainly around the most recent Saturday night dance, and included lengthy critiques of dresses (Mary had worn black) and escorts (Mary had none). The only interesting gossip she missed was about the mysterious stranger on a Harley—a motorcycle was as good as a uniform to catch a woman's eye—who had been spotted riding up and down Main Street.

That morning, Mary had awakened to unexpected flurries of snow—crazy spring weather, on the heels of the flood—visible from the double windows in her bedroom. She preferred the town sifted with a layer of white. It beat the hell out of a layer of water. The Turnleys' house looked soft and welcoming, and Boyd Turner's white clapboard house was a powder puff.

Outside, Kermit Howard was waiting. He drove the big black ambulance that doubled as the town's hearse. When she worked the early shift at the hospital, he stopped by to pick her up. This, in her job, was considered a major perk.

Unfortunately, as Mary observed later, riding with Kermit could lead to a death worse than fate. He was fast, he was reckless, and the general consensus was that he couldn't steer a horse and wagon, much less a motorized vehicle. It was so cold that the air was blue as she climbed into the passenger seat. Mary would have liked to dig her hands down into the warm pockets of her heavy wool coat. But it was more important to hold on for dear life.

Kermit skidded off, spewing ice. They passed the Martin Theatre at breakneck speed, forty miles an hour, which might as well have been a hundred on such a narrow road. If two cars traveling in opposite directions came upon each other, one would have to pull over to the shoulder to allow the other to pass. Kermit, who was dumb enough to think he could stop on ice like he could on a dry street, never allowed for approaching traffic. Nor did he consider the possibility that the new traffic light by the high school might turn red.

It did.

The only thing Kermit had going for him when he hit the brakes was the belief that ambulances were not supposed to wreck. It was not enough. The ambulance hit an icy patch near Mrs. Hunter's restaurant and started to spin like a figure skater. Mary had a queer feeling in her stomach, courtesy of the laws of gravity. The ambulance tipped, then it flipped, and finally it slid.

Mary was alive and she was conscious. But she was discombobulated. She was confused about why she was wrong side up—or at least the ambulance was—and about why her arm was throbbing and why people were running from stores into the street toward the vehicle. Only after some seconds had passed did she understand that she had narrowly missed being thrown from the vehicle and killed.

Her first instinct was to reach out and slap Kermit. This didn't make her feel as good as she had expected. Her second was disgust. Death by snow flurries would have been a fine end to eighteen years of life. She was able to climb out. Or maybe someone helped her out. That part was confusing to remember, even years later. What stuck in her mind was the crowd and the pain in her arm. She shivered under a blanket—where had that come from?—and stared at the sight of the dented mound that lay like a dark, beached turtle. Someone took her to the hospital, she couldn't remember later whether she went in a wagon or a truck, and the diagnosis was that she was shaken up. She said she was fine, but anybody could see she was rattled.

The odd dream continued. With a splint on her arm, she stood in the hospital's lofty, echoing hallway for a moment to get her bearings, a girl in a white dress with the sun shining through the tall windows behind her. The bright light blinded her to her future, which at that moment was fixing the water cooler. She didn't notice him. And she didn't realize he was the same fellow who had been riding a Harley through the streets in recent days. But he saw her.

His name was Elmer Wolverton, and he would be my grandfather. Maybe she should have run from him faster than she fled that upturned ambulance. He was too old for her. He'd been married—and divorced—twice. He was a wanderer who never stayed in one place longer than a few months. He gunned his motorcycle in town, not caring about the red light, and how could he see where he was going with the hat at such an angle?

Elmer was a novelty. Although Mary didn't know every person in Martin by name, she did know most folks by family. In a town as clannish as Martin, the inhabitants were easily categorized by surname; if they themselves weren't Dinguses or Tacketts or Lackeys or Mays or Allens, they were cousins. The majority of the population had descended from the same few ancestors who had ridden a horse through Pound Gap from Virginia a few generations back. When was the last time that Mary had seen a foreigner in this town? She couldn't remember. But she knew when she had last seen one with a loud Harley and a leather coat. Never.

Helen Jarrell's older sister Alma, Mary's best friend, had the scoop on Elmer. Alma's boyfriend, Junior Osborne, worked with him at Porter Electric, where a good repairman could always get a job. Alma introduced Mary to Elmer while she still had the sling on her arm. Double dates ensued.

Sixty-five years later, I went to see Alma to get the details. She lived in a trailer on the side of the road in the north end of Martin. The day I visited was a god-awful hot day in July. It was barely mid-morning, but the air was oppressive and heavy as a sedative. The back of my skirt was sticking to my legs. I took Alma a box of fudge and she set it on the table between us, unopened, while she searched my face for a glimpse of Mary. But I think it's just as likely she saw Elmer instead. All these years later, when she hears his name, she still wrinkles her nose at the memory of the repairman who came to town like he owned it and claimed her best friend.

Alma made different choices. She raised her four children in one house in one town. ("I was grounded for twenty years with those children, and if I left the house to go anywhere with them, I had to walk," she said. "It was an all-day trip, practically, to walk down to the hospital for them to see the doctor.") She married twice, and both her husbands were local boys.

Mary was always different, Alma said. "With Mary, everything had to be kept just the way it was supposed to be," she said. "She looked so pretty in her nurse's uniform, ironed. If you were supposed to be somewhere at a certain time, she was."

Alma remembered many things she didn't like about Elmer. He bragged about his exploits (bootlegging and motorcycle racing). He was a wanderer. He had a past. Stocky ("not my type of feller"). Too old for Mary.

"But you didn't warn her not to marry Elmer?" I asked.

"I didn't like to interfere," Alma said.

"They're both dead now," I said. "You can say what you think."

She still didn't want to interfere. But here is what Alma thought in 1937, what she still thought: "They weren't the type for each other. He was wild. And Mary was anything but wild."

Things that other people considered calamities lured Elmer. Like big floods. He had come to town directly from Louisville, where he'd been repairing commercial refrigerators in the aftermath of the most recent one. Elmer had earned a nice bit of overtime, which explained the Harley. After Louisville, he'd signed on at Porter Electric, which had sold Beaver Valley Hospital a generator some years back. The hospital's power plant had fifty-six batteries in a big glass bowl (you could see the plates in them, and a lead strap that tied them together in a series) and it powered a 110-volt generator. All it needed to run was a gallon or two of kerosene—unless there was a flood and nine feet of water poured into the ground floor of the hospital. There was nothing about that in the Delco manual. But Elmer didn't need a manual to fix anything. Herman Porter saw that right away. When Doc Walk phoned to demand that Porter send over someone sharp to make sense of the mess, Elmer got the assignment.

To get to the hospital, Elmer had to drive past Mary's house. A few days after the ambulance accident, Mary and Pauline sat at the kitchen table. Heads together, they were trying to work through Pauline's Latin homework. Pauline vowed that if she lived to be a hundred, she never would learn to conjugate. Mary believed her. Pauline was far more likely to solve the Latin problem by dropping out of high school. She was just stubborn enough to do it. Mary, who vaguely remembered earning a B-plus in Mr. Johnston's sophomore Latin class, felt it was her sisterly duty to prevent that mistake. Mary couldn't help noticing, however, that no matter how many times they tried a translation, one particularly tricky sentence insisted on coming out as "I shall be about to have been." She feared it was a prophecy.

Outside, they heard a terrible noise. Elmer was in front of the house, astride his idling motorcycle. Through the window, Mary saw it had a sidecar, as if it needed embellishment. He had attracted a crowd of kids, including Walter, who already was studying the cycle with an eye toward bumming a ride. Walter immediately grasped the true value of the nearly new 1936 model 45 Harley-Davidson with its air-cooled V-twin engine and three-speed transmission. Although the engine didn't look particularly astonishing and had unexceptional horsepower, the side-valve design made for great torque. Walter, who knew a thing or two about engines, figured this one must have cost close to $300 new. The cycle was a beauty, a true breakthrough for Harley-Davidson, for engines in general, and, if you stopped to consider it, maybe for the whole world. It had a two-into-one exhaust, a speedometer mounted to the fuel tank, and enough chrome, if the sun hit it just right, to spark a brushfire. On the road nothing could catch it.

Mary went out onto the porch. "Betty, you stay back," she called to her five-year-old sister. The kids were inching forward, bewitched by the throbbing engine.

Elmer cut the engine and called, "Do you know how to get to the hospital?"

"You don't look sick," she said.

He looked like an adventure. He had a pugnacious set to his chin, as if he'd recently been insulted or expected to be imminently. In addition to the mustache (clearly he meant to remind people of Clark Gable), his smile curled up one side of his mouth. The effect was attractive.

"Want a ride, Mary?"

The sidecar did not look overly clean (it turned out to be the place where Elmer stored his tools). A greasy wrench was on the seat. But it sounded like a more attractive proposition than a ride in the ambulance.

"Who would sit in that thing?" she asked.

She climbed in.

There weren't many places in town to go on a double date: a restaurant or two, the movies, or a dance. One Friday night Mary and Pauline stood in the doorway to the gym and squinted into dim light. Pauline saw her beau first, waved to him across the room, and disappeared into the crowd. So far the brand-new high school gymnasium had not improved the varsity basketball team's league standing to any measurable extent. But the first string of the Martin Purple Flash joked that at least their personal win-loss records had improved, thanks to the regular dances. There weren't a lot of decorations to disguise the cavernous space—nobody in Martin had money for that sort of thing during the Depression—and even if there had been, no amount of streamers or confetti would have camouflaged the scent of a freshly varnished gym floor. People donated a few chairs and card tables to grace the edge of the dance floor, and there was a punch bowl.

Mary could see Alma in a gingham dress her mother had made. She was with Junior and, leaning against the wall, Elmer. Mary headed toward them. In Martin, this constituted a double date.

Alma was compact and quick, the best dancer in town. She could follow anybody. As Tavis Flannery patrolled the perimeter of the gymnasium, slow waltzes filled the air, courtesy of a phonograph. "Blue Moon" was a favorite. As Tavis walked by, only a few went out of their way to greet him. Elmer was one of them.

Mary's parents disapproved of Elmer. It hadn't taken long after Mary's first ride on Elmer's Harley for word to get around town. Much of the news about Elmer was disturbing, and every bit of it seemed to reach Fred. It was hard to know the source of his information. He could have gotten it from the men in the yard, or from a conductor who had heard it on the platform of the depot at Allen, even at the barbershop across the street from the tracks. Maybe he picked it up at the bunkhouse, where through-freight crews laid over for an eight-hour rest, which they generally spent playing poker, eating bologna sandwiches, and catching up on gossip. Talk was that Elmer was a bootlegger, and that he hauled whiskey in from Quicksand Creek in Harlan County. Also, he liked to race cycles on the steep hill behind Powderhouse Hollow and bet on the outcome. A few years ago his father had been murdered at Garrett during a family feud that had involved Elmer.

Hesta decided not to stand in the way. If Mary had asked for her opinion, Hesta might have given it, though, and here is what she would have said: "You never forget your first love." That was the kind of pronouncement she often uttered to her daughters in a melancholy voice, with a faraway look in her eyes. Hesta's own first love, a West Virginia boy named Kenner Young, had appeared on her doorstep the night before she married Fred. He brought her a book, and on the flyleaf was written, "If you ever need me, all you have to do is call me." Hesta appreciated the romance of the gesture, but it did not sway her. Kenner Young was first-boyfriend material, period. That's how she viewed Elmer Wolverton, as well. As Mary's first real romance, he'd make good memories. But Mary didn't ask her mother's advice. Mary was eighteen, and Hesta figured that if she wanted to throw her life away, that was her business.

It was up to Fred to warn Mary. One night, before a dance, he had looked up from his newspaper while Mary was searching for a lost earring, and remarked that Elmer didn't look like the type to dance. Mary asked how Fred and Hesta had met. Fred didn't want her to change the subject, but he knew that any time a father criticized a daughter's boyfriend, she would be determined to prove him wrong. He didn't answer, and resumed reading his newspaper. When he looked up, she was still standing there, the child who always wanted his blessing. This time he couldn't give it. He knew it was useless, but he took a pull from his pipe and said, "Mary, you could burn hell and sift the ashes and not do any worse than Elmer."

Mary had never before considered the possibility of rebelling. Even now, there were so many other boys—nice boys, safe choices—for her to consider. Mary's old friend Pid Pelphrey had a brother named Redmon who came down with Pid to spend weekends at the Mynhiers' house. The Pelphreys were a fine, respectable family from Henclip. Anybody could see Redmon still had a crush on Mary—he would have had to, to explain his willingness to drive Pid all the way from the next county, wouldn't he? He was tall. He was friendly to Mary's little brothers. But, as Mary pointed out, although those qualities would have been very useful if Redmon were running for sheriff, they didn't necessarily make him a candidate for romance. She'd also shown a marked lack of interest in the classmates with whom they'd graduated, including Dick Evans, who had played the wealthy millionaire in the school play *Two Days to Marry* and who was generally a lot of fun. Nor had she fallen for McClellan Martin, a mainstay of the basketball team. Or even Otto Frazier, who'd been class president and who prided himself on dignified behavior. (What was wrong with Otto? Mary had pointed out that, for one thing, his chief hobby was hitchhiking to other towns to see motion pictures.) Those boys crashed the girls' taffy pulls or showed up under an open window at a slumber party in search of a "nice sweetheart." It was a description that fit Mary, whether she liked it or not. Of all the girls in the Martin High School class of 1935, Mary had seemed the most likely to succeed, after Ora Mae McGlothen, who had gone off to college in Pikeville. Mary might even become head nurse some day. It was hard to imagine a man like Elmer Wolverton fitting into that future.

It was Mary this, and Mary that. Elmer was crazy about her and when he wanted to meet her, he sent word through Walter, who at age thirteen enjoyed the clandestine work of delivering the lovers' notes. Elmer and Mary went to parties, where suddenly the same old hand-cranked ice cream tasted fun again. They sat in the shade of Alma's porch and pulled taffy, butter all over their hands so the candy wouldn't stick. Pid Pelphrey came to town, and one night they all went to a party together where they played post office in a closet. At one point Pid was in there with Elmer. Later, Mary tried to tell Pauline about it, but she was laughing so hard that the words came out wrong. "Elmer and Kid were pissing," she said, and they both doubled over at the image. When Mary was with Elmer, riding at breakneck speed in the hills after dark with nothing but the big round headlight to show the way, she could forget her responsibilities at home. She might prefer a life that did not require her to take care of her mother's five younger children. All it took to escape, Mary saw, was to walk out onto the hospital steps in the twilight and to listen, for a minute, for the familiar roar of the dragon as it approached.

One night in early April, Mary told her parents she was going to sleep at Alma's. There was nothing unusual about that. Alma's mother, Frances, was a warm, round woman who liked to cook for the girls. At dusk Mary appeared at the Jarrells' doorstep. She cracked the door and peered into the kitchen to make sure Alma was present—and alone—before announcing, "We need a witness. Will you come with us?"

Getting married was a crazy idea. But Mary was determined to elope with Elmer. Alma didn't want Mary to get married, partly because she herself wasn't yet married and partly because Elmer was wrong for her, it was clear. But Alma didn't like to interfere. Mary said Elmer had a car.

Elmer was the type to have a car, all right. Mary sounded so excited. It was after dark, and a ride to Paintsville, the county seat in Johnson County, would take nearly an hour even on the newly paved road. Mary said Elmer knew a preacher.

Nobody had time to dress up. The three piled into a jalopy and took off. It was too dark to see the landscape that hurtled past like a motion picture, but the windows were open and the air smelled like new leaves and fresh-turned earth. The girls' hair flicked their faces, and it was impossible not to be excited, not to feel the rush of fate and destiny hitting them on the black road. It felt as if they traveled a thousand miles, at least, from where they started. Elmer knew where to go. They already had a marriage license, and Elmer drove to the home of Burns Conley. He was minister of the Free Will Baptist Church and lived in downtown Paintsville.

Reverend Conley was not expecting them, Alma noticed, but he didn't seem to mind, either. The reverend's wife, Minty, had died years ago, but he remembered young love fondly and was glad to aid its cause. Or maybe he just believed in preventing impending sin. He was an old man with a high, wide forehead and deep-set eyes that searched their faces for doubt.

They stood in a warmly lighted room. The bride and groom arranged themselves in front of him, Alma to the left of Mary, and before a minute passed, it was I do, I do, and it was over. Getting pierced ears caused more of a fuss than getting married, apparently. It happened so fast and Alma was so upset that afterward she never remembered the moment when she signed her name as a witness on the marriage bond.

Full names of parties, Husband: Elmer B. Wolverton
                         Wife: Mary Elizabeth Mynhier
Age of Husband: 25 years; Condition: Divorced.
Age of Wife: 21 years; Condition: Single.

If adding three years to her age gave Mary a twinge of guilt, she didn't say so. They drove home slower. When they reached Alma's

Mary Mynhier
at eighteen, when
she met Elmer

Elmer Wolverton
at twenty-five,
when he met
Mary in 1937

house and the headlights shone on the chicken coop, Mary said she couldn't go home. She couldn't face her parents yet. Alma's mother took it in stride and said the newlyweds could spend the night at the Jarrells' house. But later, out of Elmer's earshot, Alma's mother hissed her disapproval of him: "That old man."

CHAPTER 6

Elmer could listen to an engine and know from the sound exactly what was wrong with a car. When he decided to go into the service-station business on Main Street, Mary thought her new husband's economic prospects were excellent. Auto repair was a growth industry; in those days, the car was evolving as quickly as the personal computer would in the 1990s. Just when a mechanic had mastered everything there was to know about how an auto worked, Buick introduced a new feature called flasher turn signals. Pontiac announced the first column-mounted gearshift, and Packard even started selling a model with a refrigeration system, air-conditioning in an auto.

Elmer confronted this progress from a crouched position. He couldn't afford a hydraulic lift, so when a job called for a mechanic to get under a car, Elmer drove the vehicle up a ramp and shimmied beneath. He listened to the engine above him for a while, and then, after he had intuited the problem from, say, an off-key pinging sound, he climbed back out for the proper tools. There was no place he felt more comfortable than under a car.

Every car had personality quirks. Elmer understood them all. Lawrence Keathley, who owned the movie theater, was always fussing over a late-model Chrysler. Other big shots, like the doctors in town, drove Buicks or Cadillacs or Lincolns. Even Dick Osborn had a Model T Ford, bought over Myrtle's frugal objections. He drove with such abandon that from the passenger seat Myrt was reduced to repeating herself like a parrot: "Dick, you're going too fast. Dick, you're going too fast." Dick, whistling, tried not to respond. "Dick, I *said* you're going too fast."

He took his eyes off the road to look at her. The car veered wildly as Dick said mildly, "Well, Myrtle, I'm not going any faster than you are." Since Dick never mastered such finer points of driving as "reverse," he was always backing the car into Myrt's roses or dinging it on a fence. Dick always looked and acted as if he'd just stepped out of a comic strip. "Hey, Lordy," he'd say, and scratch his head in consternation. It was easy to imagine a bubble above his head that said, "#$%!!" However, the collisions rarely caused major damage; Dick didn't bother fixing most of the dents.

As a rule, pricier cars returned to the dealership for service, even if that meant a trip to Prestonsburg. One notable exception was a black Lincoln Zephyr in Elmer's parking lot. It was a beautiful, streamlined car, with a stately hood that looked like a ship's prow. To the casual observer, the Lincoln didn't look as if it needed repair. The paint shone, the chrome gleamed, and the engine was as clean as the day it had left the factory. Whoever owned the car babied it; the Lincoln came in for service so often that Elmer got into the habit of moving it like a chess piece on the tightly packed lot, so he could get to other pawns that needed his more immediate attention.

One day, as he was hanging the Lincoln's keys on the pegboard in the office, he glanced out the window and saw a regular customer named Johnny* loping toward the garage. Johnny never needed gas or a tune-up or spark plugs. In fact, he didn't even own a car. He was a railroader, just like his father, and the only vehicle in which he traveled routinely was a locomotive. The reason he came to Elmer's garage was to buy moonshine.

Elmer wiped the grease from his hands, tossed the rag into the corner, and greeted him.

"Don't have any," Elmer said.

This was almost surely a lie. The soda pop freezer in the back of the garage was usually full of moonshine. Although Elmer was the best mechanic in Martin, his true calling was his night job: bootlegging. He had a gift for running liquor. Sometimes he took Mary's brother Walter along on midnight motorcycle rides up Right Beaver, across the county

---

* Not his real name.

line, into a little indentation in the hillside that was called Royal Holler. There was a cluster of company houses he remembered from the days when his family had once lived nearby. (The Wolvertons moved so often that there was barely a hollow in eastern Kentucky that they had not "once lived nearby.") Up the road past where the Wolvertons had lived briefly on a little farm, past where Elmer's brother Joe had smoked his first cigarette, was a certain shack. Another of his brothers, Mose, used to buy moonshine there, direct from the manufacturer. Elmer usually sent Walter to the door to say that Mose had sent them—an introduction calculated to save them from being shot—and to see if the moonshiner was home. Often he wasn't. To find him, Elmer and Walter hiked into the woods beyond the shack, following the bends in a nearby creek, until they reached the still. They waded through the underbrush on a narrow path, buggy and muggy and full of mosquitoes along the muddy slope. They bought as many jugs of liquor as they could carry up a steep creek bank—a strong boy like Walter came in handy here, as well—and returned to the motorcycle for a more careful, gentle ride home. Elmer had never lost a jug to the road.

Walter, who thought it was a great adventure, was happy to risk getting shot for the opportunity to ride his brother-in-law's motorcycle all the way to Harlan County. On the way back, along the old road they passed little shacks that Elmer pointed out as "ginny barns," featuring a jukebox and just enough floor space to dance and get drunk. Ginny barns came and went; the ones that stayed in business longest had proprietors who were smart enough to bribe the local cops with a bottle or two of whiskey. The establishments were always open, day or night, and some would sell a sandwich to accompany the moonshine. After a long night ride, Elmer liked to stop at one down near Garrett, which had a hot-dog grill. Elmer made Walter promise not to tell Mary.

At his garage, Elmer would decant the moonshine into smaller containers—pint jars and fifths—before he went home to bed.

"Just a pint," Johnny pleaded. He was antsy. He played basketball in high school, and when he got nervous he started to shift from foot to foot as if he were dribbling. He was taller and darker and skinnier, by far, than Elmer. But when the two stood facing each other, the first thing anybody noticed was that Johnny looked frail.

Elmer did not like him. The problem was that when he drank, he got helpless. He talked too much. He was likely to tell anybody who asked— or anybody who didn't—exactly where he'd bought his liquor and how much he'd paid (four dollars for a pint, seven dollars for a fifth were Elmer's standard prices). The last time Elmer had sold liquor to him, he had even managed to get arrested with the booze in his possession.

"Get out," Elmer said.

There was no point in arguing with Elmer. There was no point in threatening him either, especially not if you were a skinny, scared-looking kid. So Johnny didn't say, "You'll be sorry," or "Sell me some, or else," or anything like that. But his need showed in his eyes.

Elmer spit a plug of tobacco onto the ground and took a step forward.

Johnny skittered off the property. He knew better than to antagonize a member of the Wolverton family. Although Elmer had arrived in Martin as a mystery on a motorcycle, the Wolvertons had a reputation in town. They were the family that killed one another. Elmer's father had been murdered a few years back by one of Elmer's uncles—who had been aiming for Elmer. Although her brother's behavior had saddened Elmer's mother for many reasons, the violence had not particularly surprised Amanda Wolverton. As one of my relatives described the family many decades later, "Amanda had three brothers and they all were trouble. The easiest way to tell them apart was that Daniel would shoot you in the face, Ed would bushwhack you, and Charlie would kill you any way he could. Once he used a fire poker that belonged to his victim."

I wonder if my grandmother had any idea of what she was getting into when she married Elmer. He was the oldest of nine children and liked to say he was born in a tent. Whether this was true mattered less to him than having people believe it was. It was certainly true that in Elmer's youth his father worked as a cowboy in Oklahoma; with a tent it was easy to pack up and follow the herd. Now the Wolvertons followed Amanda, who currently rented a white frame house on the outskirts of Martin, in a neighborhood called Cracker Bottom. Amanda's oldest sons were prone to bar fights and to pulling guns. All the children resembled Amanda insofar as they did not smile much, neither with their mouths nor with their snappy dark eyes. Life had not given them much to smile about. As a mother-in-law, Amanda made a lasting impression, in the same harsh way that a crow attracts attention. She had coarse black hair pulled into a severe knot, an aquiline nose, and a complexion that confirmed that her grandmother had been a Cherokee. Her hands were partially frozen in the shape of claws, the result of a childhood mishap. One of her brothers had pushed her into a burning fireplace.

How the Wolvertons had ended up in Martin was a puzzle. Bake sales and church socials and barbershop gossip did not attract them. Martin was a place of PTA intrigue and of life-or-death high school basketball games attended religiously by the general populace. The Wolvertons were at home in more isolated places along the branches of Beaver Creek, on the outskirts of the mining towns—like McDowell, Lackey, and Garrett—that had earned Bloody Floyd its nickname. In Martin, Friday was tonsillectomy day and Saturday was matinee day. Children could play in the streets without getting shot because the citizenry had entered into a pact to endorse the headstrong dictates of men like Officer Tavis Flannery in exchange for order.

Elmer didn't appreciate those nuances. He'd lived a nomadic childhood; his father moved the family from state to state in an attempt to stay one step ahead of the Depression. Elmer's formal education had ended with expulsion, after a fistfight with his eighth-grade teacher. (The teacher lost the fight.) The rest of his education was self-taught. Car engines, refrigerator motors, busted phonographs—he learned to put them back together. Of all machines, he loved cars most. As a teenager, Elmer had spent a few dollars to slowly amass all the necessary components to build his own. He bought an engine, spoke wheels, a steering wheel, and when he was sixteen, he built from scratch a car that ran. It was ugly. It made a lot of noise. He loved it.

After Johnny left, Elmer went to work on a carburetor. He was so intent that he didn't even hear the men come into the garage until one spoke.

"Morning, Elmer."

He hated a surprise visit, especially from representatives of the county sheriff. The two who stood in his garage weren't in uniform, but he recognized deputies when he saw them. Bootleggers made it part of their business to know by sight the scads of deputies whose primary duty was to catch them. With shakedowns and bribes, deputy was a full-time job.

Elmer looked up briefly.

"Got a minute?" the talkative deputy asked.

"No," Elmer said. "Fella wants the car by noon."

Elmer never promised a car by noon. In fact, he never promised a car at any specific time or on any specific date. He worked on a car until it was fixed, and a customer could collect it then and not a moment sooner. Everybody in town knew this policy. A few seconds passed. The deputies didn't move and Elmer didn't put down his wrench.

"The thing is," the deputy said, "we got a report to check out."

Elmer stood. "What kind of a report?"

"Illegal sale of alcohol."

"Not here," Elmer said. He made an elaborate show of looking over his shoulder to inspect the far corners of the garage. All he could see was a big tin building with a sliding door. It was clean, not cluttered, with all the tools in their place. Elmer had two potbellied stoves, for heat and to speed the drying of paint. He had an air compressor. Along one wall was a workbench. The garage was quiet, not a place where people went to socialize or to have a conversation. The only people who stayed around Elmer's garage were customers, for repair or booze.

"Mind if we have a look around?"

"Hell yes, I mind," Elmer said. "I have a business to run."

"How about take a rest and show us around."

"You got a warrant?"

They did.

"What's in the cooler?" the deputies asked.

"Look yourself," Elmer said. His head disappeared under the hood.

The deputies exchanged looks. They were uneasy looks. Although they represented the law and therefore considered themselves well within their rights to rummage around a man's private property, the law was a technicality compared to the reality of the situation. Poking through Elmer Wolverton's garage—which could only rile him up—wasn't a job they relished. Elmer was an exotic species; he hadn't grown up in or around Martin, hadn't attended school with the deputies or any of their brothers, hadn't joined a local church or the Masons' lodge or the golf club over at Allen. They didn't know enough about him to know how far they could push him without provoking real trouble. All they knew was what everybody in town knew, that the Wolverton boys had never backed down from a fight, not since the day when the family had first been spotted in Floyd County, arriving in curious style in 1929. In those days, the unpaved roads up Left Beaver branch were so rutted and treacherous that the Wolvertons—who had ridden the five hundred miles from Detroit in a caravan of cars—had driven along in the creek bed. They'd simply picked a low spot where the bank wasn't too steep. In the creek, which was nearly dry, the main impediments besides rocks were holes deep enough to swallow a wheel. More than once, a farmer with a mule had to aid the cause. The obstacles hadn't daunted the Wolvertons, who attracted a number of spectators interested to see the very first autos to navigate that isolated region. Elmer had driven the lead car.

The deputies walked slowly to the cooler. They lifted the lid. Inside, they confronted the evidence: dozens of bottles of soda pop, stacked in neat rows. Orange Nehi, strawberry pop, Coca-Cola.

"It's a nickel apiece," Elmer called. "You need a bottle opener, let me know."

The talkative deputy blushed. He was the one who also had a temper. He didn't relish having to go back to the sheriff's office to report having been made a fool. Plus, he'd already mentally spent the commission he'd earn off Elmer's fine. So he asked bluntly, "Where'd you hide it?"

"Hide what?" Elmer said.

"Open the trunks," the deputy said. He gestured to the parking lot, where nearly a dozen cars had been angled in to fit like so many jigsaw pieces.

"Which one?" Elmer asked.

"All of them."

Elmer took his time walking to the pegboard to get the keys. "You're wasting your time," he said. It wasn't so much a commentary on the proceedings as it was a warning.

"Open them."

One by one, Elmer unlocked the trunks—a Ford, a Chrysler, another Ford—to reveal contraband no more damning than the odd spare tire.

"That's it," Elmer said.

"What about the Lincoln?" the deputy asked. He pointed to the Zephyr, which had no earthly reason to be parked in the far corner of a local garage instead of on Harry Ranier's Lincoln lot in Prestonsburg.

"Sticks out like a sore thumb," the other deputy agreed, admiring the ostentatious hood ornament.

"Now we got a chorus," Elmer said.

"Open it," the talkative deputy said.

"Can't," Elmer said. "The guy didn't even trust me with the keys." The pegboard was empty.

"We want to see what's in that trunk," the deputy said.

Elmer shrugged.

"Get a crowbar," the deputy said.

"Don't have one," Elmer said.

"You don't have a crowbar? You're a mechanic without a crowbar?"

"It's the damnedest thing," Elmer agreed.

The deputies had a crowbar in their trunk.

Elmer stood with his hands jammed in the pockets of his overalls, watching them slip the prongs under the lip. The trunk lid was heavier and thicker than they expected; they scratched the chrome and tore the car all to hell before it popped. It was the sort of extensive damage that even a talented bodywork man would have to spend hours fixing. It was the sort of time-consuming repair that any garage owner would begrudge doing for free.

Inside was treasure—a dozen or more clear glass jars full of clear liquid. The talkative deputy unscrewed a lid, dipped a finger, sniffed, and tasted.

"Will you look at that?" Elmer said, as if marveling at a particularly miraculous sunset.

"You're under arrest," the deputy said.

"It's not mine," Elmer said.

"It's your garage," the deputy said.

Elmer shrugged and went to get his jacket.

He spent the rest of the morning in county jail, sitting on the edge of a cot in a cell and contemplating with great interest the dirt under his fingernails and the dirt lodged in the cracked calluses of his hands. After lunch, the deputies told him the judge had been located. Elmer appeared before the bench, pleaded not guilty, heard the county judge say, "Guilty," and agreed to pay a fine of $100. It was a lot of dough; if he'd been arrested for public drunkenness, he'd have gotten off for $20, and even driving under the influence wouldn't have cost more than $50. But bootleggers could easily afford $100. He slowly counted out bills.

An hour later, he was back in business.

At the garage, he walked deliberately into the office. He closed the door and sat in the desk chair and stood up again. He kicked the metal wastebasket as hard as he could. Even if he hadn't been wearing work boots with a reinforced toe, the vicious force of the blow would have crumpled the metal like paper. But it was probably the work boots that gave the wastebasket enough added velocity to fly up into the air and slam into the wall next to the pegboard.

Elmer took the Lincoln's keys out of his pocket and walked to inspect the damage. It gave him a sick feeling in his stomach. He hadn't been so powerless since the night his dad died.

The last surviving witness to James Wolverton's murder was Elmer's younger brother Joe. Seventy years later, he was eighty-one years old and living in Birmingham, Alabama, when I phoned to ask him to show me the spot where it happened.

"I haven't been back to Garrett in sixty years," he said. There was a small silence on the line. Then he said, "Can you meet me there in early October?"

Garrett was a town that felt the effects of the Great Depression long before the Depression officially started. The town was dependent on the coal mines for its livelihood; when that industry went sour in the 1920s, life turned desperate in Garrett. Decades later, things hadn't improved.

My uncle Joe had a big, bouncy American sedan. In it, we sidled down Garrett's main street, parallel to the railroad tracks that used to bring passengers and supplies to town. The tracks looked lonely and forlorn. At a ramshackle brown, two-story house, Joe stopped. "We lived there for a while, after the old man broke his leg in the mines and he wanted to be compensated and they said no and blackballed him," Joe said. "So he took to bootlegging when we lived in that house. He took an old dynamite box and cut off the top to make a dry sink. He hid his whiskey down in the box."

Joe passed more dilapidated buildings and crossed the tracks— "Used to be stores along here, and a restaurant"—to get onto the old highway. About two miles south of town, he braked and made a sharp right turn onto what appeared to be a sheer drop off the side of the road. If anybody else had been driving, I would have been alarmed. But Joe, who bore an uncanny resemblance to my grandfather, also drove like him. He rode a car the way other men ride horses: as if communicating with a living, breathing creature that could answer back. We dipped and were on a steep lip of a meandering dirt road. Weeds grew alongside. Beyond was a precarious relic of a swinging bridge. The bridge was barely wide enough for a car. We swayed across.

"This is where we moved later on," Joe said. "My dream for Christmas was to have a little red Radio Flyer wagon. I used to look at it in the catalog. Never did get it. There never was money. I made my own instead. I used roller skates for the wheels."

We passed grayed buildings that looked like heaps of scrap lumber. None was familiar to Joe. A mile farther, the road ended at the railroad tracks. Now there was nothing to see but underbrush and weeds alongside the trestle. We'd reached a dead end.

"We must have passed the house," Joe said, executing a smooth K-turn. We backtracked to the first ghost house on the left. Joe shifted into park and squinted to bring the past into focus. Finally he said, "It used to have a front porch."

Across the road, the house where Elmer's sweetheart lived in 1932 had disappeared. He searched his memory for her name. "Pauline Owens?"

I calculated the distance between the two houses—a couple of hundred yards at most—and thought about what had happened in the road between them. We were parked pretty nearly on the spot where James Wolverton was shot.

"There was no snow," Joe said. "It was very cold, though. And it was about dark."

That long-ago evening, Amanda's brother Ed—he was the sneaky one—walked down the road toward the Wolvertons' house. He'd been feeling sour even before he started drinking, and hours later had worked himself into a black disposition. His main grievance was his nephew Elmer.

Seventy years later, the details of Ed's complaint are heartbreaking in their trivia. Elmer, who was twenty-one years old, had embarrassed Ed's son in public—over a baby-sitting debt to Elmer's sister. Elmer had threatened to whip Ed's son if he didn't pay. Ever since, Ed Thomas had plotted revenge against Elmer.

We sat in the car. I imagined Ed's eyes adjusting to the dusk. Ed could see his breath. He also could see into Pauline Owens's house across the street, where light from the front window cast a glow into the road. Inside, Elmer stood framed in golden light, hanging curtains for his girlfriend. Ed would have had plenty of time to contemplate the excellent view of Elmer as bull's-eye. Ed could see in but Elmer could not see out. Ed probably could have walked right up to that window and pressed his face to the cold glass before Elmer noticed a surprise visitor.

Maybe Ed wanted to test the theory. As he walked toward the house, one of his nieces came out onto the porch. Rexine was sixteen years old and understood the danger immediately. She ran, but not fast enough to head off Ed before he reached the Owens house. He climbed the steps and pulled his gun. Ed always carried a pistol.

What happened next became part of the official court record. As Ed aimed at Elmer through the glass, Rexine grabbed her uncle around the waist. She reached for Ed's gun. She started to yell. The two tussled for the pistol, knocking into the porch railing and wrestling down the steps to the street.

The younger Wolverton children, including Joe, came running onto their porch in time to see Ed and Rexine cursing at each other.

The Wolvertons' front door opened again. James walked out.

"Ed, we don't want to have any trouble," James said.

James stepped down from the porch to the street. Ed glanced up to see his brother-in-law walking, slowly, with one hand outstretched for the gun.

"Ed, you should go home," James said.

Normally James's moderate manner had a calming effect on his in-laws. But this time, Ed jerked away from Rexine, leveled the pistol at James, and pulled the trigger.

It shocked everybody. What made Ed shoot? The best explanation he could come up with, years later, was a lie. "Self-defense," he would tell a jury.

At the sound, Elmer dropped a curtain onto the floor and ran into the street. Amanda ran from the kitchen, holding a spoon, to see what the fuss was about.

The bullet knocked James down. For a moment, everyone was frozen in place, as if they were posed in a snapshot of a distant land no one believed in.

James rose. He turned toward the house. He walked at a steady, un-hurried pace, as if he were returning home from a shift in the mines, or had forgotten his pipe, or just wanted to get his fiddle. Nearly every Saturday night and Sunday afternoon, James sat on the porch to play old country songs like "Maple on the Hill," "Cripple Creek," and "Boil Them Cabbage Down." When James sang, the words came out like, "Bile them cabbage down, boys," and in that twang it was possible to hear his longing for a different kind of life. Passersby walked up and sat on the steps to listen, without saying hello or nodding. It was as if they were enchanted. James liked waltzes better than anything, tunes like "Anniversary Waltz," and "The Blue Danube," and "The Missouri Waltz." His music coaxed the neighbors into a curious kind of a dance. Men hopped around without partners, knees pumping to their chests in a motion that James called a "hillbilly jig." They danced until the music stopped. Sometimes they danced all night.

Tonight James walked up the porch steps. His disappearance into the house broke the spell on the onlookers. Ed shook off Rexine, and walked quickly down the road toward the railroad tracks. By the time James emerged from the house with a rifle, Ed was gone.

James collapsed again, on the porch. A bloodstain appeared on his right side, near the waist, a dark soaking mess that spread and spoiled his clothes. Elmer grabbed his father's rifle, but before he could chase Ed, Amanda said, "No, let's take care of Jim."

She sent one of her boys for Doc Walk. She told the others to carry their father to the bed. By then, James's overalls were drenched and blood puddled on the floor. She told the girls to find clean rags and to tear them into strips. She told her husband he would be fine.

An hour later, Doc Walk arrived, tied his horse to the porch rail, and stomped into the house.

After a quick examination, Doc Walk told James the wound was most likely superficial. He changed the bandages, which were soaked already. James looked weak but nodded.

On the porch, Doc Walk told Amanda the bullet was lodged "right close up to the spine," too close to remove. He said it had hit a big artery. Then he left.

James bled to death that night. He was thirty-seven years old.

My uncle Joe, who was eleven years old the night his father died, left Kentucky for good before he was twenty. After the war, he became an electrician, moved north, and raised a family in a different kind of a town that people called a "suburb." Nearly seventy years had passed since the day he had climbed the hill to the graveyard, a pallbearer barely able to keep up with his older brothers as they carried his father's casket up a steep incline. As we walked up that same dirt road now, wet leaves slicked the walkway and a dismal layer of fog hovered. The air was muggy. Joe climbed the hill as if it were flat. At the crest, there was no sign for the old cemetery, just a few haphazard rows of headstones listing this way and that. He searched for landmarks—a certain tree, a ragged iron fence, a concrete crypt he remembered—and walked without hesitation to a spot in the center of the graveyard. Years earlier, before the trees grew so tall, it would have commanded a fine view of the rolling hills and valleys of Right Beaver branch. Joe stared at the weeds and the dirt and the clotted leaves caught in the high, stringy grass. There was no marker. "There's our dad," he said.

At the garage, Elmer contemplated the damage done to the Lincoln. He slid into the driver's seat—the leather upholstery was smooth and smelled expensive—and gripped the steering wheel briefly. He could just drive the hell out of here and never come back. He had that choice.

The Lincoln could wait. Instead he drove uptown looking for Johnny. Through a restaurant window, he saw him at a table near the ice-cream freezer. Johnny was eating a burger.

Elmer opened the door, which announced his presence with a bell that had a misleadingly cheery jangle, and walked to the table. He picked up Johnny like a kitten. With one hand, Elmer lifted him by the nape of his neck.

"Snitch," Elmer said.

Johnny said no, he wasn't, he didn't even know what Elmer was talking about, why was Elmer mad all of a sudden, leave me alone. Besides, it wasn't his fault; he only snitched on Elmer after the cops caught him with some whiskey and told him they'd let him go if he revealed his usual source. It was nothing personal; he hadn't snitched on Elmer for revenge. He was used to bootleggers' refusing to sell to him.

None of this talk calmed Elmer.

Fighting back wasn't an option for Johnny; hitting Elmer would be about as effective as smashing a fist into the chrome grille of the Lincoln Zephyr.

"Snitch," Elmer said, while he considered how to remedy the situation.

With his other hand, he punched Johnny in the face.

Still holding him, Elmer walked to the ice-cream chest. As if there were no hurry, he opened the lid and dropped in Johnny, who hit his head hard. The impact knocked him unconscious.

Elmer flipped down the freezer lid. All that was visible of Johnny were his legs and feet, dangling.

"He'll melt your ice cream," Elmer said to the proprietor.

Elmer walked back to the service station. One by one, he moved the cars in the lot, until he had enough open space to maneuver the Lincoln into the garage. He climbed underneath. He lay on the cement for a while, listening to nothing.

From above, he heard the voice of one of his best customers.

"Elmer?" It was more of a growl than a voice. "You in here?"

He slid out from beneath the car and stood to face his best customer.

"I don't have any 'shine," Elmer said to Officer Tavis Flannery. "Come back tomorrow."

CHAPTER 7

W*alter scrunched up on the cracked leather of a passenger*
seat, his window rolled down to compensate for the driver's lack of a recent bath. Every time the car hit a bump, it rattled his teeth. Hitchhik-
ers had no right to complain. Walter, who for the past few minutes had
been counting squashed windshield bugs, turned toward the open air,
gulping in smells of summer and baked dirt. As a perfume, it was
preferable to perspiration. The car rounded a bend, and there was
Pound Mountain, a substantial wonder of the natural world that separated Kentucky from Virginia, extending for more than one hundred
miles in either direction. Such a severe geographic impediment explained the isolation of Kentucky's hill towns. As recently as the nineteenth century, even some of Virginia's most soil-starved farmers had
been reluctant to brave the mountain; the only route through it that
anybody knew of was Pound Gap, a natural fault where sheer walls of
exposed sandstone brushed against the sky. At the foot of the mountain,
on the Kentucky side, lay Jenkins, a coal town built practically on top of
an old Civil War battleground. Down the main street, into the heart of
Jenkins, rode the hitchhiker. If he'd chosen to climb the mountain, he
could have seen Virginia. Instead, Walter asked the driver to let him out
at the corner.

"By the rec hall," he said.

At fifteen, Walter was reckless. He would do nearly anything or go
nearly anywhere, anytime, just for the novelty. He had never been to
Jenkins before, had never seen the fancy redbrick building to which he
was gesturing so confidently, and, now that he thought about it, had

never had the slightest urge to even visit Letcher County. As far as he was concerned, that was no reason not to come. He lived by whim. Once he had hitched all the way to Virginia and back for pie. In comparison, traveling fifty-five hot miles from Martin to a coal town that was just like every other coal town was sensible. His purpose was greater than pie. Mary lived here.

"Here?" the driver asked.

Not exactly. Mary and Elmer lived somewhere on the outskirts with the rest of the miners' families, in a narrow hollow lined with rows of shotgun houses that even the inhabitants had a hard time telling apart. Although they'd moved here months ago, after Elmer had gotten restless and closed down his garage in Martin, Walter was vague about the exact location. But "here" was close enough.

"Thanks."

Walter swung lightly from the car, a lanky boy with neither luggage nor cash to encumber him. It was past noon; the sandwich he'd crammed into his pocket at dawn was a dim memory.

A coal company had built Jenkins overnight. Did a nice job of it too. This Main Street was grander than Martin's, wide and paved and lined with maples. Along with the usual features of an eastern Kentucky downtown—post office, beauty shop, and restaurant—Jenkins boasted a vine-covered drugstore and a two-story jail with a peaked roof. The rec hall was three stories high, with a bowling alley and hotel rooms on the top floors. Ten thousand people lived in town. Most worked in the mines. Bosses lived in gracious houses in a neighborhood called Lakeside Drive. The rest weren't rich enough to live in a "neighborhood"; they lived in "sections." There was Goodwater Section, Gaskell, Burdine. Mary's section was Wheaton Hollow. From there, it was an easy walk to Mine Shafts Nos. 3 and 4.

Walter saw the turnoff from Lakeside Drive, just where Mary had described it, a steep road that headed in the opposite direction from the mansions. He walked slowly, searching each two-family house for clues to his sister. She remained elusive; he didn't see a trace in the identical front porches or the blank windows. The only sign of personality flapped on clotheslines. Sheets, shirts, aprons—everybody's were different. It was laundry day.

He heard cursing. It was familiar, comfortable cursing, delivered in the half-amused tone of someone who was used to winning arguments with inanimate objects. He rounded a bend and saw Mary threatening a washtub.

She was on her back porch, standing—or rather hunching—over a witch's cauldron. Steam rose from the water. Her hands were red. She scrubbed a pair of Elmer's heavy work pants. She scrubbed hard. Every bit of her attention was focused on how much she hated those pants. She didn't mind letting them know how she felt either. It was over between her and the pants, whatever they'd once shared was dead as far as she was concerned, on account of the pants' betrayal. They'd gotten dirty—no, filthy—and now they were trying to sully her too. The black water was Mary's lost afternoon. It took her ten minutes or more of rubbing a single pair of pants against a washboard to remove all evidence of the previous day's underground shift. It took a second tub full of fresh hot water to rinse and wring. Each week there were five pairs of pants, five shirts; the day was nearly over before bed linens and baby clothes even came under consideration. Mary wasn't lazy. She'd been doing laundry since she was old enough to reach the clothesline. But she'd never felt the full responsibility for clean clothes until she'd married. Nor had she given a second thought to the messy, complicated process of running a household. In Hesta's house, daughters were trusted agents who had been put on the earth to do their mother's bidding. Their duties were discrete. They scrubbed if Hesta said scrub. They wrung if Hesta said wring. But the burden of coordinating the chores—of ensuring the simultaneous magic of clean clothes and hot meals and dusted furniture—had remained Hesta's alone. Now, for the first time in her life that Mary was eager to understand how Hesta performed a curious alchemy to transform chaos into order, her mother was in a distant town, fifty-five miles away. It was a long fifty-five miles.

Mary blamed the pants. She wrung and flung them, and they landed on a nearby pile of similarly sodden and renounced fabric. Water ran from pants to the edge of the porch, dripping a sad commentary about the state of her homemaking skills onto the weeds below.

"Wash mine next?" Walter called out from thirty feet away.

She turned, not trusting her ears, and smiled wide—for just a second—at the sight of him, as cocky and disheveled as ever. She noticed at that moment that the day was bright, the sun was warm, and the baby was napping.

"Mine could use a bath," he said, gesturing toward his dusty knees.

"What in the hell are you doing here?"

"I've come for something to eat," he said.

She laughed. She couldn't help it.

"You'll eat when we eat."

Two years of marriage had not noticeably changed Mary. She was still pretty, Walter thought, generously overlooking her chapped hands, sweaty ringlets, and missing earring. She'd cut her curly hair short to make it easier to take care of. Her oldest dress was splashed with soapy water. She still looked too thin to be hauling a heavy washtub out of a house on her own. But the only concession she'd made to the day's heavy workload was a lack of lipstick.

She said, "Go inside and grab me another bucket of hot water from the stove."

Walter had a policy about chores. He didn't do them. It wasn't that he preferred idleness; he was always up to something. But since he'd been a child, he had preferred activities that sent him sneaking around the edges of acceptable behavior. He liked to get away with things, always had, from the time he was six years old and spent the nickels Fred gave him for candy on chewing tobacco instead. Somehow Walter managed to evade the consequences for even the worst of his actions, like the time he had accidentally chopped off his cousin Jim's finger. It happened after the two boys, while trying to figure out how to break a piece of tobacco into two, had decided the solution was for Jim to hold down the tobacco while Walter swung a double-bitted ax. A doctor sewed Jim's finger back on and in the confusion, it wasn't until years later that someone bothered to question Jim's cover story about how the ax had slipped while he was doing his chores. Certainly, no one had suspected Walter of voluntarily chopping wood.

"It took me the better part of the day to get over here," he said. "Aren't you glad to see me?"

He tried to look as tired as possible. He didn't have to pretend much. On the highway, people had been good about picking him up, but most weren't going very far. In between rides, he'd waited as long as thirty minutes before he saw a car. He'd made a game of it, trying to guess from the sound of an approaching engine whether the vehicle that was about to come around the bend would be a rattling old Model A or a smooth new Cadillac with leather seats. Delivery trucks were another story. Most companies didn't want the drivers to pick up anyone, so the ones most likely to pull over were men who owned their own pickups. These days there was enough auto traffic to ensure that Walter rarely had to climb into a horse-drawn wagon.

"You do look tired," Mary said.

Walter hoped she'd suggest a nap. She didn't.

"Go inside and grab me another bucket of hot water from the stove," she said. "That'll wake you up."

She'd turned hard. Marriage had ruined his own sister; what a shame, Walter decided. Living with a man like Elmer had broadened her vocabulary. "Goddamn" was a new word for her, its appearance in conversation having been linked to the first time Elmer hadn't shown up for supper. "Sonuvabitch" was terminology that emerged around the time she realized that her husband was prone to disappear for more than a meal; unannounced absences that stretched from days to weeks were natural for Elmer. What she hadn't figured out, during the first two years of her marriage, was why she remained devoted to the god-damned sonuvabitch. Upon his return, when Elmer would offer no ex-cuse other than a terse "I went with the motorcycle club to Virginia," Mary stormed. She cursed. But she never walked out. Now, as she tipped the washtub over the edge of the porch (at least she didn't expect Walter to break his back with that!) a grimy, dark soup of coal dust and squashed insects splashed the dirt below.

Mary knew Walter had no intention of pitching in. His expecta-tions—mischief and loafing—were the same on any day. He was unre-liable and he was evasive. But somehow the same qualities that were such a drawback in a husband seemed rakishly charming in a younger brother. When she'd turned and seen Walter coming lightly up the road with the promise of adventure, Mary had never before been so happy to see someone in her family. The only concern was whether Hesta knew where Walter had gone. And if not—as was likely—who would she blame for her son's disappearance? Mary, probably. Walter could do no wrong. One time, after he'd hitchhiked all the way to Virginia to visit a newlywed Pauline in a different coal town, he'd shown up at the very moment his sister was removing a lemon cake from the oven. Walter ate most of it—he later estimated it must have weighed twenty pounds—and washed it down with sweet milk. He asked for pie, a follow-up request that sent Pauline straight to the nearest phone to report his whereabouts to her mother. Hesta still hadn't forgiven Pauline for kidnapping Walter.

Mary didn't even know how to bake a pie. But she told Walter he could make himself a sandwich.

"Bake me a cake?" he asked.

"No," she said.

"It doesn't have to be lemon," he said to show he wasn't picky.

Mary spent the first hour after Elmer failed to arrive home for supper studiously not burning the beans as Walter entertained her with the gossip from home. Hesta had recently had another baby. Ann was the tenth and final Mynhier child, smart enough even in infancy to know how to get on Hesta's good side. She cried rarely. She sat as placidly as a theatergoer in the kitchen, observing the chaotic plot of the Mynhier family as it unfolded. By 1938, a baby needed something special to charm an old hand like Hesta. Ann was wily enough to avoid precociousness; she walked late.

But there was even bigger news from Martin. Doc Walk Stumbo had been sent to jail, and not just any jail; he'd been sent to a federal penitentiary for pocketing thousands of dollars of federal aid money. Although everyone in town had known about his shenanigans, no one expected him to get caught. Doc Walk in prison constituted a cataclysmic, seismic shift in the social fabric of Martin. The details kept Mary's mind off Elmer's tardiness—if in fact he planned to come home at all—for at least another hour. Although Doc Walk's recent legal travails had been entertaining the county for some months, it was hard to believe he could end up in prison. His life had been a textbook example of the advantages of lineage. His father was a farmer descended from Stambaughs prominent in eastern Kentucky for generations. He'd been raised like Queen Victoria; his destiny was to rule. By the time he was twenty-three, Walker Stumbo had a medical degree and had been performing surgery in a makeshift lean-to near the depot. He'd soon moved on, to ruling the grand operating suite and state-of-the art laboratory at his hospital. Every time Doc Walk rode his horse up to his personal hitching post by the hospital's front stoop, he was reminded of his two greatest advantages. He was by birth a Stumbo, and by temperament a Stumbo who capitalized on opportunity.

In the end, his entrepreneurial nature had done him in. His problems started after he got greedy. From his vantage on the relief commission, he had been struck by how much money was available for the taking. All a person had to do to get a fistful was to fill out two pieces of paper—Form No. 6 and Form No. 7, they called them—and file them with the proper authorities. The commission had a tall, tall stack of the forms. Form No. 6 was a slip of paper a poor person was supposed to present to a participating merchant to request food or clothing. Form No. 7 was the one a shopkeeper subsequently filled out and mailed to Louisville to request reimbursement. Doc Walk saw how efficient it would be to bypass certain steps of the process—the steps that involved distributing merchandise to actual poor people—to claim reimbursement for an enormous amount of money ($381,212.66, it would total in the end), which he figured nobody in Washington would ever miss. Doc Walk gave Form No. 6 to store owners, who listed nonexistent merchandise they said they had supplied to fictitious needy customers, whose signatures they forged. The merchants then mailed Form No. 7, to file a claim for reimbursement, and, after the checks arrived, split the proceeds with relief commission members like Doc Walk and the mayor of Prestonsburg. The manager of the Kroger Grocery and Baking Co. was in on it. So was the general manager of Mayo Cash Grocery and the grocer who ran the Great Savings Store. It was a simple plan, and for eighteen months seemed foolproof. Then the government got wind of the scheme, dubbed it a conspiracy, and indicted Doc Walk and his cronies on twenty-one counts of "purloining, embezzling and misapplying" federal funds. The trial lasted nineteen days, the longest in the history of the Eastern District Court in Kentucky. Even after a jury convicted Doc Walk and sixteen other defendants, no one believed he would go to jail. Minutes after the verdict was delivered, he announced his intention to appeal the case and declared, "This is one man that is not guilty."

A few months later, a federal court of appeals affirmed the convictions. So Doc Walk appealed to the U.S. Supreme Court. A few months later, the Supreme Court declined to review the case. With his options running out, Doc Walk decided the best strategy was to beg the trial judge for leniency. Doc Walk made a list (in which he referred to himself in the third person) of all "the cogent reasons" he did not deserve to go to jail. "They rest, broadly speaking, in the extensive service he has rendered and is now rendering to the citizens of his community," he wrote of himself.

The way Doc Walk saw it, he single-handedly rescued Floyd County from the medical Dark Ages. Before he went to college, the area's only doctors were self-taught farmers like Isaac Goble, a Civil War soldier who served in the infantry's hospital department and who had never read a book on anatomy. Doctors like Yates, who practiced in Louisa in the 1840s, and Cushion, who went to the Falls of Tug a decade earlier than that, dug roots outside a patient's door to brew their medicines during a house call.

"It is not without difficulty, however, that this subject is approached. To proclaim one's own virtues is, for obvious reasons, neither a pleasant nor an easy task," he wrote. "However, trusting the court will not consider it immodest, but rather the result of an existing exigency to do so, petitioner will briefly review the work to which his life has been devoted."

The application for leniency had been widely circulated in town. Some of the more outlandish paragraphs, the ones that made it sound as if Doc Walk was applying for sainthood rather than parole, people practically knew by heart:

> He was born in Floyd County, Kentucky, on May 15, 1885, long before Eastern Kentucky had been visited with development or improvements in the way of railroads, highways, schools, hospitals or other institutions. The whole section was then virtually a frontier, a wild country, remote from the outside world. He and his brother, Ed Stumbo, early perceiving the suffering and hardships

endured by the masses of the people of that section, through lack of medical treatment and hospital facilities, started out to equip themselves to help remedy the situation. Their opportunities were limited. They were forced to work out most of the necessary funds. Under the most trying circumstances they finally succeeded in completing their medical educations at the University of Louisville, Ed Stumbo graduating in the class of 1905 and petitioner in the class of 1907.

They promptly returned to their own hill country after graduation, and commenced the practice of their profession of medicine and surgery amongst the mountain people. To better care for these people, they built a public hospital, one of the very first, if not the first, to be erected in Eastern Kentucky. Later, they built another (which was burned), and then another, a large institution known as the Beaver Valley Hospital, making three and the *only* public hospitals in the County. Ed Stumbo died in 1929, as a result of injuries received when his horse fell while he was out on a *charity* call over mountain trails.

These facts are common knowledge through this whole region. They will not—cannot well be—denied by even the petitioner's most bitter political enemies. The truth thereof may be readily established beyond doubt.

Doesn't it seem at least paradoxical that one who has generously given and ever shown solicitude and devotion to such an unfortunate and indigent class of people, should change almost overnight, after more than a quarter of a century in their service, and conspire to help rob them?

Put that way, it did seem at least paradoxical. On the off chance that the judge needed more convincing, Doc Walk had followed up with a dramatic public demonstration of his commitment to Floyd County's indigent. He had placed an advertisement in the local newspaper, offering to perform free tonsillectomies on local children. (He was known for grand gestures; during the years he owned Beaver Valley Hospital, freshly slaughtered meat from his farm traveled to town by train nearly every day, arriving precisely at 11:17 at the hospital. Crates of beef and mutton and pork were unloaded for the hospital's cook, who had recently started serving lunch to anybody in town who looked hungry.)

Curiously, the judge remained unmoved. Before Doc Walk could get his tonsil clinic off the ground, he was sentenced to two years in a federal penitentiary in Georgia. He took a bus to jail. But he didn't climb aboard in defeat, didn't trudge up the steps with stooped shoulders or a low-hung head. He didn't consider the situation ruinous. He leaned out the window to say good-bye to his wife, who stood on the pavement sobbing into a handkerchief. As Annie looked up, tears streaming, he called out in a voice the whole town could hear, "Honey, don't worry. If I like the place, we'll buy it."

Mary was laughing when Elmer walked in.

"I thought you were dead," she said.

"Not yet," he said. "Hello, Walter. What's for supper?"

"I haven't decided if we're going to have supper," she said. "I burned the beans. I might just bake a cake."

Mary couldn't deny her essential nature. She was the accommodating one. As a girl, she made her siblings' lives more comfortable. And from the day she married, she smoothed Elmer's way in the world. She indulged his whims even when they required her to become a reluctant nomad. Elmer refused to stay in one place for more than a minute. He moved more times than Hesta, and for flimsier reasons. Basically, Elmer itched to get out of town. Any town. He couldn't say why. He took Mary first to Louisville, where he collected his belongings from his former landlady on South Second Street. Mary enjoyed that part of the adventure, and for the rest of her life would be caught humming under her breath the chorus "Eight more miles to Lou-ee-ville, hometown of my heart." From there, they went to stay with Elmer's mother (who by then had returned to the outskirts of Garrett) and later to Paintsville, far enough from Martin to make visits difficult but close enough to make her hanker for them. In Paintsville, Mary kept house, waited for Elmer to come home from his job as an appliance repairman, and had a baby. Mary named her Margaret after the delivery nurse (there was no question of the physician's being similarly honored, his surname being Picklesheimer). Then it was back to Martin, where they lived across the street from Hesta in a two-room house so tiny that her brothers dubbed it "the doll's house." This was the first year of her marriage.

Living proximate to her mother proved problematic. Hesta, who all her life would share anything she had with her children during hard times, expected the same generosity in return. Mary may not have minded when Hesta took her new curtains off the windows to rehang them at home. But Elmer did. A soft lamb's-wool sweater Mary had been given by her friend Faye Boyd Dingus was last seen on Hesta, who stretched it fatally. Mary never complained because she hated to quarrel with her mother, but Elmer had no qualms. He didn't know what made him madder, that Hesta took from his house or that Mary looked the other way. When cornered, Hesta changed the subject to Elmer's womanizing. Hesta said that if Mary believed the only reason he left was to camp out with his motorcycle buddies in some strange farmer's tomato field, she was a fool. Hesta pointed out that the *other* members of the motorcycle club traveled with their wives and girlfriends.

Mary was relieved when Elmer wanted to move again. Elmer's younger brother Joe, who had aced high school chemistry, helped him pass a state licensing test that made him eligible for a mine foreman's job. Elmer earned a piece of paper that proclaimed him legally capable of reading a gauge that measured underground methane gas levels. It wasn't a college diploma, but in the mines the certification qualified him for management. They moved to Jenkins, a company town where jobs were plentiful and foremen in demand.

Coal was the one thing eastern Kentucky had that the rest of the world wanted. Mining was a miserable living, but Elmer had no apprehensions about the job that every man he'd ever admired—his father, his brothers, his uncle D—had held. It was fate. The earliest European settlers had practically tripped over the black clods that littered their fields. They noticed rich veins that marbled rocks, and while they may not have realized they were in the presence of one of the most lavish concentrations of natural resources in the United States, they recognized it for an astonishing natural occurrence. The settlers suspected a man could dig a thousand feet deep and still uncover yet another layer of coal. Even before the Civil War, businessmen were shipping bushels out of state by steamboat. By the turn of the twentieth century, a savvy entrepreneur named John C. C. Mayo was riding around in a buckboard wagon to persuade his neighbors to sell something he called "mineral rights." Mayo's wife accompanied him, wearing a dress that had coin-sized pockets sewn into the lining. She jingled from the twenty-dollar gold pieces, which Mayo doled out to persuade farmers to hear his sales pitch. Mayo bought miles and miles of mineral rights, paying fifty cents or a dollar per acre and later selling them to coal companies for double or triple the price. By the time Mayo died in 1914 (when Elmer was barely three years old in a faraway state), railroad tracks crisscrossed even the most isolated valleys and hills, and the serious business of transporting nearly 11 billion tons of coal had begun. Some farmers' sons—like Elmer's father—became miners. Other farmers' sons—like Fred—became railroad men. And they started in earnest to strip the riches from the mountains.

The big picture did not greatly interest Elmer. What attracted him to the mines was the danger of working in a cave. And why not? He amused himself on weekends with the most hazardous of local sports, hill climbing. He and his buddies pointed their cycles upward to scale the mountainsides as zealously as if they were scaling Pikes Peak itself, where the sport had recently been invented. Sharp rocks, tree stumps, and underbrush defined the route. Cycles frequently flipped. Most Sundays, Elmer came home beaten and bloody and immortal. He wouldn't be satisfied with less peril the other six days a week. It was satisfyingly risky to work underground, where coal cars could derail or uncouple and crush a man (in Floyd County, fatalities averaged three a year). Machinery could malfunction and take out an eye (eye injuries: thirty-four). A man could fall from a perch, a ledge, a tipple (sixteen injuries a year). Explosives could backfire (rarer). The biggest daily risk Elmer faced was renegade rock; sixty times a year a chunk fell onto somebody's face. Surviving each shift proved his invincibility.

Elmer was a foreman in one of the biggest, most productive, most famous coal towns in eastern Kentucky. In Jenkins, he told Mary, they loaded by hand and so the air down there wasn't too dusty. If she had to be a miner's wife, Mary knew her husband could have chosen far worse locations. At least he hadn't suggested moving to Harlan County, where

strikes and violence over the United Mine Workers' attempts to organize miners had erupted in bloodshed and had led to a courtroom battle that had earned the county a nationally known nickname. In contrast
to Bloody Harlan, Jenkins was a model town, one that the Consolidated
Coal Company built to make life so convenient that day-to-day living
barely distracted anyone from the work at hand. Jenkins had streets and
houses and stores laid out in a neat grid to make it handy to shop, and
sturdy houses to keep out the cold and heat, and schools and churches
and a hospital. Nobody ever needed to leave.

Indeed, Mary might not ever have escaped if Elmer had not picked
the wrong place to eat his lunch one day soon after Walter's visit. That
morning, Elmer had pulled on his last clean pair of pants, tucked in his
work shirt, and buckled on a heavy leather belt. From the belt hung a
light, a rescue kit, and a metal cap crimper. With the crimper, which
looked like a pair of pliers, he could attach a fuse to a blasting cap. He
took his lunch bucket and headed off to the mine.

Underground, he felt like a damn rat. Nobody with claustrophobia
could stand the mines. He spent the morning on his knees, scuttling
through cold puddles. The only light came from the carbide lamp on his
hat. He practically had to be an engineer just to operate the light. It had
a flint on the side. He put water on the top and carbide on the bottom
and adjusted the mix. Too much water would ruin the lamp and the rest
of the day would be dark. Half a dozen men worked for Elmer on the
long wall, driving back ever deeper into the base of the mountain, blasting the world away to burrow straight into the clammy blackness.
While the crew worked to open a tunnel wide enough to work in, Elmer
made sure they were leaving a generous margin of coal along the tunnel's perimeter, "pillars" that along with a few timbers would support the
rock "roof." The pressure on the pillars made it easier to loosen the sur-
rounding coal. Later, they'd reverse direction and work their way back
toward the entrance, removing the pillars and allowing the roof to collapse. It was dangerous work, and a constant worry. Every few minutes,
he checked methane levels. Elmer also made sure that the motormen
took their cars to the right destination to load. After each coal car was
full, Elmer's crew tossed in a handful of shiny silver-and-red metal scat-
ter tags to christen the load as Consolidated's. The tags said CAVALIER.

By lunch, he was exhausted and filthy. He settled back against a damp wall. Beneath a dripping slate overhang, he unwrapped his sandwich. He didn't want to touch the bread with his hands, which were coated in coal dust. He didn't want to taste grit. So he handled it gingerly, folding back one edge of the paper as carefully as if he were stripping a petal from a daisy. The grainy black dust was under his fingernails. It was lodged in the creases of skin on his wrists and on his neck. He felt it in his lungs.

He didn't hear the slate loosen above his head. Elmer took a bite—bologna—and straightened his cramped legs, because it might be his last chance to stretch before his shift ended. He swallowed. A big chunk of ceiling fell. It hit his leg. Elmer yelled at the impact. He spit bologna and bread before he was aware of what he'd done or of who had cursed. His own voice was strange to him. His crew ran up in time to see him lift a chunk of rock from his leg and hurl it at the wall. He yelled again. He didn't try to stand.

Someone called for a rescue crew. His leg hurt badly just above the ankle. The pain would have persuaded him to wait even if he hadn't been issued a cardboard-covered book titled *Manual of First-Aid Instruction for Miners,* full of advice about how to react to an emergency. Like a lot of other foremen, he had studied the 221-page instruction booklet, printed courtesy of the federal Bureau of Mines to inform him that he should wait for the first-aid men. "Do not attempt any unnecessary movements of the patient's body or limbs," the manual instructed. Elmer had read the manual expecting that someday he would have to dispense first aid. It never had occurred to him he might be the patient. While he waited for help, he reviewed the checklist he had memorized, and realized much of it was not applicable: Don't fail to remove false teeth from an unconscious person. Don't put a quid of tobacco on a wound. Don't tie knots over the eyeball.

Above ground was a first-aid station stocked with a supply cabinet. As per the Bureau of Mines' instructions, the cabinet held twelve sterilized forty-inch triangular bandages, a dozen smaller sterilized compresses, six packages of picric-acid gauze, two ten-yard spools of adhesive tape, and six splints, among other things. But none of that stockpile—not the fifteen-foot-long gauze roller bandages, not the aromatic spirits of ammonia, not the tourniquet, and certainly not the teaspoon—would do him any good down here.

Pain interrupted this train of thought. He tried to ignore it. Don't burn a patient with an unwrapped hot-water bottle or other heated object. Don't wash wounds. Don't tie knots over protruding bones in compound fractures. The list was not calming. Although he was not normally given to queasiness, he was on the verge of making an exception by the time the stretcher squad arrived.

The captain knelt and ripped Elmer's pants leg from the ankle to the knee. The leg was swollen and purple. With textbook precision, the captain bandaged two splints to the leg.

"Prepare to lift patient," the captain said. The squad took positions, kneeling beside Elmer's knees, feet, and shoulders.

"Lift patient," the captain said.

Elmer felt himself rise into the air and slide smoothly onto the stretcher.

"Forward march," the captain said.

Elmer barely felt the stretcher sway as they carried him toward the tunnel. A few seconds later, as the squad fastened the stretcher to an empty mine car, Elmer said, "Thanks, fellas."

He bumped along for miles, it seemed, as he clutched the stretcher's frame. He saw daylight. The rescue squad lifted him again.

"Load ambulance," the captain said.

After another ride, he arrived at the company hospital on the hill. There a doctor used to diagnosing much worse confirmed the leg was broken. He called Elmer lucky.

Mary was stirring beans when she heard a noise outside. A wagon, pulled by a mule, stood outside the front door. Elmer emerged, splinted and swearing.

"I was sure you were dead," she said as she flew out the door.

"This time I am," he said.

Two men helped him into the house. A third carried his crutches. Elmer was pale. He looked terrible.

She helped him to a chair.

"Dinner?" she asked.

"Whiskey would be better," Elmer said.

The incident changed Elmer's mind about working in the mines. After the worst of the swelling went down, he and Mary loaded their belongings and their baby into the back of Elmer's car. They stopped to drop off the house key. When they reached the outskirts of Jenkins, they didn't look back. A few miles north of Pikeville, they saw the first road signs for Martin. When they arrived, Mary was surprised to see that a town without Doc Walk managed to look remarkably peaceful. On the surface, nothing had changed. Nobody had even bothered to change the MARTIN POP. 860 sign to 859.

CHAPTER 8

One June day while the rest of America enjoyed wedding weather, the windstorm that heralded Doc Walk Stumbo's return hit Main Street. Sudden rain on a Monday afternoon was the only warning. As shoppers scuttled under awnings, the first powerful gust whipped skirts and stole hats. Pedestrians reflexively grabbed door handles to avoid taking flight. This egged on the wind. With a captive audience huddled under eaves and overhangs, the bully flung raindrops sharp as fleabites to punish anyone who had put faith in short sleeves. The temperature dropped ten degrees in ten minutes as handbills were torn off light posts to flutter like a thousand handkerchiefs waving good-bye to a lost world. Trees curtsied, bushes shook with shock, flower stalks snapped. At Beaver Valley Hospital, curtains flapped crazily as nurses ran to shut windows. At Dermont's, a clerk hauled from the sidewalk sacks of potatoes, their burlap already soaked dark.

The wind swept through town with a mighty, unshakable authority that had otherwise been missing since Doc Walk Stumbo went to jail. It announced its intent to change the nature of things by snapping limbs from oaks. It rattled the brand-new panes of glass at the high school. It sent dogs beneath porches and children into the nearest neighbor's house. As the angry air blew through the depot, candy wrappers scampered under an idle caboose.

Near the depot was a little frame building on which a modest sign said VELVA'S BEAUTY SHOP. The emporium was one of many salons in Martin, where hair care was a booming industry. Vernice Hall Stamper

had Granny's Beauty Shop, which gave machine perms. But real inno-
vation would come to Martin from the Twin Modernistic Beauty Shop,
owned and operated by the Slade sisters (who boasted two chairs to cut,
four dryers, and a shampoo bowl). The Slade twins trained in Chicago
at the Wilfred Academy of Hair and Beauty Culture, enduring a year
and a half of exile and the elevated train to the Loop—which scared
them to death—to learn the latest techniques. Returning from their pil-
grimage north, the Slade twins introduced razor cuts to Martin.
Women came from as far away as Mud Creek for the twins' cold wave
permanents. A carload would pull up to the Modernistic, clamoring for
electric-roller treatment; a little light went off when the wave was done.
By contrast, Velva Preston was a traditionalist who championed a weekly
shampoo and set for her regulars. Far from craving change, Velva's customers asked only that things stay the same. The wind did not approve.
With terrible power, it scooped up Velva's building and tossed it like a
ball of paper. Velva and her daughter Donna Jean were unharmed. The
salon's equipment was less fortunate. As for the beauty shop, it looked
like a heap of old lumber lying near the depot, a pile of boards and broken windows abandoned in a ditch.

The wind had made its point. Later a cluster of the curious surveyed the scarred hole where Velva's Beauty Shop used to be. Splintered
board and shards of glass were sprinkled almost delicately over raw,
black earth. The rest of the town looked scoured—and expectant.

The town didn't have long to wait for change to arrive by way of
Georgia, where it had been biding its time in a federal penitentiary. Doc
Walk Stumbo returned in the same condition in which he had left—
ready to run the place. The most famous man in town was also now its
most infamous felon. During his absence, details of his life in jail were
discussed tirelessly among customers who stopped at the newsstand on
Main Street for a bag of popcorn and a conversation. In jail, Doc Walk
sold cigarettes to other inmates. Further, he had been said to remark
that there was more money in tobacco than in tonsils. His self-esteem
had not suffered on account of his being convicted of illegally pocketing
federal money. Nor had his personal finances.

Martin had a very short list of hometown heroes. Smalley Crisp qualified, for valor on horseback. At the turn of the century, Mr. Crisp had dutifully journeyed over the mountains, braving snakes and squirrels, to retrieve the mail from Prestonsburg. But aside from a short-lived period of glory (when briefly the Bucks Branch post office had been rechristened "Smalley" in his honor), Mr. Crisp had lived a long and peacefully uneventful life operating a water mill. Upon dying a mere seven days before his ninety-third birthday, he had left as a legacy his ten children, also blessed with longevity, and the skeletal remnants of the mill. After him, the most colorful historical personage was Mrs. Susan Martin Cox, onetime proprietor of a small boardinghouse near the depot. A C&O manager who lodged there long ago named the depot "Martin" in honor of her home cooking, paving the way for her name to supplant Smalley's on most local maps by 1926. These days, however, no one could remember what had made Susan Martin Cox's biscuits so memorable; her recipe was lost to history.

Among contemporary heroes, nobody was half as flamboyant as Doc Walk. Others were more widely liked, including entrepreneurs like Lawrence Keathley, who owned the movie theater. Keathley was revered both for his business acumen (he sold smelling salts at any scary double feature) and for his decision to increase the supply of strawberry pop on matinee days. No moviegoer went thirsty, even during the final reel, and for that the populace felt grateful. But Lawrence Keathley was a temperate, restrained fellow, not the sort to stride down Main Street in jodhpurs, cussing and aiming spit plugs of tobacco at stray dogs. That level of entertainment only Doc Walk could provide.

Luckily for his audience, prison did nothing to dampen Doc Walk's colorful personality. And why should it? Martin was not a town to hold a grudge against a felon. "Jailbird" was just another job description, and not an uncommon one. With Kentucky's state prisons bursting at the seams, nearly everybody had a relative or two who had served time. Statewide, violent crimes were so common that Kentucky's population boasted the nation's highest proportion (30 percent) of inmates serving sentences for murder and manslaughter. That statistic made a fraud conviction sound like a trifle.

During his incarceration, Doc Walk's neighbors had amused themselves with speculation about his return. As a felon, Doc Walk had been stripped of basic rights of citizenship. He was barred for life from holding elected office, a harsh comedown for a former judge. What would he do instead? The talk over at the Utilities Elkhorn company store, where manager Floyd Skaggs presided over a daily exchange of both scrip and gossip, was that the government hadn't caught Doc Walk unaware. A man that cagey would have had to have a premonition. People figured he'd prepared for the worst long before formal charges ever were filed. Talk in the company store was a barometer of prevailing sentiment; Utilities Elkhorn handled good brands (Levi's, Florsheim) and therefore attracted an intellectual crowd. In the back of the store, near "Shoes Counter," the consensus was that he had stashed money somewhere, probably buried at his horse farm: "The government will never get his cash." Debate about the amount was heated, and the discussion in "Notions" along the store's long walls focused on precisely where he might have buried cash. It was easy to picture him with a shovel, a stocky, solitary figure digging by the light of a full moon. Nobody believed mere prosecutors could get the best of Doc Walk.

Some talk was negative. The Pikeville doctors who had bought Beaver Valley Hospital felt tricked. They resented how Doc Walk had reneged on his promise not to compete against them by building Stumbo Memorial Hospital. He wasn't present to physically compete by seeing patients at Stumbo Memorial, but that seemed a small point, given that Annie Stumbo was on the scene. Beneath her sweet nature and carefully waved curls, Annie was a shrewd businesswoman. While her husband was "away," as she'd put it delicately, she'd "leased" the operation of Stumbo Memorial to some out-of-town doctors who "managed to keep things running." She checked in on the hospital from time to time—from nine to five most weekdays—just to make sure.

Doc Walk got paroled after serving less than half of his two-year term. And just like that, he was back, clumping down Main Street in his boots, scattering chickens and children and anybody else senseless enough to stand in his path. He looked as grumpy as ever, and was no less likely to curse or bark orders. Soon after, one of Elmer's younger brothers had the misfortune to become his patient.

—

Loren Wolverton was the least likely member of his family to end up at Stumbo Memorial. He never got sick. In the fifteen years since he'd been born a twin on March 26, 1923, nobody could remember his ever seeing a doctor. It was impossible to imagine him confined to the claustrophobia of a ward lined with iron beds—or laid up inside any building, for that matter. He lived almost entirely outdoors. He skipped school so often in favor of hunting or fishing that Elmer said, "He wore his books out, all right, but he did it by sitting on them on the creek bank." Although nearly all of Amanda's children were anachronisms in a modern world, relics from a time when one's ability to navigate obstacles like the public school system was less crucial to survival than a dose of frontier fortitude, she said that Loren would have benefited most from being born a century earlier. We would have had another Daniel Boone on our hands, Amanda said. Loren was hardy.

Loren's twin was a different story. Oren and Loren were technically identical. Both had dark brown hair and slim builds and seemed interchangeable—until they started talking. As soon as Loren opened his mouth, he became noticeably better looking than Oren, who skulked like a shadow. Loren led. Oren was grateful to him. Loren was the one who suggested hunting as an alternative to attending school, the one with the foresight to hide a single-barrel gun in the bushes the preceding night, the one who showed Oren where to stash his books under a bush, the one who whistled to Rhoda the dog to follow him up the mountain. Oren scrambled behind Rhoda.

Loren was the only Wolverton with expectations. Poor as he was, he believed that anything out there in the world should be free for the asking. If he could get something, he took it. The concept of prior ownership he ignored. And he often got away with it, on sheer audacity. When he was twelve, he learned to drive by "borrowing" an old car that belonged to his older brother Mose, sneaking off at night while Mose worked the second shift in the mines. How Loren got hold of the key no one ever knew. Speculation was that he must have stolen that too, long enough to make a duplicate. Loren also filched replacement gaso-

James and Amanda Wolverton (at left) and another
couple in Oklahoma, shortly before Elmer was born in 1911

Three of Elmer's
younger brothers—
Joe, Oren, and
Loren—in Martin
in the mid-1930s

line, using a hose to siphon a gallon or two at a time out of another tank. The cover-up was successful. Mose never caught on; he bragged about what good gas mileage the car got.

Risks were meaningless to Loren because he believed he'd win any gamble. This lent him a certain charisma that made him exotic among Wolvertons. In a family like Elmer's, self-confidence constituted charm. Loren's aplomb lent him power over his siblings, who regarded him with awe and, in the case of his sisters, with adoration. He was their pet. In the neighborhood, he bossed everybody around. He corralled other kids to carry out his schemes. Everybody went along, maybe because they were just as happy as Oren to have a leader. Or maybe because it tickled them to think they could subvert authority in even a small corner of the world. If in the morning Loren suggested stealing copper from a nearby coal mine, by the end of the day a ragtag assembly line would be chopping purloined metal cables into chunks to sell. And if the sheriff eventually found a hundred pounds of copper under the Wolverton house (sitting beside a drum of gasoline), Loren didn't feel defeated. After all, the coal mine decided not to prosecute such a young boy. The Wolvertons got run off and ended up in yet another hollow. But Loren had stashed away six cents for every pound the junk man bought.

Loren was the one who wanted to bike to the movies on a cold, foggy October afternoon. It was an activity he would have endorsed without a second thought even if the theater in Garrett hadn't been showing a western he'd wanted to see for months, *Six Shootin' Sheriff,* starring Ken Maynard (who always wore a white hat as big as all outdoors) as a former jailbird seeking revenge against the scoundrel who had framed him. As the sun went down, Loren and Oren and a third boy set off on a single bike toward the highway. The twins' older brother Joe, pedaling a second bike, balanced a passenger on his handlebars. Near the theater was a shortcut over the railroad tracks. Joe was a junior in high school, the only Wolverton to have studied and loved geometry, and he instinctively veered off at an angle to take advantage of the turnoff over the tracks. But Loren, far ahead, continued along the highway, disappearing around a blind curve in twilight.

Seconds later, Joe heard an explosive bang, as if a truck backfired. A minute later, he arrived at the theater. A minute after that, he started to wonder where his brothers were. He headed back to the highway.

As Joe rounded the curve, he saw a delivery truck lying on its side, pushed up against a big rock at the edge of the road. A sign on the truck said EASTERN KENTUCKY PACKERS (PAINTSVILLE). A crowd was gathering. As Joe skidded short, he saw the truck's door open into the air, and out climbed the driver. He took one look at the wrecked vehicle and ran away.

Lying in the road near the truck was a bike. It was crushed and twisted, the front wheel still twirling idly. A few feet away lay Oren, and a few feet beyond him lay the boy who owned the bike. Both were conscious but moaning. By the time Joe reached them, Oren was being helped to his feet. Oren held one hand cradled in the other and flinched when anyone tried to touch it.

"Where's Loren?" Joe asked.

He lay crumpled near the rock, which the truck had hit at high speed. Up on two wheels, the driver had tried to steer clear of the hillside and had instead run into the boys' bike—and over Loren's leg. Loren was in shock. His eyes were open but he didn't speak, he didn't try to get up, he just shivered beneath a coat that somebody threw over him while the crowd waited for an ambulance.

That night at the hospital, an unfamiliar doctor examined the boys. The doctor was a surgeon from Michigan, hired by Annie during Doc Walk's recent absence. Oren had a bruised hip and a broken hand. But Loren was in worse shape. His leg was broken, multiple fractures, the surgeon told Amanda, adding that the boy would have to stay in the hospital while he healed.

Weeks turned into months. All winter Loren lay in bed at Stumbo Memorial. The open wound refused to heal. It was impossible to put a cast on it. The nurses tried to keep him quiet, so the leg could lie rigid. The surgeon said to be patient. But the wound festered. By February, it was still red and angry. It was a long winter, affording Loren plenty of time to stare at the ceiling and consider fate. The only thing he talked about was how he couldn't wait to get out of the hospital. He wanted to go hunting.

One day Doc Walk and the other doctor got into an argument—

nobody ever accused Stumbo of being an easy man to work for—which resulted in the immediate and final departure of the surgeon, who was last seen carrying a suitcase on his back, headed to Michigan.

Doc Walk came into Loren's room to examine him, the boy's first encounter with Stumbo since the night his father had died.

Doc Walk unwrapped the dressing, assessed the stench, and grunted. He lifted the leg, none too gently, to get a closer look at the scabbed area. He said, "Gangrene, boy."

Loren hoped he'd heard wrong.

"You have two choices," Doc Walk said. Prison had not softened his bedside manner. "Either the leg comes off, or it gets worse. And then you'll die for sure."

An operation was a gamble. Surgery carried the risk of further infection, not to mention the unpleasant prospect of trusting oneself, helpless and unconscious, to the mercy and skills of Doc Walk. But Loren didn't hesitate. Although the last diagnosis he'd heard Doc Walk deliver had been to his father ("You'll be fine. Get some rest") hours before James Wolverton had bled to death, Loren wanted to be cured and he wanted to be cured fast. He couldn't bear the thought of languishing in bed throughout the spring.

"I'll take the operation," Loren said.

Doc Walk congratulated him on a good choice.

Doc Walk operated the next Monday. Loren was in surgery for hours. Amanda and Joe waited in his hospital room, beside the empty bed. They drank coffee and talked quietly, but afterward could never remember the topics. Finally a surgeon named Dr. Wicker came into the room to say that Loren was recuperating in the recovery room. Dr. Wicker, who had assisted Doc Walk in surgery, said the amputation had taken so long because Doc Walk had to perform it twice. The first cut hadn't been high enough to remove all of the gangrenous flesh.

Long after suppertime, Loren was carried into his room. He recognized his mother.

"I'm glad that's over," he said. He closed his eyes.

Amanda and Joe went home to sleep.

Soon after, Loren slipped into a coma and died. At eleven o'clock, someone from the hospital came to the Wolvertons' door with the news.

Joe and Amanda returned to the hospital. Doc Walk wasn't there, but the nurses said Loren had lost too much blood. The surgery was too traumatic for his system, the nurses said.

Doc Walk never offered a fuller explanation. But he confided to Dr. Wicker that he felt responsible. The only communication on the subject that the Wolvertons received was a bill in the mail. Amanda never replied. Annie Stumbo never sent a past-due notice.

CHAPTER 9

World War II sneaked up on Martin. *That is not to say the* town was completely unaware of the problems overseas, just that in the late 1930s Europe seemed irrelevant. Those troubles were so removed from everyday life in the mountains that they seemed more like a made-up story than an actual threat. How could abstract headlines like GERMANS OCCUPY SUDETENLAND compete with the immediacy of such earth-shattering events as Doc Walk's return from jail (which had occurred around the time the Czech government resigned)? The same month the Soviets were expelled from the League of Nations, a thirty-inch-long copperhead was discovered lurking on the banks of nearby Mud Creek. The snake, not the Soviets, made the front page of *The Floyd County Times.* Rationing began in Britain as Florence Crisp was polishing her silver in preparation for a PTA tea, a success at which the troubles in England were not remarked upon. The Nazis invaded Denmark and Holland the week after Mrs. Greer's third-grade class raised the most money for the school's annual Easter party and egg hunt. Holland surrendered to the Nazis. Belgium surrendered to the Nazis. The Germans marched into Paris. None of these catastrophes managed to shake the general feeling that war in Europe was not Martin's business.

A peacetime draft got the town's attention. Less than a month after the first British air raid on Berlin, the United States government passed the Selective Training and Service Act of 1940. What that signified, to Martin, was a threat to every family's established, insulated life. All men between the ages of twenty-one and thirty-six had to register, and in Floyd County that added up to 6,108 farmers, miners, brakemen, shopkeepers, doctors, teachers, and lawyers—more than 11.5 percent of the county's population. If all those men were called to serve, who would be left behind to harvest crops and to dig coal and to file lawsuits against one another? Who would be left to slaughter hogs?

My grandmother's older brother Red, a butcher, was among the first to report to the newly established office of Local Draft Board 45, which had commandeered as headquarters a classroom in the high school. He joined a long line that stretched out the door, down the hallway, and outside onto the steps. He spent the better part of the day waiting for a physical exam and filling out forms. The draft board's physician, Doc Callihan, took one look at Red and said, "Fit." Red's classification: 1-A. He was available for immediate service.

The lottery came next. In Washington, numbers were drawn from a fishbowl. Quotas were set; by the following summer, the state of Kentucky would have to supply 9,154 healthy men to the peacetime conscription army. The government said draftees would have to serve one year.

Fred Mynhier feared the situation would get worse. Around the time the lottery got under way, German troops entered Romania and Italy invaded Greece. Loopholes helped some men avoid the draft, but Red didn't qualify. He wasn't married, like Elmer, who had been classified 4-A. (Although Elmer's lottery number—2,546—was one of the first called, Elmer would not be among the early draftees.) Men with jobs deemed "essential"—coal miners, steelworkers, and some railroad men—also were being passed over. So were farmers. Red needed an essential job.

Fred asked Hesta if she'd like to move. As if he had to ask. She had her eye on another house on Main Street, closer to downtown, where the novelty of electricity had just been installed. Big changes were under way, streetlights and paved roads and talk of a local telephone exchange. The phone company was running lines to connect all the houses in the county by a thin wire. Even indoor plumbing was on the verge of becoming more than a rumor at some houses. Hesta asked Fred which house he had in mind.

Fred said he'd like to move out of town, to Cow Creek. Hesta wondered if she'd heard wrong. He might as well have said Mars. Cow Creek was an isolated settlement, farmers mostly, a few miles north of Martin, accessible via a one-lane gravel road from the Prestonsburg highway. The vicinity's only excitement had occurred in the eighteenth century. A local historian named Henry Preston Scalf had recently turned up the story of a group of hunters who, while traveling along Johns Creek, had stumbled upon a family of three bison. The startled animals tried to escape downstream. The site where the hunters overtook and shot the bull became Bull Creek. They killed the calf along another stream (now: Calf Creek). A hundred and fifty years later, the significance of moving to the area where the family matriarch was overpowered was not lost on Hesta.

Time had not caught up to Cow Creek. The area remained bucolic, with a few houses and adjacent fields perched along the winding road. Pastures rolled and a creek burbled through fertile bottomland. The same families had been living on Cow Creek for generations: the Gobles, the Harrises, the Burchetts, the Woods. There still was no town to speak of, just a post office established in 1904—the postmaster was a Goble—and a general store, both squatting at the mouth of the creek. A quarter mile down the road was the Freewill Baptist Church, built by its congregation in the early 1930s. The bus from Martin passed the Cow Creek turnoff twice a day—once early in the morning, once late in the day—on the way to Prestonsburg. Cow Creek residents so seldom wanted to leave that there was no official bus stop. It was necessary to flag down the vehicle. Fred said a man named Mosely wanted to rent out a house. He showed Hesta the newspaper ad. Hesta wondered what the family would do on Cow Creek. Fred suggested growing corn. The house came with a good, level field of black bottom soil. Hesta looked doubtful. Fred clarified: Red could grow corn. He'd become a farmer.

A farm was nothing more than a very big vegetable garden. This was the theory by which the Mynhiers hoped to achieve success on Cow Creek. After years of hoeing and weeding and raising feed corn in neatly planted rows outside the kitchen door, they knew the rudiments of agriculture. The trick was to apply their knowledge on a grander scale to the weedy, overgrown field across the road on the creek bank. They also planned a second, smaller crop of corn for their hillside.

They got a plow. Then, from a neighbor, Fred bought Bob to pull it. Bob was a common brown mule with no distinguishing features. But my grandmother's brothers soon learned that in a lineup of mules, Bob would have been easy to identify. He was the worthless one. Even in a strain known for stubbornness, orneriness, and laziness, his behavior was remarkable. Nobody had informed Bob that his was a breed known through history for endurance in the field, for stoic strength in the face of a heavy workload, for carrying more weight than a similarly sized horse. Bob had little knowledge of and less interest in the glory his nobler ancestors earned by carrying armored knights into battle and by pulling artillery equipment across Civil War battlefields. Bob was not a mule you could picture earning a legendary place in American history by hauling borax out of Death Valley. If the subject was raised, Bob looked away.

Some mules love attention. Not Bob. Some mules have personalities more like a dog's, eager to serve and to earn praise. Not Bob. Some mules are so sure-footed on a rocky trail that riders trust them more than horses. Not Bob.

Laziness was not Bob's only personality flaw. A normal mule who had been raised to work would respond docilely when the prospect of labor was put to him. Bob was not normal. He liked to stand quietly in the barn or the pasture, trying not to attract attention. The only effort he voluntarily would exert was to avoid work. If a human approached him to broach the topic of chores, Bob bit or kicked. He was not above trying to crush a bridle-toting child against a barn wall.

Bob's personality improved after he met Red Mynhier. He weighed nearly three hundred pounds, with about two hundred seventy of them allotted to muscle. Red was used to getting his way. The day he decided to change Bob's shoes, he expected no complaints. But Bob kicked his right rear leg, hard as he could, into Red's leg. Red swore and staggered back to steady himself against the fence before he turned and kicked Bob in return. Red had better aim and a meaner streak. He got Bob in the ribs. Toppled on his side, braying in shock, Bob kicked the air, causing a ridiculous scene. By the time the mule righted himself, he no longer entertained fantasies of being the boss. With new shoes, Bob compliantly turned the weeds in both the big field and on a steeper hillside behind the house. He didn't complain. The rest of the family believed that if Red had said to Bob, "Iron my dress shirt," the mule would have used starch.

The move to Cow Creek was successful as an agricultural experiment. My grandmother's brothers harvested and sold four hundred bushels of feed corn. The crops paid for rent and food. To supplement the income, Fred kept his railroad job. Walter drove him to town in an old '29 Rockland touring car purchased from Elmer for twenty-five dollars. It had nineteen-inch wheels, wooden spokes, and a steering wheel that looked like a wagon wheel.

In the fields, the younger boys were responsible for hoeing and weeding. It was blister-provoking work that never let up. For Jack and Walter, the summer of 1940 was one of long hot days, followed by long muggy nights. After dark was when Cow Creek seemed the most distant from Martin. The sky was blacker, and the bulk of the mountains seemed closer.

For girls, Cow Creek was lonelier. My grandmother's little sister Betty, who turned ten the year the Mynhiers moved out of town, had to be content with just one girl who came by. Betty spent far more time walking around with one of Mary's children on her hip than she spent playing. There was nobody to make teams for kick the can or any of the other games she was used to playing at dusk. The only twilight magic Cow Creek had to offer was music on the battery-powered radio. Most nights, Betty sat in the front room to listen. She turned the volume low after her parents fell asleep.

Jack sat on the front step one night, past ten o'clock, straining to hear a melody, because the radio faced considerable competition from crickets. The mountains were so close that Jack heard sounds he never would have noticed in town. Rustling was so loud that Jack suspected a regional convention of every fox, raccoon, and squirrel in eastern Kentucky. But if sound was magnified, sky was minimal. On Cow Creek the tall mountains' peaks limited the view of the heavens to one small slice of stars. In the narrow valley, the moon disappeared behind the hills early, and Jack for the first time truly understood what "black" meant.

Dim light spilled from the front window. Jack absently petted Ranger, a yard dog that had never looked in a mirror and therefore mistakenly believed himself to be as big as the hound dog Joe. Ranger considered himself much larger than, say, a chicken, which explained why he so fearlessly menaced the local poultry. He got by on bluff.

In the night, distant noises were close. Jack heard Joe bark. But he didn't know immediately that the hound was a good quarter mile away, near the top of the mountain behind the house. All he knew was that it was a remote sound, the bark, and when it transformed into a bellow— Joe had a lot of different barks—Jack knew Joe was hunting. Often he brought home a fox, a raccoon, or, less fortuitously, a skunk. Given the volume, tonight Joe was hunting something big.

Jack listened as Joe's barks changed in pitch, and in direction, becoming louder. The dog was steering his prey down the mountain. No matter where he flushed an animal, Joe tried to maneuver his quarry toward the front yard, where he hoped an audience consisting of everyone in the family would convene to admire his ingenuity.

As the hunt neared the house, the crackle of underbrush became a crash as Joe and his intended victim rushed past chestnut oaks, white oaks, hickories, beech, and dogwood trees. More than a hundred species of tree are native to Kentucky, and it was a good bet that as the animals rushed pell-mell past black locusts, white walnuts, mulberries, sourwoods, and hackberries, they were breaking low-hanging branches off most of them.

The barks got louder. The barks got more urgent. Jack grabbed hold of Ranger to keep him from getting hurt.

Two shapes—Joe and something else that was nearly as big as the black hound—burst past the tree line and into the yard. As they flew into the circle of light from the house, Jack observed something he had never before seen: a live, angry bobcat.

Hunters near Martin bagged one now and again to drag home the carcass as a trophy. A live bobcat was a different story. It was fury and muscle. It looked like an overgrown house cat with a docked tail, longer ears, and a worse attitude. It was two feet long, at least a foot tall, tan-colored—and all teeth. A single dog, even a twice-as-big hound like Joe, couldn't handle it alone.

Ranger struggled against Jack, desperate to help Joe. The two dogs were used to hunting as a team. Jack released Ranger. As the bobcat rushed by the steps, the little brown dog surprised it, jumping on its neck as it raced by.

The animals passed the steps in a blur. In the glow of lamplight, the bobcat reared, shook off Ranger, and, having determined that the little dog blocked the path to freedom, turned its full attention to the job of killing Ranger. As Joe snarled and rushed the bobcat, it yowled murderously and lunged at Ranger. The little dog parried, but Joe took a swipe of claws to his ribs and started to bleed badly. The bobcat cuffed Joe again, and now his ear was bleeding. The hound staggered.

Two dogs were not enough dogs to win this fight. Jack jumped from the steps and ran toward the bobcat—he was terrified of the wild animal but more scared still that it would kill Ranger—and managed to grab Ranger by the nape of the neck while aiming kicks at the bobcat. All he could think about was what would happen if the bobcat ripped open Joe's stomach.

"Get out of here!" he yelled. "Get out!"

Jack's voice disoriented Joe. The dog stopped, confused, for a second, which was long enough. The bobcat saw an opening. It burst free of the dogs, the yard, and the light and crashed off into the cornfield. Jack, still holding Ranger, staggered across the grass toward Joe, who looked as if he had an ill-advised urge to give chase. Jack dropped Ranger to the ground and grabbed Joe.

The commotion woke the family. The screen door slammed behind Red, who came running down the steps, shirtless and disoriented. Behind him was Fred in pajamas, Hesta in a robe, and Betty, still hearing music.

They surveyed the scene: Jack knelt in the grass with a torn pants leg. Jack held Joe. The yard was torn up from a fight. Joe was bleeding. There was a lot of blood.

"What the hell was that?" Red asked. He gestured toward the cornfield.

"Joe jumped a bobcat," Jack said.

Red snorted. Common sense told him not to believe it. "It must have been a fox," he said. "There aren't any bobcats left around here."

"Could a fox tear up Joe like this?" Jack asked.

Red was not an ideal brother. He resented his younger siblings, particularly Jack, because being around them made him feel he didn't fit in. Red had dropped out of school long before completing grade school. Now here he stood, challenged by Jack, the clever one who had skipped two grades, the boy who made the honor roll every marking period and who expected to go to college.

Red's derisive look said all the education in the world didn't stand up against common sense. Red made a show of kneeling in the grass to examine the dog's wounds. Joe's side had long cuts; his ribs were visible through torn flesh. Deep tooth marks were in his head. Half an ear was ripped.

"Hell's fire, it was a bobcat," Red said over his shoulder to Fred and Hesta. It wasn't praise for Jack's quick thinking or bravery. It was a fact.

"The cat was trying to cut his stomach open," Jack said. "I kicked it."

"It takes three dogs to handle one," Red said, as he gently leaned over Joe.

"It never expected more than one dog, or it would have climbed a tree," Jack said.

Fred said they'd better patch up Joe. Betty brought the iodine, a salve, and tape. Red said the bobcat would have killed the dog—probably would have killed both dogs—if Jack hadn't been there to break up the fight. It still didn't sound like praise, just another fact. Red held Joe still while Jack patched him up. Fred warned Jack never to go out into the hills without a shotgun. Then he turned off the music and went to bed.

CHAPTER 10

While the Mynhiers were fixated on the finer points of how to coexist with the wildlife on Cow Creek, back in town Doc Walk became preoccupied with rebuilding his political empire. Fate labeled him a felon, and he could live with that tag. But being barred from holding office as a consequence was unacceptable. A future without political clout was a gloomy purgatory. Walker Stumbo had devoted his life to building and wielding influence in one small, geographically isolated corner of the universe. Give it up? Never. In his youth, he had worked to get other men elected. Fresh out of medical school, he'd carried jugs of whiskey on horseback along with medical supplies; during a house call he was as likely to dole out moonshine on behalf of a local candidate as to dispense salve for a wound. He was willing to pay a high price for votes. Once, he had even offered to perjure himself on the witness stand in a murder case for the sake of politics. Subpoenaed to testify against a cousin accused of murdering an inconveniently impregnated sweetheart, Doc Walk had offered to change his testimony and to deny under oath that he had received an incriminating letter from the defendant "if backers for a certain candidate for judge would back off their support." Let others judge his behavior amoral. Politics was the only religion in which he wholeheartedly believed.

In eastern Kentucky, such faith was common. As early as the nineteenth century, the commonwealth had encouraged the emergence of petty power brokers like Doc Walk. In the decades after Kentucky achieved statehood, lawmakers created many, many separate counties, each an incubator of patronage. By the mid-1880s, when Walker Stumbo was born, the state had become "the second most constitutionally subdivided state in the Union per square mile," according to Robert M. Ireland, a history professor at the University of Kentucky who in 1976 dubbed the state's 120 mini-fiefdoms "little kingdoms" in a book of the same name. Walk Stumbo saw the benefits of living in a dirt-poor county; it was a magnet for government money. The trick was to have the authority to dole out the money. The men most likely to surmount the poverty and isolation of Floyd County were the ones who got elected commissioner or judge or sheriff or clerk, offices from which they funneled funds directly to family and friends. They knew not only how to work the system, but also held the power to scrap it to create a new hierarchy in county government if they preferred. They were a de facto ruling class, an elite in a county where most residents were more likely to fall into such categories as "starving farmer" or "exhausted coal miner."

Walk Stumbo was king of Floyd County for many years. He lost his throne overnight. After Doc Walk went to jail, E. P. Hill, Jr., replaced him on the bench. Hill Junior was the well-connected son of another judge ("Senior"). Junior quickly grew into his new role. In robes, he was dour and looked as if he was doing his best to fulfill the considerable responsibility of upholding the public's trust. Off the bench, Junior oversaw half a million dollars in federal funds earmarked for building new roads throughout Floyd County—a pile of money that in an earlier era would have been Doc Walk's to divvy up by handing out contracts to loyal supporters to clear, to excavate, to lay pipe, to grade, to drain, and to surface.

Not that Doc Walk technically had loyal supporters anymore. The Democratic Party got a new chairman. The party had filled the position with a sober, dark-suited non-felon named J. D. Fitzpatrick, who lived in Prestonsburg and was vice president of the local Bank of Josephine (named after its founder's wife, whose portrait hung near the tellers). The party's Prestonsburg faction considered this a big win. They would have preferred nearly anyone to Doc Walk, who had never genuflected toward the county seat. Doc Walk made no allies in Prestonsburg by building the county's first hospital in a town as minor as Martin. Years later, he might have been forgiven, if he had not chosen to build Stumbo Memorial, the second most popular hospital in the area, so far away as well. As far as Prestonsburg was concerned, good riddance.

Doc Walk appeared unfazed by his new humble position. He quietly went about the business of doctoring. Maybe "quietly" was the wrong word. But he did it with a minimum of fuss. To mollify the doctors who owned Beaver Valley, he "sold" Stumbo Memorial to another doctor who was secretly in his employ. He magnanimously offered to buy back Beaver Valley—for a generous $5,000 more than the current owners had paid. They were so happy to be rid of it that they also signed an agreement not to compete against Doc Walk in Floyd County for ten years. One hot summer morning, Doc Walk tied his horse for the first time in five years to the hitching post in front of Beaver Valley Hospital, a building coincidentally located in the exact geographic center of the county and its fifty-three voting districts. That day, he performed seven abdominal operations. From the top-floor operating room, he could look out in the direction of every voting district—and of every voter.

The next surprise came from the governor. After receiving mailbags full of letters from both local and national officials, pleading on Stumbo's behalf, Gov. Keen Johnson restored Doc Walk's citizenship rights. The governor was convinced by letters from such influential men as A. B. "Happy" Chandler, a former governor of Kentucky, who wrote to point out that since his release, Doc Walk had been a model citizen. From Washington, D.C., Governor Johnson received a letter from the chairman of the Department of Justice's U.S. Parole Board, who affirmed that Doc Walk had been a "model prisoner while in the penitentiary." Not to be outdone by big shots, Floyd County's officials also had taken up pen. The clerk of the circuit court, the clerk of the county court, and even the sheriff sent accolades. It seemed that every precinct committeeman, every local minister, and perhaps every patient who had successfully survived an appendectomy wrote to extol Doc Walk's virtues. The letters have not survived in the state archives, but the order, signed "Keen Johnson, Governor" with a flourish of ink, has been preserved for history:

By virtue of the authority vested in me by the Constitution and the laws of the Commonwealth of Kentucky, I, Keen Johnson, Governor of the Commonwealth of Kentucky, do hereby restore the said

Dr. W. L. Stumbo to all the rights and privileges of a citizen, including the right to hold public office.

The rest was easy. Afterward, Doc Walk walked around shaking hands and mentioning, to anyone who might have forgotten it since the last time he had broached the subject, that there was no longer a legal barrier to bar him from politics. He kept a low profile until the next local Democratic Party convention, when the issue of who should run the party arose. Doc Walk waited patiently for the ideal solution to occur to the assembled committeemen. The strategy worked. With a vote scheduled, the pragmatic banker J. D. Fitzpatrick foresaw the inevitable. Chairman Fitzpatrick withdrew his name from consideration. In a panic, the Prestonsburg faction scrambled for another candidate, nominating a Salisbury (the Salisburys had commanded a powerful bloc of their Left Beaver neighbors' votes for nearly a century). But the anointed Salisbury withdrew his name as well, remarking resignedly to the assembled Democrats: "It's all cut and dried."

He was right. The vast majority of the 106 Democratic committeemen and women in the county's fifty-three precincts voted for Doc Walk. It was as if they were hypnotized. As a consolation prize, the banker Fitzpatrick was named to run the highway department.

Barely were the votes counted before Democratic county chairman Walk Stumbo announced his next move, by way of an inconspicuous item in the newspaper that carried the headline "Political Announcements." It read, simply:

FOR SHERIFF

I HEREBY ANNOUNCE MY CANDIDACY FOR

SHERIFF OF FLOYD COUNTY,

SUBJECT TO THE ACTION OF THE DEMOCRATIC PARTY

AT THE AUGUST PRIMARY, 1941.

DR. W. L. STUMBO

Doc Walk was audacious enough to believe he could become the first convicted felon sworn to uphold rule and order—not to mention the traffic laws—in Floyd County. He wanted the job because being sheriff was arguably as good as being county judge. The sheriff controlled a slew of deputies and exerted influence over the county jailer. The sheriff's office had broad discretion about where and when and on whom to serve warrants. The sheriff collected taxes (kickbacks were not uncommon). Although incorporated cities had their own police forces, the sheriff had jurisdiction to enforce any laws he pleased everywhere else in the county. Doc Walk liked a job with leeway.

His candidacy incited outrage among some of his fellow citizens. This he'd expected. For years, they'd put up with him and his difficult personality, with his horse in the aisles at the general store, with his assumption that he ran the world. His latest show of arrogance was more than some could stand.

Within weeks, the race for the Democratic nomination for county sheriff had a long list of candidates. Doc Walk faced so many competitors that it was hard for the average voter to keep everyone straight. Unlike past elections, when opponents had deferred politely to Doc Walk, some of these looked difficult to beat. Among them were the brother-in-law of the sitting sheriff, a former county schools superintendent, and a former county sheriff who was ready, he said, for another term. But of all the candidates who confronted Doc Walk, the one who gave him the most trouble was a political novice named Boone Arnett, who lived in a little town called Cliff. The residents of Cliff had no downtown to speak of; they did their shopping in Prestonsburg. But they had their own mountain—it was called Abbott, and they farmed at its base—and they had a proud history, having been a regular stop for the steamboats that had ferried freight up the Big Sandy to Catlettsburg during the previous century. Cliff had a post office, a general store, and a freight station, which were sufficient to give residents a sense of their rights. Cliff deserved better than a felon for sheriff.

Boone Arnett believed Keen Johnson had made a mistake. One early spring day, Arnett filed a lawsuit charging that a governor's whim was not sufficient to restore Doc Walk's eligibility to run for public office. Without a presidential pardon, Doc Walk had no standing, Boone Arnett charged. And with a world war on the horizon, it was unlikely that Franklin Delano Roosevelt would have time to review the case.

Arnett's lawsuit was a noble effort. But that was about as far as it went. In the state capital, an assistant attorney general spoke on behalf of the governor when he cited the state constitution and said, "All courts recognize that the qualifications of . . . an office holder are determined by state law." In Prestonsburg, Special Judge W. P. Mayo heard the case after Circuit Judge Henry Stephens (who was a cousin to one of the other Democratic candidates for sheriff) was disqualified. Judge Mayo, also a Democrat, supported the governor's decision, quoted identical sections of the state constitution, and said he wished Doc Walk well with his campaign. In June, an appeals court declared Stumbo's candidacy legitimate.

Doc Walk's opponents shifted their arguments to the court of public opinion. Throughout the summer of 1941, a barrage of negative anti-Stumbo ads appeared in the newspaper. On July 10, a candidate asked: "Can we afford to put into the sheriff's office W. L. Stumbo, who relishes and craves power?" On July 17, another pointed out to the voters: "Dr. Stumbo as you know has two hospitals to look after and it looks like he has enough to do to keep them going and he does not need the Sheriff's office as he would not have time to give it the attention it needs." Barely a week after making it through that long, comma-free sentence, readers were treated to this salutation from one of the candidates:

TO THE PEOPLE OF FLOYD COUNTY:

IF I AM ELECTED, I WILL GIVE THE

OFFICE PERSONAL ATTENTION,

AS I HAVE NOTHING ELSE TO DO.

I WILL NOT BE SHAKING THE PEOPLE DOWN.

JOHN STEPHENS

A few days before the Democratic primary, all pretense of civility was dropped. A quarter-page ad, printed in bold type, grabbed readers' attention. It said:

AS FOR DR. W. L. STUMBO, HIS RECORD IS THERE FOR YOU
ALL TO READ, TO PERUSE, TO REMEMBER. SURELY YOU
CANNOT FORGET IT! ARE YOU WILLING FOR HIM TO

HANDLE ALL THE TAX MONIES OF FLOYD COUNTY? ARE YOU
WILLING FOR HIM TO HAVE SOLE CONTROL OVER THE LAW
ENFORCEMENT FORCES OF THIS COUNTY?

The paid political advertisement was signed "Campaign Committee for Taylor Stumbo," an opponent of no close relation to Doc Walk.
Taylor Stumbo posed a special threat, not because he was a popular former county sheriff, but because he had an identical surname. The two
Stumbos were bound to confuse a percentage of voters.

Doc Walk, who maintained a public silence for all the months after
he announced his candidacy, calculated that the time had come to get
vocal. He was ready, having already quietly printed campaign posters to
succinctly convey his position on the whole mess. He passed along the
word to his supporters, and overnight the posters appeared throughout
the county: in shop windows, on the sides of buildings, nailed to trees
and lampposts. The posters featured a big photo of Doc Walk, posing in
the operating room in his scrub suit—and mask!—and bold type ran
across the page: "Don't believe all those things you've been hearing. You
get out and vote for me." That did the job. In the primary, Doc Walk
beat Taylor Stumbo by 609 votes to win the Democratic nomination for
sheriff.

Before he became a felon, the party's nomination would have assured Doc Walk's eventual election in a county that was controlled by
Democrats. But a funny thing happened to Doc Stumbo after the primary of August 1941. For the first—and the last—time in his life, he
faced a serious challenge from a Republican.

Perk Dingus, his opponent, did not look from a distance like sheriff material. He was a railroad man who had never run for office. Most
people would have described Perk as crotchety and quick-tempered.
But my great-grandfather Fred liked him. Perk was a fair brakeman (not
the sort to make mistakes that led to a runaway) and a good, solid
neighbor. Physically, Perk was in no shape to chase the county's crimi-
nals. At 250 pounds, he huffed and puffed. He didn't owe political fa-
vors. He didn't hold personal grudges against Doc Walk (they were
cordial during the campaign, and their families remained so for years af-

terward). He didn't have greater political aspirations. To his wife, Kitty, he said simply, "They asked me to run, so I will."

He had no illusions about his prospects, he told Kitty: "I know not many Republicans get elected." But he had a sense of duty and felt the obligation of standing up for what he believed. When party leaders came to Perk, he knew there weren't many other Republicans who would be willing to put their name on the ticket against Doc Walk. For that reason, if no other, he said yes.

Perk was not a natural campaigner. Whereas it was said Doc Walk would pull out a hundred-dollar bill and hand it to any man who looked hungry, Perk didn't have the instinct, even in front of a crowd of voters, to pull out fifteen cents for a beggar. Whereas Doc Walk was larger than life—"He was the type of person you didn't think would ever die," Walter Mynhier remembers—Perk got flustered. Sometimes he worked in the yard; there he was quick to jump on brakemen who he didn't think were responding fast enough to signals.

In the weeks leading up to the vote, Perk ran what could only be called a low-key campaign. If people approached him on the street and asked him directly if he was running, he admitted that yes, he was. Otherwise, he didn't bring up the subject. Meanwhile, Doc Walk pumped hands and passed out promises to every voter he encountered.

On Election Day, the Board of Elections hired guards to prevent tampering with the ballot boxes. By evening, as early results were counted, most of the Democratic candidates saw they would win easily. By ten o'clock, E. P. Hill, Jr., knew he had won another term as county judge. Soon after, A. B. Meade accepted congratulations for being re-elected county clerk. Jailer, tax commissioner, coroner—all those races were called before midnight and all went to Democrats. As the results came in, the only race that couldn't be called was for sheriff. Doc Walk paced his office, puffing on a cigar, mulling over the bits and pieces of information his supporters brought him.

Early reports put him ahead in District One. Someone said he had a 105-vote lead. But the results from Right Beaver—hard-core Dingus territory—started to come in, and Right Beaver was going for Perk. Later reports put Perk ahead by 70 votes. As counting continued, rumor had it Perk was falling behind. With ballots from seventeen of fifty-three precincts tabulated, Doc Walk was ahead by 102 votes. Sometime after midnight, with the outcome unknown, counting was suspended until morning.

The next day, when the results were announced, Doc Walk had won by 393 votes, the slimmest margin of victory in any race in Floyd County.

Doc Walk called it a close call, accepted congratulations, and went to see patients at Beaver Valley Hospital as if it were just another workday.

Then a curious thing happened. Nine days later, less than half an hour after he finished performing an operation, he went into the hospital kitchen for refreshment. While standing at a counter and eating a slice of watermelon, he collapsed.

Annie Stumbo was getting a manicure in her nieces' beauty shop when the phone rang. Sis Slade answered. The call was from the hospital; an ambulance driver was coming for Annie and it was an emergency. Sis said okay, hung up, and finished the manicure without another word. Annie always wore Windsor, which was barely any color, anyway. What good would it do Annie to know bad news five minutes sooner? Martin Mayo came roaring up in the ambulance before the polish was dry. He screeched to a stop in front of the Twin Modernistic Beauty Shop and ran inside yelling, "Miz Stumbo, Doc's sick! Come quick!"

As soon as she reached the hospital, she knew he was gone. Doc Walk lay in a bed, gray-faced and unresponsive. The oddest sight in the world was to see him helpless. No one had ever imagined the doctor as patient. Pikeville's best doctors were on their way, rushing from the next county. But after they arrived, there was little to say to her but how sorry they felt. Through the night, Annie sat up in Doc Walk's office, at his desk beneath his medical school diploma, which hung next to a framed copy of his favorite poem, "In Kentucky." A judge named Mulligan had written the poem and read it aloud at a banquet of legislators in 1902. Doc Walk particularly loved the last stanza:

In Kentucky;
Mountains tower proudest,
Thunder peals the loudest,
The landscape is the grandest—and

Politics the damnedest—
In Kentucky.

Walker L. Stumbo died the next morning, at 11:40, less than two weeks after he staged the greatest political comeback of any Floyd County politician, before or since. He was fifty-seven years old. A few weeks later, Annie was sworn in as Floyd County's first female sheriff.

CHAPTER 11

The big one they called Red? He just sticks out in my mind for some reason.

—JOHNNIE B. STEPHENS, JULY 2003

R*ed was the most memorable Mynhier. Hesta's oldest child* stuck out in everybody's mind. Many decades later, people who have forgotten the rest of the family can still conjure a mental image of Red. He barreled down Main Street in bib overalls, a force of muscle and belligerence. His horizon-blue eyes were as likely to look through his neighbors as at them. The only soft spot he had was for a girl named Faye Chaffin. She was twenty-three and he was seventeen when they met in the post office. She was a tiny thing, just five-foot-two and never in her life weighed over a hundred pounds, but the minute he met her he declared his love. It just came out of him like something he couldn't control. She tilted her head back to look up to meet his eyes and laughed at the idea. He didn't laugh. He said he would marry her. Something about the way he said it made Faye think twice. Something about Red always made people think twice.

No wonder Johnnie B. Stephens, who no longer remembers the rabid dog that crouched beneath her house and menaced the whole town, can still picture Red. He was as unaware of his notoriety as he was of the extraordinary physical strength that earned it. Red could lift a horse off the ground to win a bet, and he could push wheelbarrows full of wet cement up a steep ramp fast enough to keep three bricklayers busy. On Halloween, teenage boys came to the door to ask, "Can Red come out?" They wanted him to lift cars so they could put pop crates underneath. He was so unaware that his power was unusual that he taunted anybody weaker for being lazy. Red's nickname came from his hair color, which since his childhood had been cause for conversation not only because it was a brighter, more intense hue than any other redhead's in town, but also because people noticed it separated him so clearly from his dark-haired siblings. This observation did not please his mother.

Keeping a secret in a small town is never easy. Hesta, more furtive than most, was successful for years at hiding truths large and small from family and friends. Secrets are funny; they can confer power or, like Hesta's, they can bequeath to their guardians terrible feelings of vulnerability. Not a day went by without Hesta's worrying that someone would discover her family skeletons. Even her children weren't told that a favorite "aunt" was really a cousin, the illegitimate daughter of Hesta's sister. Nor did they know that their Grandpa Kelly had another family from a first marriage. And for years, nobody suspected that Hesta had an even bigger secret: Red. The most memorable Mynhier boy wasn't really a Mynhier at all.

RAYMOND TALBOTT—Born 1917.

CASE INVESTIGATED, FEB. 12, 1937

The above named child was placed with Mr. and Mrs. Fred Mynhier on March 24th, 1917. Mynhiers at that time lived at Quincy, Kanawha County. Some two years later they moved from Quincy. From a party in Quincy I learned that the mother of Mrs. Mynhier, a Mrs. E. M. Kelly, lived at Hugheston. I found Mrs. Kelly at Hugheston. Mrs. Kelly states that she is expecting a visit from her daughter, Mrs. Mynhier, and at that time she will have Mrs. Mynhier write us regarding the adoption. I left an envelope.*

* From the adoption agency's case file.

Young and unmarried in 1917, Red's mother had wanted to keep him. Her name was Harriett Talbott, she was eighteen when he was born, and she lived with her parents and three younger brothers and sisters on the family's farm in Ohio, across the river from West Virginia. Harriett came from a long-established local family. Her grandfather had been a steamboat captain and her uncle Ezbai was owner of the Sistersville Ferry Company, which carried passengers back and forth between the two states. But the child's father had deserted Harriett. She had no money to raise him on her own. Her parents were not wealthy. She gave up the baby after two months.

In those days, orphanage officials from Charleston took whistlestop tours, visiting poor, hungry little towns throughout the state. The trains returned to Charleston with pint-sized passengers: children whose parents had perished in the influenza epidemic; children whose parents, having lost their coal mine jobs, could not afford to feed them; and children whose mothers, abandoned by their fathers, wept bitterly as they handed over their babies on the station platforms.

Harriett wrapped Raymond in a blanket and gave him to N. O. Sowers, the director of the Davis Child Shelter. She signed a release that said, "Being solicitous that my child Raymond Talbott born Jan 10 1917 should receive the benefits and advantages of the Children's Home Society of West Virginia, a corporation organized under the laws of West Virginia, and said Home Society being willing to receive and provide for him a Christian home where he will be loved, trained and educated, so as to be fitted for the requirements of life, I do hereby surrender him." Her parents signed their names beneath hers.

Three days later in Charleston, Hesta saw him, an infant with hair as red as her own. She and Fred had been married for three years; she feared she was barren. Her doctor had done nothing to relieve those worries. The caseworkers watched her watch the baby. They were trained to be wary of prospective parents. To get the baby, Hesta had to reveal personal, private information. The children's society wanted to know where Fred worked and how much money he made. The caseworkers wanted to know where the Mynhiers lived, what type of home they had, and whether it was clean. But the instant Hesta saw that redheaded baby—he was so tiny—she decided she'd do whatever it took to get him. (She had a hunch plenty of applicants were rejected, an intuition confirmed many years later by the historian Stan Bumgardner in his 1996 book *The Children's Home Society of West Virginia*. Bumgardner, who sifted through decades of case files, came across one letter from a prospective parent who had written, "Please do help me I beg of you. I hope how soon i can get a baby Plase help me I am lonsom." On the applicant's letter, Bumgardner noted, "A case worker wrote, 'temperamentally unsuited to handle child.' ") Hesta worked hard to appear temperamentally suited. She spoke nicely to the caseworkers. The Children's Home Society had many orphans to place. Hesta and Fred got custody.

The baby's legal name remained Raymond Talbott, and Hesta was told not to change it until the adoption became final. She agreed. She signed papers. She walked out of the building with him. Then the first thing Hesta did was change his name. He became Raymond Frederick Mynhier before he even knew he had a name. The next thing Hesta did was to cut off communications with the Children's Home Society of West Virginia. She and Fred made no attempt to legally adopt the baby, possibly because going to court cost money. Or maybe Hesta wanted to forget he wasn't hers.

The baby brought her luck; the next year she gave birth to Mary. Hesta's paranoia took over. What if they learned she had had a baby of her own and tried to take back Red? She schemed. She would never give him up. She didn't relax even after she and Fred moved to Paintsville, Kentucky, where nobody knew any better. One day in 1920 a census taker came to the door and started asking snoopy questions. Hesta's guard went up. Born in Kentucky, she said. Both my children were.

So began Hesta's life on the run. Were the authorities hunting for Red, wondering what had become of little Raymond Talbott? She never knew, but she had her suspicions. At the butcher shop, a casual comment like "Where'd your boy get that red hair?" would send her home in a panic, ready to pack the dishes and leave town. She tried not to live in one place long enough for too many people to start wondering about why Red didn't resemble the rest of her children in either looks or personality. After Red showed a disinclination to enroll in school, she didn't press the matter. The fewer schoolteachers and public officials who knew him, the better. Red wanted to spend every day in the hills.

Hesta and her three children— Pauline, Mary, and Red—visiting the Paintsville graves of her two younger sons in the mid-1920s

Lori Stephens next to the C&O Cafe near the Martin depot in the 1920s (Courtesy of the Stephens Family Collection)

Hesta let him. He hunted and trapped in the creek for muskrat. He got an otter once in a while. He sold pelts to trappers. Once a hawk swooped in to take Red's bait and got a leg caught. Red wanted to tame it for a pet, but as he tried to put a bag over its head, the hawk jabbed him. The beak broke the soft skin between his thumb and forefinger, and continued through his hand and out the other side. Red broke the bird's neck with his other hand. After he arrived home with his story and with his hand wrapped in a rag, Hesta began to hope he would one day be able to take care of himself.

The Mynhiers' clandestine adventure lasted nearly twenty-one years. They got caught on the eve of Red's twenty-first birthday, when a plain white envelope addressed to Mr. Fred Mynhier arrived, addressed to Box No. 432 at the Martin Post Office. Even after all those years, Hesta recognized the handwriting, although she'd seen it only once before, a signature scrawled beneath a line of print that said, "Mother of said child, Harriett Talbott, duly surrenders the said Raymond Talbott."

Harriett Talbott had searched for years for her son. She wrote to say that she was married now, that she had sufficient means to pay for a good education for Raymond, and that she'd like to regain custody. She asked if he still had red hair. With the letter came a court summons.

Hesta did not write back. She went on the defense. She decided that Fred should be the one to travel to West Virginia to explain to a judge why Red had disappeared without having been formally adopted. Fred was mild-mannered, he was moderate, he was likable, and he was a model father.

Then she had to tell Red the truth. That's what Fred called it: the truth. As far as Hesta was concerned, the only truth was that Red was her son, she'd raised him, and that was the end of the story. But Fred said since Red was nearly twenty-one years old, he had a right to choose.

Hesta knew Red would choose her. Red was invariably loyal to his parents. He gave half his pay to Hesta and did more than his share of chores to ease Fred's burden. One time she got terribly ill—pneumonia—and for days, weeks maybe, it was unclear if she would survive. The doctor came and went. It was expected, as Hesta lay bundled beneath the blankets in her high-necked maroon nightgown, tossing and delirious, that her daughters would sit with her. Mary and Pauline, grown women by then, fed their mother broth from a spoon, smoothed the sheets, and laid cool cloths on her forehead. The unusual sight was Red, hunched at her bedside and doing the same. Normally he'd rather kill someone than show emotion. He held Hesta's hand while she had feverish dreams. In one, an angel called but Hesta said, "I can't go now. I have children to take care of." When Hesta woke, she said she knew she would live, if only for her children's sake. Then she asked Red if he had been getting enough to eat. He had.

The day she decided to tell him about his birth mother, she surprised him while he was washing up after work.

She was not the type to sugarcoat. "I picked you out in an orphanage," she said.

Red looked confused.

"I picked you because you had red hair like mine," she elaborated.

That was as much as she could bring herself to confess.

Fred filled in more of the details, and after ascertaining that his son had no desire to meet his birth mother, traveled alone to the court hearing. A judge listened to the story and reviewed the recent notes a caseworker had made upon being asked to follow up on the boy's file after twenty years of dormancy:

One year and three months after the Mynhiers took Raymond, Mrs. Mynhier gave birth to a baby girl. Since that time in the 20 years there have been 7 children born to the Mynhiers. However, Raymond has grown to be a fine young man, does not know that he is an adopted child. The oldest girl was in training for a nurse. Raymond is learning the butcher trade.

While awaiting the judge's ruling, Hesta guarded Red jealously. She hated to let him out of her sight. If Red started off to a job, Hesta was likely to insist that one of her other children accompany him.

Red didn't need the help. He was a talented butcher. The work came easily to him. He'd been practicing since boyhood, when he sneaked off to the woodshed with Mary's dolls to chop off their heads.

One day in early winter, as the first snow of the season—flurries mostly—blew through the air, a sour-hearted C&O engineer named

Charlie Caudill hankered for beef. Red, who charged four dollars to slaughter a bull and dress the meat, packed a gunnysack. He had knives, a saw, a rope, and a Y-shaped harness sturdy enough to hoist a Model T Ford into the sky. He swung the bag over his shoulder and headed for Caudill's.

"Go along and help your brother," Hesta said to Jack, who was half Red's age and far less than half his size.

It wasn't a pleasant prospect. Even more unappetizing than the gory proceedings was the prospect of spending a day with Red. Whoever Hesta sent along to "protect" Red worked like a slave. Red issued orders to build a fire, to boil big tubs of water, to hand over a certain knife, and to stay the hell out of the way. And he wanted it all done at once.

But when Hesta made up her mind, there was no room for negotiation. Jack pulled on his coat.

Red never wore a coat. Jack followed him down the yard and past the family pigpen. Red was almost ready to butcher the Mynhiers' winter supply of pork, a Hampshire hog that had grown from a piglet into a monster in less than a year, abetted by kitchen scraps. He was vicious. Hogs get that way if they're penned; they'll kill and eat a small child if they get a chance. Anybody who had ever been sent to slop the Mynhiers' hog (Jack, mostly) looked forward all year to Thanksgiving ham. Red had a smokehouse, too, where he relied mainly on hickory and sometimes dogwood for flavor. He had his own method of sugaring and salting a ham. Caudill would pay Red in beef as well as cash, and that additional meat would serve as insurance in case the weather got too bad to butcher the family hog.

Red strode ahead, ignoring Jack. He took big steps, loping along in his boots, shirtsleeves pushed to his elbows. By the time Jack caught up at the edge of the pasture, Red was standing near the pen into which Caudill and his son had driven the bull. The prospective victim, black like an Angus but not as fat, wasn't fully grown. But at eight hundred pounds, it outweighed Red somewhat. Red was taller by a head. If the animal had been castrated, it would have fattened faster, and the meat would have been more tender. But Caudill, who kept a number of cows, generally only had one male at a time. It remained a breeder.

The bull had a pair of long horns that curved forward. Caudill had warned Red about those horns. The bull had developed a habit during the previous summer of chasing the kids who crossed the pasture to swim in the creek. Caudill, who didn't like children and was prone to shooting a gun into the air to frighten even the smallest trespassers, hadn't discouraged the aggressiveness. But as Red eyed the animal, he concluded the bull was all bluff.

Red turned away. He liked to follow a certain procedure. First, he needed a fire. The Caudills had gathered wood. Red stacked it just so. Together he and Jack balanced a tub on a metal stand above the wood, and Red lit the fire. As flames rose, Jack filled the tub from a hose. Red told Jack to look for more wood. They would require endless buckets of hot water.

Nearby, the bull watched. Cattle can actually be very smart; they panic easily. But if the fire meant anything to this bull, he didn't let on.

As the woodpile started to hiss and smoke, Red turned his attention to the bull. Red liked to kill things. He never explained why, but anyone could see it in his eyes. His two choices were to shoot the bull or to poleax it. In either case, he'd aim for the middle of the forehead where the skull was thin. To imagine the spot, picture an "X" drawn from the base of the horns to the eyes. Right behind the skull was the brain; if he hit it dead-on, the animal would die instantly. With an animal this big and this unpredictable, it was far easier to shoot than to try to smash the flat side of a blade into the sweet spot. A less competent butcher might hit the bull too low, right between the eyes, for instance. That wouldn't kill the bull; it would just give him a bad case of painful sinuses. He'd be a mad, upset, stampeding bull. For this reason, poleaxing was a distant second choice. Red picked up his rifle.

One shot was all Red ever needed. Some butchers tethered an animal tight against a tree, to limit skittishness. But Red never bothered. He was a good shot and, most important, a fast shot. When he aimed at an imaginary bull's-eye on the forehead, the bullet went home. The bull toppled, already dead. Usually this unfolded as smoothly as ballet. Lightly (for someone so large), Red walked up to the wooden fence. He picked an angle that allowed him to look straight at the bull. He shouldered the rifle and from a distance of four feet—

Cursed.

At the last instant, the bull turned away.

The bull couldn't go far. There wasn't much room to maneuver in the temporary holding pen, just enough space for the animal to shift his weight, move slightly, and present a glossy black profile.

Red readjusted his stance. He walked a step closer. From a no-miss distance of three feet, he lined up the target, and locked blue eyes onto black. He raised the rifle, sighted down the barrel, started to squeeze the trigger, and—

The bull turned away.

It didn't try to run. It didn't try to escape. It didn't try to hide. It just turned its head.

Another man might have admired the animal's survival instincts. A man who'd never had his hand run through by the beak of a hawk might even have marveled over a bull smart enough to try to outwit death.

"The SOB," Red said. For the first time, he noticed the snow, noticed the cold.

Red didn't deal gracefully with obstacles. He was not a natural negotiator. He had more in common with the bull he was about to kill than with many men. Faced with an impediment, he never looked for a way around it. Instead, he lowered his head and crashed straight ahead into the center of the problem.

"Goddamn bull knows a gun," Red said. "He must have seen another one killed that way."

Red aimed again. The bull turned again. Red saw Jack watching. Before Jack had enough time to really register the fact that there was an obstacle, Red removed it in his usual way. He shouted, "You SOB, I don't need a gun for you!"

Red dropped the rifle. He reached over the fence, grabbed a horn, and forced the bull's head down. With one hand, he twisted the massive neck to one side. Now he had a good angle. Red balled his other hand and punched the bull between the eyes. His fist hit the bull like a boulder. The bull's eyes crossed, he went to his knees, and rolled to his side, out cold.

After I heard this remarkable story, I wondered how much force it takes to drop an eight-hundred-pound bull to the ground. Jack, who witnessed the incident, has known since he was a boy that it was possible for a bare-knuckled man to punch a bull unconscious. I never doubted it, either. If Jack said something happened, it happened. But the story sounded so fabulously implausible that I wondered just how strong Red Mynhier really was. Was he the only man who ever lived who could do it? The consensus among those who knew Red was yes.

What I confirmed, from cattle handlers and professors familiar with animal anatomy, was something I already assumed. Red was an unusual man. Consider this. A strong fellow who holds a rock (or any other kind of heavy, flat object) in his hand could stun a bull with a blow. Not a twelve-hundred-pound bull, probably. But a young animal in the eight-hundred-pound range? Even a well-placed karate chop would be enough. These days, when the humane method of slaughter involves a stun gun to the forehead, it has been widely documented that the thin part of the skull in front of the brain is particularly sensitive to attack. A single, strong electrical impulse will kill a steer immediately. But Red didn't use electricity or a blunt object. His hands were huge, and from the heavy work he did, rough as emery paper. The skin was like dry leather. When he cheated at canasta, his fingers covered the whole deck, so he could take as many cards as he wanted. With hands like that, the force of a fist hitting the bull was enough. His fist was as strong as a rock. "I'm not saying he couldn't have done it," one expert told me. "I'm saying I would have liked to see your uncle Red's hands."

His knuckles weren't even bruised. Red opened the pen's gate, stepped inside, and slit the stunned bull's throat. It happened so fast that it took Jack a few seconds to understand what he was seeing. Blood gushed onto Red's clothes, covering his arms to his elbows, splashing his pants. Quickly Red looped a rope around the dying animal's front legs and a second around the back haunches, to make sure it stayed down. Even after a bull is dead, its legs can kick reflexively. He kneeled against its hot side, and watched the snow turn red. Slowly, the breaths of both the man and the bull slowed. Soon the bull's torso stopped heaving. Its tongue hung limp and its eyes stared at nothing.

Red wiped his hands on his overalls. Now he felt hot. He stripped off his shirt and looped a harness around the carcass. With a pulley, he slowly hoisted the bull over a strong branch of Caudill's old oak. It was impossibly heavy work, and steam rose off Red's body as he pulled. But he made it look not only reasonable for one man to do a job meant for at least two, but easy, as well. He raised the bull, and the black weight swayed, like a lazy pendulum, at the end of the rope.

Gutting and skinning was a slow process. Red made a cut stretching from the soft part of the belly all the way to rib cage. Then he carefully slit the skin—the hide could be tanned later to make winter coats—the rest of the way. He worked like a confident surgeon. He was messy, but methodical. Blood splattered everywhere, yet the situation was completely under control. Jack brought an empty tub for the entrails. Red patiently worked the skin off the bull, starting at the hind legs, until he could remove the hide in one piece.

Decapitation was a challenge. Red used a knife to slice down to the spine, then he hacked away for a while with a cleaver. Then he sawed, his muscles bulging with the effort as bits of bone and hair caught in the blade disapprovingly.

Over the next hours as Red worked, blood dripped into the snow and Jack poured pails of hot water to wash away the brilliant puddles. Jack became so hardened to gore and muck that he watched with clinical detachment as Red dragged the head out of the way.

"What are you looking at?" Red asked.

"Nothing," Jack said.

Red split the carcass into two sides of beef and carried them to a raised wooden platform built for the last bull. There he carved the meat into precise cuts that he divided into two piles, one for Caudill and one to take home as part of his wages.

That evening, Hesta met Red and Jack at the door. "You're late," she said. "I was getting worried." She shot Jack a sharp look to say she hoped he'd taken good care of Red.

Eventually, another envelope arrived. Inside was a piece of paper that set Hesta free. The judge had ruled that after all these years, the Mynhiers could legally adopt Red. The paper said, "It is hereby adjudged, ordered and decreed that said prayer for adoption is hereby granted and that Raymond Talbott shall therefore be known as Raymond Mynhier." Hesta kept the good news in her lockbox, proof that no one could steal her son away.

Was Red's birth mother resigned to his loss? Harriett died in 1982 without ever seeing Red again, but I found the phone number of one of her nieces. "We never knew Harriett had that baby," her niece said. "It doesn't sound right. Harriett mentally wouldn't have been able to keep him. The story was that she had a fever when she was four and was never right afterward. It was the family making excuses, excuses for her. Harriett would not have been financially able to offer anything to anyone. She was a black sheep." Hoping to jog a memory, I recounted the details that my family took as faith, that Red's birth mother's married name was Scott and that she had been living in Ironton, Ohio, when she tried to get him back, but Harriet's niece said those facts didn't fit her aunt. Starting to doubt the adoption agency's records—perhaps Red wasn't a Talbott, after all?—I said that the reason my great-grandmother wanted that particular baby so badly was because he had hair just like Hesta's. "Red hair?" Harriett's niece asked. "Red hair sort of pops up every once in a while in the Talbott family. Harriett had a brother, Corwin, with red hair. Corwin was an unusual man." I asked what was unusual about him. "Well, Corwin was very big, and he was extremely strong. He had huge hands, and I know it sounds hard to believe, but Corwin used to do things like lift calves into the air." I said it didn't sound strange at all.

The Talbott family lost Red to Hesta. But if she thought she'd thwarted all efforts to take him away, Hesta had reckoned without the army. As Fred feared, Red earned no exemption. He was drafted in 1941, along with nearly 120 other local men who got a notice in the mail. He was to report for military service within sixty days. In the meantime, he had to ride a special bus to Huntington, West Virginia, for a physical exam to make sure he was strong enough to serve.

By the time Red's orders to report for duty arrived, Fred and Hesta had moved back to town. They didn't talk about the situation, although Fred's stooped shoulders and Hesta's new and nervous, birdlike habit of smoothing Red's collar revealed worry. The morning Red had to leave at 6:30, Hesta made eggs and biscuits and sausage gravy, but for once he didn't eat much. The family wanted to see him off, but he said no, he'd go alone. They watched from the windows as he walked in everyday civilian clothes toward the bus stop in front of Martin's Drugstore, where the other recruits were gathering.

A few days later, Fred sat in the living room listening to the Philco on a Sunday afternoon.

"Hell's bells!" he yelled. "We'll be at war now!"

Hesta ran in to hear what the fuss was, in time for the news services' first sketchy reports of the Pearl Harbor attack. The rest of the children—Jack and Walter and Betty and Billy and Ann—wondered what was so exciting. One look at their parents and they turned somber too. They listened to the announcers' scratchy voices all afternoon and tried to decipher what the words meant to their lives. There was no discussion about what this would mean for Red. In front of Hesta, a topic like mortal danger was off limits.

CHAPTER 12

*A*fter Red went to war, Fred bought an American flag from Grigsby's Five-and-Dime and hung it on the front door. Hesta, like other mothers whose sons were in the service, added a forty-ninth star to the flag in honor of her son. A second flag flew from the roof. On a windy day, Hesta could see it flapping from as far away as the post office, where she forced herself to walk each afternoon, dreading the possibility of a telegram inside Box No. 432. As early as Christmas Day of 1941, the prospect became all too real after a West Prestonsburg mother became the first in Floyd County to learn her son was missing. Navy fireman Walter Karr was lost, the telegram said. His mother held out hope; it was Christmas, after all.

Martin mobilized. Rationing, scrap-metal drives—Floyd County was prepared to do its part. Sacrifice was second nature in eastern Kentucky. Within days of the Pearl Harbor attack, local farmers, 2,300 of them, pledged to aid the war effort by increasing production well above the new quotas. President Roosevelt wanted 10 percent more eggs; Floyd County farmers promised their chickens would lay 464,190 dozen in 1942—a 28 percent increase. The president asked for more pork and Floyd County promised 6,934 hogs, along with 2,099,954 gallons of milk and 4,045 head of beef cattle.

Even the dabblers began to take their vegetable gardens seriously. Dick Osborn saw an opportunity. On acreage he owned on Mulberry Hill, near Ice Plant Hollow, he raised tomato, onion, and potato starts. He nailed a sign to the side of his pickup that said S. D. OSBORN— PLANTS FOR SALE and loaded hundreds of seedlings onto the tin truck bed. He drove up Left Beaver, parked in front of the general store, and sat, whistling, next to the truck. Eventually somebody came up to ask, "Do you have any plants?" In answer, Dick nodded toward the sign. After closing the deal, Dick stuffed the money behind the driver's seat. Dick's next stop was the post office, where he parked in front and whistled to attract tomato lovers. By the end of the day, Dick had stopped in front of enough general stores and barbershops to supply the entire county with the makings of salad. On the drive home, he continued to whistle, oblivious to the biggest obstacle that stood between him and a clear profit: his poor driving skills. Approaching the Arkansas Curve at the north end of Martin at a speed more suited for a straightaway, he went off the road, bounced into bottomland, and emerged shaken to see one of his parishioners walking nearby. "Brother Dick, you appear to be all right, the Lord must have been with you," the congregant said.

"If he was, he must have had a rough ride," Dick said.

That night Dick returned home with dry lips from all the whistling and with four or five hundred dollar bills behind the seat. The cash he relinquished to Myrt. She knew how to hold on to it. When she and Dick went into Miz Hunter's restaurant, they ordered a single bottle of orange pop to share. Afterward, Dick might smack his lips and say, "That was so good I could drink a *whole* one." But he knew better than to try. Myrt kept close track of every nickel in her Blue Horse composition book.

Annie Stumbo's tenure as sheriff was forgettable. Although she would live another forty years on her own before dying at ninety-nine, after Walk died she found she couldn't run anything anymore. She agreed to be sheriff only as a temporary figurehead until another election could be scheduled. The situation would have turned into a real crisis if not for her sister. Lula Slade, who in her youth had broken wild horses in rodeos out west, knew how to take charge in an emergency. Lula put her own businesses—the gas station, the restaurant, the towing service, and about ninety-seven others—on hold and went over to Lackey to oversee operations at Stumbo Memorial. Lula instructed her husband, Edgar—who had been a certified public accountant at a mine in Weeksbury before she'd met him, bewitched him, and erased all memories of his native Michigan from his consciousness—to go to Prestonsburg to run the sheriff's office, and so he did. From the day Edgar met Lula Elliott, that had been it for him. Pumping gas, directing deputies, it was all the same to him so long as she was happy.

Red's unusual skills translated well to war, although no one would have known it from his letters. He wrote to Faye Chaffin that he was still planning to marry her as soon as he got home. He wrote to Mary, "Dear Sis, I am fine and thinking of you." He stuck to platitudes even when describing a new outfit called the Rangers for which he'd volunteered to train in the British Isles. He didn't add that it was one of the more dangerously thrilling assignments that he could have drawn or that the 1st Ranger Battalion was an elite force of commandos who were learning to lead sneak attacks. His subsequent descriptions of training glossed over the speed marches, the live fire (to simulate combat experiences), the swim in icy water while carrying a heavy pack, and the time he almost fell from a rope swing high above a stream (considered good practice for amphibious landings). He figured Hesta didn't need to know he was being trained to fight ahead of everybody else.

The news from Red became increasingly vague. His letters arrived in envelopes stamped WAR & NAVY DEPARTMENTS V-MAIL SERVICE OFFICIAL BUSINESS. He didn't say that he was headed to North Africa to participate in the invasion of that continent. But his mother couldn't help but notice the scrawled return address at the top of the page: "Somewhere in North Africa." He rarely wrote more than "I am all right. That is all that counts. I remain your son, Red."

Later, his family feared Red was in Sicily because "Italy" began to appear at the top of his letters at about the same time that details about the Allied invasion began to trickle stateside. The 1st Ranger Battalion led the invasion into Sicily to gain an Allied toehold in Italy; soldiers swam ashore at three A.M. to land on a beach booby-trapped with mines. Moving north, as the Allies stormed a nine-mile stretch of beach, the Rangers occupied the hilly, forested terrain at Anzio. The region, with a maze of canals and irrigation ditches, was within striking distance of Rome.

Soon after, things went very wrong for the Rangers. Within days, as forces continued to push inland, the Rangers were sent ahead to infiltrate German forces and wrest control of a nearby small town called Cisterna as backup infantry moved in from both north and south. At 1:30 A.M., the Rangers began their stealthy approach along a six-foot-wide drainage ditch. But the Germans ambushed them at dawn. German artillery units surrounded and trapped the Rangers within eight hundred yards of the town. After hours of heavy fighting and failed attempts to rescue the overwhelmed Rangers, the Allied forces gave up the battalions for lost. Only 6 of the 767 men in the two battalions made it back from enemy lines. For weeks, no news of the disaster reached the United States until the Associated Press got wind of the story.

> NAPLES, March 8 (AP)—A grim secret kept for more than a month has been placed in the record of heroic but hopeless "last stands."
>
> It concerned two lost battalions of Rangers who set out on what for them was a routine assignment to "raise hell" in Cisterna at 1 A.M. on Jan. 30. By noon of that day, they had been swallowed into oblivion.
>
> Even now, all that is known is the fragmentary picture framed by a few who returned and a German announcement at the time that some 900 had been captured. The Germans said that about 100 had been killed and many more had been wounded.

Hesta was frantic to learn that so few of the men in the 1st Battalion survived the Cisterna battle without being captured. For days afterward, soldiers straggled back, one or two at a time, to safety. Was Red among them? What did it take to survive? One who made it back was a Ranger named Ben Mosier, who dove into a cold, cold river and swam away from the Germans. Mosier was a superior athlete, in top physical condition. Before the war, neighbors in Mosier's hometown of Ashtabula, Ohio, had expected him to become a major league baseball player. Another Ranger named Arnold Davis avoided detection by rolling beneath the treads of German tanks as they climbed a rise. A third, Thurman Ellis, remembered decades later that it took a cool head: "There were ditches like, called canals, and we headed back that way until we ran into the Third Division."

Hesta and Fred scoured newspapers and magazines for clues. They learned that the Rangers had walked into a "death trap," as *The Saturday Evening Post* put it, because the Allies had underestimated the strength of the Germans who had arrived to fortify an airbase near Cisterna.

Worrying about Red was a full-time job. Yet Hesta had even more cause for concern: Walter had also enlisted, prompting Hesta to cry for days. She saved a can of fruit cocktail—his favorite—in the cupboard and forbade everyone from opening it. She sewed another star to the flag on the front door. She shared Walter's early hopes that he would be assigned to a stateside railroad unit because he'd gotten experience working as a fireman for the C&O. She wrung her hands throughout the entire twelve weeks Walter spent in basic training at Aberdeen Proving Ground in Maryland. But there wasn't much she could do after that, not when he wrote home to say he was being sent north to a point of embarkation—to New York City, and on to a ship bound for Europe. For weeks afterward, she heard no further news from Walter.

Jack, too young to enlist, worked after school at the Standard Oil filling station on Main Street. One day the phone rang while he was counting the day's cash—it was coins mostly, from customers who had paid twenty cents a gallon for gas, and not too many coins either, since rationing allotted most people only five gallons a month. The station's rotary-dial phone was still a novelty, one of a handful in town. It was a marvel of technology, far more sophisticated than the magneto phone it had replaced, which had required cranking and a ring-off for every call. The new phone automatically disconnected if you replaced the receiver on its hook. It had its own dedicated four-digit phone number, 2832 (dial "8" first to call Prestonsburg), and, most notably, a very shrill ring. It startled Jack.

It rang again.

Jack's boss, Morg Turner, had installed the phone for the convenience of customers. The phone didn't receive many calls, however, maybe half a dozen a day, because few customers had home phones on

which to place a call to inquire about a carburetor. So although the
Southern Bell Telephone and Telegraph Company had spent the better
part of two years installing a dial system to ensure that Floyd County's
service was "the most modern available," as they put it on the brochures,
most of Morg Turner's customers continued to behave as if Thomas
Edison had never been born. If they needed a fender fixed, they
dropped off the car, waited a decent interval, and eventually walked
back to the service station (or sent a child) to see if the work was complete. Morg, who paid four dollars a month for his business individual
line, still felt he'd made a good investment in community relations. Not
only was he a prominent local businessman (his family owned coal
mines, as well) but he also was a member of the local draft board. As
Morg passed judgment on his best customers' sons—pronouncing them
fit for active overseas duty, in most cases—he felt a keen need to stay on
friendly terms with his neighbors.

"Standard Oil," Jack said into the receiver.

"Long-distance operator."

Long distance was not unusual. Phone service arrived in piecemeal
fashion in eastern Kentucky. Due to the vagaries of the wiring system,
any call that didn't originate smack in downtown Martin was likely to
be routed through the central Paintsville switchboard in the next county
before wending its way back to town. Placing a call from Martin to
Maytown, a mere eight miles away, was a leisurely process.

A phone call qualified as an event. The Standard Oil phone was the
first Jack ever used. Learning to operate it had been as complicated as
learning to park cars.

"Yes?" he asked in a professional tone.

"I have an overseas call for Hesta Mynhier," the operator said.

This was too much for Jack. He forgot to be professional.

"I have an overseas call from Walter Mynhier for Hesta Mynhier,"
the operator repeated. "Is she there?"

The operator knew as well as Jack that Hesta was not at the service
station. The operator may have been stationed twenty miles from Martin, but the nature of her work gave her intimate knowledge of both the
town's physical layout and its residents' personal habits. She knew exactly how many phones were in Martin, and had memorized frequently

called numbers such as Beaver Valley Hospital's (2141) and the Twin Modernistic Beauty Shop's (2176). She knew how long she could expect to have to hold the line open while the person who had answered a call went to look for the person to whom it was directed. She knew that most long-distance calls went either to the Keathleys' theater (2921) or to Morg's service station; their central locations provided the speediest access to phone-call recipients. The only wild card in this equation, as far as the operator was concerned, was Hesta, a woman not often on the receiving end of a long-distance call. The last time that Hesta got an overseas phone call was never. So while the operator may have suspected that Hesta was across the street at the post office picking up the Mynhiers' mail—it was that time of the afternoon, after all—she had no prior knowledge of how fast a woman like Hesta could run.

"She's at a neighbor's," Jack said. He didn't know if that was true, but he had to say something. "I'll have to go after her."

The operator said that was fine. She'd hold the line open. After all, who knew when a serviceman headed to battle might get another chance to phone his mother?

Patriotism had played no part in Walter's decision, soon after his eighteenth birthday, to serve his country. He enlisted on practical grounds. After some unfortunate events at home, he was not at all reluctant to go to war to avoid the consequences. He enlisted to escape a young lady he was dating intermittently, after she informed him of her plans to file a paternity suit against him. She had gone to see the sheriff. After a night in jail, Walter stood in front of the county judge's bench, desperate to steer clear of what he considered an unfair life sentence. Walter told the judge the baby was not his. The judge gave him a choice: take the bus or the baby. Walter already had had rudimentary military training that had whetted his appetite for more; when he was thirteen, he'd attended a Citizens Military Training Camp at Fort Benjamin Harrison in Indiana. He told the judge he'd take his chance on the army. And in the early morning light, Fred had walked Walter down the hill to catch the next vehicle bound for Fort Thomas and basic training.

Walter believed being killed on a foreign battlefield was a lesser evil than settling down and raising a family. Walter had reached the conclusion, a few months before arriving in England—where he had stood for hours waiting for his turn at a phone, one of a long line of men with identical hair length, their necks displaying the angry goose pimples of the recently shaved—that no matter what happened next, he was better off in the army. Given the climate at home, he believed his chances in battle in Europe were slightly higher than his current odds of surviving Martin.

Jack laid the receiver on the scarred desktop and took off at a run. Barely was he out the door (and wondering: should he look for his mother at the grocery? at her friend Juanita's house?) before he saw Hesta walking along Main Street, headed toward home. She was a few steps from the front porch when Jack started to yell.

Hesta considered no news good. Under other circumstances, it would have been a comical moment, Jack's flying down the middle of Main Street, waving his arms and calling, "Mom, Mom!" as if he were a shipwreck survivor hailing a distant trawler. From a distance of half a block, he could see she had recently visited the post office. Thankfully none of the envelopes she clutched was yellow and edged in black. But her expression was full of dread.

"Mom, come quick!" Jack yelled. "You have a phone call from Walter!"

Hesta wasn't a woman to react spontaneously to joyous news. She was more apt to sniff it suspiciously. She didn't do anything reckless like throw the mail into the air or shriek, "Praise the Lord," or start crying. Instead, she put the pile of envelopes on the front porch, grabbed hold of her skirts, and started off in the direction of the service station.

How fast could a woman like Hesta run? It turned out the answer was very fast, if her son was waiting on the other end of a transatlantic phone connection. She could set a new land-speed record without thinking twice. She passed by Jack in a second, her hair flying from its bun, and did not bother to look for traffic before she crossed Main Street. Jack took off after her—he was afraid she might fall—and by the time he caught up, she was in the service station office, picking up the phone's receiver.

"This is Hesta Mynhier," she said, not caring that she was panting.

From there, it was still a complicated process to actually get Walter onto the phone. It may have taken only a few seconds, or it may have been minutes—it felt like weeks, as far as Hesta was concerned—from the moment when the operator in Paintsville said, "Hold on, please," to the instant when another operator came on the line, speaking in a British accent. She was holding a line open for Walter.

"Mom?"

The line had plenty of static, and he was as far away from her as anyone ever had been. But Hesta could see him as clearly as on that morning when he had stood before her in uniform, as tall and as handsome as anyone, and prepared to wave good-bye. Upon departure, Walter became the hero of the family. His favorite song was "When My Blue Moon Turns to Gold," and in his absence, the family almost wore out that record playing it on the phonograph and crying over it.

"How are you? And where are you?" she asked.

He said he was fine, but he couldn't say exactly where. He couldn't tell her he'd sailed from New York City to Glasgow in a boat that pitched and moaned on high seas while the men played poker belowdecks. He couldn't describe how he'd traveled south from Scotland by train in fancy passenger cars with velvet curtains. He couldn't tell her he was currently stationed forty miles south of London, awaiting orders. And he certainly couldn't say that soon he would be bound for the D-Day invasion of Normandy, because he didn't know it yet himself. The details he would learn later, while standing alongside some of his buddies from the 42nd Rainbow Division, holding on to the side of a small boat as it rode the night waves toward a beach lit up like day by gunfire. He didn't know, when he was talking to his mother, that at Normandy he would go ashore and fight the Germans face to face. Or that one of the best buddies he'd made since enlisting—his name was Sandy Martin, and he served in the 5th Infantry Division—would die in that battle. The last view anyone would have of Sandy would be of a wounded soldier propped against a tree and waiting for the medics to load him onto a ship bound for an English hospital. Some things Walter would never understand, like why Sandy never made it to England or why two of Walter's other best friends from Martin—James McGlothen and Wiley Elliott—wouldn't make it home, either. James would be killed in the Pacific, Wiley in Belgium. Their families would get telegrams in yellow envelopes.

"We miss you so much," Hesta said.

Walter said he missed home, too.

"We worry about you," Hesta said.

"Don't you worry," he said.

The conversation continued in that vein for about ten minutes. Hesta asked Walter if he'd heard anything from Red. Walter said no. The last nine minutes of dialogue mimicked the first. Luckily the operators were patriots; it was a major technical feat to keep open the line for so long. Jack stood in the doorway, watching his mother hunched over the desk where he spent so many hours smoothing out the mundane mechanical problems of his neighbors' vehicles. Hesta was conducting what might be her final conversation with her battle-bound son on the same premises where Jack had solved the mystery of Old Doc Mayo's erratic engine. Doc Mayo had reached an age that made him reluctant to get dressed in the middle of the night to deliver a baby—"Tell them I'm not home," callers who phoned after supper could hear him hiss in the background—and had even less patience with his problematic Graham Supercharger. It was a spacious, high-powered sedan that had cost big bucks. Unfortunately, it was fussy, with an engine that died every time Mrs. Mayo drove it. The Mayos sent the car to the Standard Oil for a tune-up to correct the unfortunate predilection, and back again a couple of days later for another (free) after a repeat incident. But even a third adjustment (at no charge) failed, Mrs. Mayo had reported sorrowfully to Jack one day at the pumps. As he filled the car with gas, she went inside to report to the mechanic. Jack was cleaning the window glass when he saw her purse inside the car—hanging on the choke knob on the dash. The choke was pulled all the way out. Subsequent questioning revealed that Mrs. Mayo always drove with the choke pulled out; she liked to have a place to hang her purse. While the mechanic was explaining that this caused the carburetor to flood and kill the engine, Doc Mayo happened to drive up in his other car. He insisted on paying for the two extra tune-ups. The car never flooded again.

Hesta sat in a gas station, jammed against the wall beneath a calendar and an electric wall clock. Beyond the back wall was the restroom. Through the window, directly in front of the office, were the gas pumps. It was the most ordinary view. But it was the most extraordinary moment Hesta had experienced in months. Walter was alive!

Finally, she said, "You take care of yourself."

She hung up.

"He'll be going into danger now," she prophesied to Jack.

Soon Hesta's conversation would belong to everyone. A serviceman's call home was rare news, good news, and everybody spread it. Walter Mynhier was in Europe and the boy was alive as of four P.M. local time. That qualified as an urgent bulletin.

Hesta considered the news a mixed blessing. Walter was alive. But he was poised to head into combat. She could feel it.

So much of the war lay ahead of her, so many terrible days. Hesta didn't yet know it. But she sensed it. She stood heavily, as if a woman of her age could move only slowly and deliberately and after careful consideration of the consequences, and walked home.

CHAPTER 13

"*Mary! Mary! Come quick!*" *With the windows open, the* voice carried, very clearly, from Ora Mae's house across Main Street to the house that Mary and Elmer rented. The voice was high-pitched and sharp and panicked. Except for that, it sounded just like Ora Mae.

In all her life, Ora Mae had never panicked. She took control of a situation—but nicely. She was firm, she stood her ground, but she didn't make enemies. She and Mary had that in common, as well as the coincidences that had brought them together as girls. Ora Mae's family moved to town the same year as the Mynhiers, and for the same reason: a good job on the railroad. Ora Mae's father took the job of Left Beaver section manager over the protests of his wife and six children, who had not wanted to move east from Winchester, Kentucky (paved roads), to Martin. Compared to the curriculum in Winchester, in Ora Mae's opinion Martin's high school had offered nothing—absolutely nothing—that she had needed for college. But she had had no choice but to make the best of things. (Later, Ora Mae said the best thing she learned at Martin High School was Mary's name; they stayed friends for life.) Ora Mae managed to extract every bit of value that the school offered. She made A's, played on the girls' basketball team, and gave the principal helpful suggestions on how to broaden the course offerings beyond Latin, geography, and geometry. Eventually she graduated with the label "Most Likely to Succeed," an acceptance letter from Pikeville College, and firm plans to become a schoolteacher. In town, it was generally agreed that Ora Mae was far too pretty to teach school; she was small and slender and dark-haired, the sort of ambitious girl who was expected to move to a big city to find a new life. But Ora Mae wouldn't leave her family. She came home with a degree and persuaded the county schools superintendent, whose name was Town Hall, to hire her to teach. That first year she had forty-two students in her combined first- and second-grade class; Ora Mae wrote their names in a ledger because it was the only way to keep track. Her goal was to teach every one of those forty-two to read and write fluently by the end of the year. The principal said gently, "Ora Mae, that's not possible." When she went home at night, she cried in frustration, afraid he was right. But by June, every first grader could read at least one of the ten stories from the second-grade primer *Friendly Village*.

"Mary!"

Mary flew out the door and down the porch steps and into the street before she even thought about whether she'd left anything on the stove—she hadn't—or where her own children were. By the time she crossed the yard and gained the road, she'd taken a mental inventory: Margaret and Judy were next door with Hesta. Jo was in the crib. Ten steps later, as she hit Ora Mae's front walk, she called to Betty, whom she saw coming down the street with friends, "Listen for the baby, she's asleep."

Mary pushed open Ora Mae's screen door. The front room was empty.

"Ora Mae, where are you?"

The frantic voice called from the bedroom. "Mary, he's dying!"

Mary found Ora Mae leaning over the bed, on which lay her new baby. Dickie was a little doll adrift on an ocean of a mattress. Mary's first thought was to worry that he would roll off the bed. Her second was to realize he couldn't. Dickie was limp and pale and blue around the lips. He was not breathing.

"He's turning black," Ora Mae said.

It was an exaggeration, but Mary wasn't about to argue the fine points of Dickie's complexion, not when his skin tone was obviously headed in the wrong direction.

"I just found him like this," Ora Mae said.

Mary tried to calculate how many valuable seconds had been lost already. Many. But maybe not too many.

As Ora Mae watched, Mary slipped her hand under Dickie's neck. She lifted his head. Dickie didn't respond. She put him over her shoulder, surprised to realize she already had forgotten how little an infant weighed. A sweet smell of baby prompted her instinctively to pat his back. Nothing. She sat on the bed with him across her lap and swept her finger in his mouth. Nothing. Then around his tongue. Nothing. She hated to look up because she would have to meet Ora Mae's eyes.

Dickie had been born prematurely. Ora Mae's oldest boy, Jitter, was the healthiest toddler in town. Who would have expected anything different the second time? But Dickie had had trouble from the start. When he slept, he forgot to breathe. After the doctors in town had advised taking him to a specialist, Ora Mae and her husband, Bill, had gone to Lexington for a consultation. But after they'd returned home, the baby still suffered from spells of apnea.

Even in the worst crisis, a person noticed the most ordinary things. A clock ticked on a night table. A breeze rustled a curtain. A sound— laughter—wafted in through the window as children played in twilight. The ordinary world was priceless. Routines that seemed humdrum an hour ago—dishes soaking in the sink, children playing in the dusk and pretending they didn't hear Mary calling to come inside and wash up before bed—were beyond her reach. What wouldn't she have given, at that moment, for the monotony of scraping supper off dirty plates? What wouldn't she have traded for the safety of boredom?

"I found him like this," Ora Mae repeated. Ora Mae, who never cried, started to sob. Ora Mae, whose students so loved her calm, sensible sweetness that they squandered their recess to pick bouquets of wildflowers for her, was lost. Ora Mae, who accepted wilting bunches of dandelions with grace and who kept cool water on her desk to revive vases of bachelor's buttons, violets, and clover, seemed beyond help and possibly beyond helping Mary.

"Ora Mae, come on," Mary said. She never spoke sharply to Ora Mae. This was the tone that she reserved for Elmer after one of his mysterious disappearances. It had the desired effect. Ora Mae stood.

Mary grabbed a blanket that smelled of new baby and, as she trotted out the door, expertly swaddled Dickie in mid-motion. "Bring Jitter."

Parked outside was Ora Mae's car. Mary did not know how to drive.

"The hospital," Mary instructed as she climbed into the passenger seat with the baby. "Drive as fast as you can."

All the way down Main Street, Mary jiggled Dickie and patted his back and egged him on. Breathe, Dickie, breathe, as if all he needed was heartfelt coaxing.

Word traveled faster through town than any car. Later, Ora Mae wouldn't remember seeing or passing anybody she knew, not from the time she and Mary left the house—certainly she hadn't made a phone call and hadn't asked anyone else to run to the service station to make one for her—to the moment when they pulled up at the hospital. Yet Dr. Claude Allen was waiting by the front door.

Young as he was, Claude Allen was on his way to becoming "Doc Claude." Plenty of other doctors in town would have liked to fill the breach left by Doc Walk Stumbo's death, but Claude Allen was the one most likely to assume the role of chief medical authority. If it was a burdensome position for someone barely out of residency, he didn't let on. And when his patients started to address him as Doc Claude, he didn't reject either the honorific or the implied comparison to Stumbo. With his easygoing manner, there was no risk of confusing the two. One generation younger but a hundred years more modern, Claude dosed patients with kindness as well as medicine. Where Doc Walk had been brusque, he was gentle. Where Doc Walk had condescended, he empathized. Where Doc Walk had rushed, he sauntered. Now his eyes were worried but his voice was teasing.

"Girls, why do you do this to me?" he said. "I was just about to take my break."

"Hush, my baby's in trouble," Ora Mae said, but Claude was already gone, halfway down the hall with the baby and calling over his shoulder for oxygen.

With its cool, polished floors and its sterile odor of order, the hospital exuded an authority greater than any other public space in Martin. Some towns have courthouses whose grave faces impose civilization. In others, grand cathedrals' spires cast shadow on sin and doubt. Others have imposing libraries whose hushed stacks persuade patrons that they've arrived at the heart of knowledge. Martin had the hospital. In a town with no resources to speak of, no money to spend, no sense of entitlement, and no plans for a better future, the hospital was the epicenter of power. It was the only place where Mary could go to put herself in the hands of something smarter, braver, and more benevolent than herself.

As quickly as the calamity had occurred, it was over. Less than a minute later, as Ora Mae entered the examining room with Mary at her heels, they could hear Claude talking. He was talking to the baby. Not at the baby, but to the baby. Dickie's eyes were open and his chest rose and fell evenly. His lips were starting to look a little pinker. The nurse took his pulse (he had a pulse!) and he screwed up his face and let out a wail (he wailed!), and it was so clear that he was alive—and that he would always be alive, would grow to manhood and would marry and would have children of his own and would outlive his mother as the good Lord had intended—that Ora Mae had to take hold of the bedrail to avoid collapsing in relief. Claude Allen looked up.

"Ora Mae, don't you worry," he said. He remembered. "Where's Jitter?"

"He's running around here somewhere," Ora Mae said. She already had Dickie in her arms, and was inspecting him for signs of wear. She was herself once more, the schoolteacher who stood her ground against all kinds of bullies, including impending death. She was the same Ora Mae who had looked up from the blackboard one day to see Miss Gusfield (who lived behind the school) push open the classroom door without bothering to knock and barge in to demand, "Ora Mae, do you know why I'm here?" She was the same Ora Mae who had said drily, "Come on in and tell me, I'm sure all the children would like to hear as well," and who had patiently endured as Miss Gusfield blurted: "Your children are picking flowers from my rosebush through the school fence." She was the same Ora Mae who had glanced briefly at the little water glass on her desk that held a posy before asking sweetly, "But why in the world would you think it's my children?"

With the return of Ora Mae's composure, Mary lost hers. She leaned against the wall looking spent. One look from Claude was enough to remind her to sit down. She sank into a hard chair.

"Why don't you just put the boys to bed here and stay the night?" Claude said to Ora Mae. He said it casually, as if it were the simplest idea in the world, as if he'd thought of the plan for his own benefit instead of to aid Ora Mae, who would have no one at home for hours to watch Jitter.

"Well," she said. She looked uncertain. "If you don't mind fooling with Jitter in the hospital."

"Ora Mae, I'm not going to fool around with anyone," Claude said. "I'm going to work on this baby, and I'm going to bed myself."

After he left the room, Ora Mae hugged Mary. "What are you going to do?" she asked.

"I'm going to drive your old car home for you," Mary said, and Ora Mae was too distracted to wonder how.

In the hallway, Mary paused to peer closely at the car key, as if by examining it she could persuade it to explain the mysterious relationship between clutch and brake pedal.

"Are you all right?"

Claude was in the hallway. He had asked the question lightly, but it addressed all the issues she'd been trying to avoid. She wasn't all right, and hadn't been since the birth of her own son.

Elmer Wolverton, Jr., was Mary's fourth child, born the previous February. She had been so sick during the pregnancy that she didn't remember much about the birth, just that the baby had seemed fine at first. Then he developed jaundice. The jaundice got worse. He became listless. He stopped eating. He lived four days.

Afterward, the doctor who had delivered the baby told her and Elmer something was wrong with the baby's blood. Elmer wanted more of a technical explanation; it shouldn't be easier to understand how to fix a car than how to fix a baby. But the doctor didn't know much more about it, except to say that sometimes a mother's blood was incompatible with her unborn child's.

Her daughter Jo had been so sick too. During that earlier pregnancy, Mary had been exhausted and weak. With Jo, she'd gained so little weight that she was able to wear Pauline's slightly bigger dresses instead of maternity clothes right up to the end. After Jo's birth, Mary stayed in bed while Pauline fed the baby milk from a dropper.

"Jo lived," Claude reminded her.

"I'll be fine," she said.

Jo had lived. But barely. An unhappy pattern had developed with each of her pregnancies. Margaret, the first baby, had thrived. Judy, the second, had been healthy. Jo, the third, had barely survived. Elmer Junior had died. It was impossible to ignore a trend like that.

In his coffin, Elmer Junior wore a white gown, his face as peaceful and smooth as a china doll's. The funeral home had sent a man to take a photo of him in his casket, where he floated on a satin cloud. The photo was printed on heavy paper the size of a postcard, and on the flip side was a place for an address and a greeting. To whom would she have mailed such a thing?

"Get some rest," Claude said.

Somehow Mary got Ora Mae's car back home without a dent. She could smell clutch burning, so she told herself it was lucky that Elmer wasn't around to see her destroy a perfectly fine machine. She persuaded herself as she walked into the house that it was the smell of hot rubber on metal that made her feel so sick to her stomach, not worries about Elmer, who had finally been drafted and sent to San Luis Obispo for basic training, and not worries because she was again pregnant.

At the age of twenty-one, my grandmother had been on the verge of a predictable life. She had two healthy children, a husband who didn't drink too much, and no greater expectations. Then in 1941 her third pregnancy delivered her from boredom—and almost killed her. Pregnant with Jo, Mary got dizzy and saw spots. She was nauseated for most of the nine months. Her vision blurred. She had headaches. Toward the end, she could not feel the baby move.

The baby was my mother. My grandmother named her Frances Joan, but she became Jo from the beginning, during those worrisome days when Pauline coaxed the sickly infant to take another drop of milk, come on, Jo, you can do it, one more, Jo, one more. The baby was mostly unmoved by these entreaties, a listless, jaundiced little thing that appeared as inclined to die as the runt was in a litter of kittens. Pauline was never one to give up. She made the baby a personal project, wrapped in blankets and kept in a little box by her side day and night. Pauline would have done no less for a kitten. And so, by the time Mary had recovered enough to take over, Jo had been persuaded to live. Her difficult entrance into the world was considered an isolated incident—until eighteen months later when Elmer Junior was born in a similar, but slightly worse, condition. "Slightly worse" was a euphemistic way of saying no one could save him.

As soon as she got word Elmer Junior had died, Amanda Wolverton had come to town to take charge. In the tiny kitchen of Mary's house, Amanda had bathed the baby as gently as if she were afraid of waking him. Mary had watched her mother-in-law's gnarled fingers delicately handling her son, unable to believe that any of this was happening. Mary had touched with one finger the pad on which the baby lay. She had touched his leg. She had started to cry, and that was how Margaret, who was five, had known her baby brother was dead instead of just sleeping. He had looked so peaceful in the gown that Amanda had chosen, each button carefully and precisely buttoned.

Dr. Claude Allen tried to reassure Mary. But he sensed a troubling pattern. Mary's problems were a medical mystery. He investigated accordingly. Now as the months of her fifth pregnancy passed slowly and she lay in bed with chills (or alternately, with a fever, because whatever ailment she had was one so contrary it couldn't make up its mind whether to burn her alive or freeze her to death); while she nursed terrible headaches in dark rooms; while she tried not to dread what lay ahead, Claude Allen reviewed the medical literature. He was not of the old school that had educated Doc Walk. Claude was a recent graduate of the state's finest medical school, and he had completed a rigorous residency in Charleston, West Virginia. He would not lightly accept a patient's fate. His training had prepared him to believe in science instead of bad luck.

Claude Allen read about a recent medical discovery. In 1940 and 1941, two articles in the journal of the Society for Experimental Biology and Medicine described a study conducted on rhesus monkeys. The researchers had discovered a blood protein in some, but not all, of the monkeys. After exposure to Rh-positive blood, Rh-negative monkeys began to manufacture antibodies that destroyed the others' red blood cells.

Mary wondered what monkeys had to do with her. Claude explained that her blood was Rh-negative. Her husband's was Rh-positive. Elmer had passed that trait to each of his offspring. By Mary's third pregnancy, she had received enough exposure to Rh-positive blood to prompt her body to produce antibodies that destroyed the fetuses' red blood cells in utero. The incompatibility led to a condition called "erythroblastosis fetalis," which caused severe anemia in a newborn. The condition, the doctor told her, was what had killed Elmer Junior.

Mary asked if there was a cure.

Claude told her he had found one instance in the medical literature of a similar case in which a blood transfusion had been performed on a newborn. The procedure had been successful, but it had been an isolated incident, in a case that occurred a long time ago in a teaching hospital in a faraway city.

Mary asked if her next baby would suffer from erythroblastosis fetalis. He said he didn't know for sure. He said he hoped not.

The second statement was true.

—

The children when born appear to be quite normal but die a few days later after birth as the result of a grave and progressive [jaundice]. . . . The disease begins on the first or second day of life and rapidly increases in severity.

—A. P. Hart, M.D., "Familial Icterus Gravis of the
New-Born and its Treatment," published in the
Canadian Medical Association Journal, 1925

In May 1944, the Germans surrendered in the Crimea, Hesta received a Mother's Day greeting from Red, somewhere in Europe, saying cryptically that he was fine, and Mary's fifth baby was born.

Arriving at seven o'clock in the morning on May 30, Barbara Sue Wolverton looked perfectly healthy. In the delivery room Claude said, "It's a girl," and handed off the baby to a nurse to clean and weigh.

Exhausted from the labor, Mary floated in a morphine haze. "How is she?"

"She looks beautiful," he said, which was true.

The delivery room smelled strongly of rubbing alcohol and fresh laundry. Mary went to sleep.

Soon after, Claude visited the nursery. He stood over the crib and watched the baby sleep. Her breathing was even. Her color was good. Her fingers were curled into a fist. She looked like a textbook specimen of a robust, normal newborn. He reached into the crib, picked up the baby, and under the lights peered more closely at her face. He saw no sign of jaundice, no yellowish tinge to her skin, not even on the tip of

her nose. He unwrapped the blanket. The baby's liver did not feel en-
larged. There was nothing definitive, certainly nothing he would have
noticed if he weren't on the lookout, when the baby woke. The whites of
her eyes were very white. The baby cried, and instantly a nurse appeared
at his side, arms out for her patient. Even the most protective nurse in
the nursery would never publicly question a doctor's prerogative, but the
look on her face said it all: Why are you making this baby fuss?

The nurse noticed the troubled look on his face. Does she need anything, Doc?

"Yes" was the answer.

> The disease begins on the first or second day of life and rapidly in-
> creases in severity. . . . If treatment is not instituted the jaundice be-
> comes progressively more intense, the baby becomes drowsy, and
> frequently signs of meningeal irritation develop with characteristic
> crying and whining. . . . Death follows in a few days from collapse.
>
> —HART, 1925

By the next day, the baby's urine had bile in it, her tongue was furry,
and her skin was yellow with jaundice. Doc Claude watched helplessly
as she refused to eat. Elmer had permission to come home on leave. He
traveled straight through on a train, and by the time he arrived, Claude
Allen said there was nothing to do but to send the baby home.

"Cure her," Elmer said. He'd just seen Mary, who was still weak and
still hospitalized. Elmer feared that if the baby died, so might his wife.

"There's nothing more we can do," Claude Allen said.

"Try," Elmer said.

He did not share the rest of the town's awe for doctors and hospitals.

The doctor said he understood how Elmer felt, but that the only
case on record of a similar patient successfully treated was nearly twenty
years old, and had involved a blood transfusion.

Elmer asked about a blood transfusion. How did that work?

Claude explained that it wouldn't work, not at a tiny private hospital in a dirt-poor town in eastern Kentucky in 1944. The only time it
had worked had been in 1924 in a big teaching hospital in Toronto.

Elmer wanted to know what they knew in Canada that they didn't know in Kentucky.

Claude was sorry, but in Martin he didn't have the necessary resources or the equipment. The success in Toronto might have been an isolated incident. It could have been a fluke.

Elmer wanted the details. So Claude told him that a physician at Toronto's Hospital for Sick Children had noticed a troubling pattern in a family's history—six of seven newborns developed severe jaundice and died—and deduced that a toxin in the blood was destroying the baby's liver cells. The physician had recommended drastic treatment: exsanguinate 300 cc of the baby's blood while simultaneously transfusing slightly more blood from a healthy male donor. The baby recovered. By the following morning, the baby's jaundice was disappearing; after three days, it was gone. The key to the procedure's success could have been the exsanguinations; three previous transfusions that were not accompanied by exsanguinations had failed.

"Give her my blood," Elmer said. It was a mechanic's solution.

But Claude just shook his head no. It was the small-town doctor's only answer. He discharged the baby.

The next day, the baby was worse. Elmer took one look at her weak, yellowed scrawniness and went for help. He wrapped the baby in a blanket and put her in a basket with a handle. He carried the basket to his truck and put it on the passenger's seat. He drove to a pediatrician in Paintsville. There, he begged doctors to give her a transfusion of healthy blood. They did. She did not improve. Next, he asked them to remove all of her blood and replace it with a transfusion of his. But they said they didn't know how to do that nor if such a procedure would work.

Barbara Sue died on June 3. A day later, she was laid out in the parlor of Mary and Elmer's little house on the edge of Newt Stephens's cornfield. The whole town came to pay respects. Philip Wicker, the high school principal's son, came with his mother holding tight to his arm. He was eight years old and didn't want to file somberly past a coffin, but his mother had given him no choice but to pay respects; Mary and Elmer were renting the house from Philip's aunt Eva.

"We need to stop by," Philip's mother had explained and so now he stood, inside the parlor, fidgeting while his mother spoke to Mary. Mary was pale, not at all like the version of herself that Philip was used to seeing in town. She looked as if she had been distraught, but now was calm enough to thank Philip's mother for coming by. Philip wandered past the casket. He looked in and thought the baby could have been asleep except that flies were trying to settle on her. It horrified him.

Mary didn't see the flies. She didn't see anything. She didn't care about anything, never would again. At the wake, after she told Elmer, "We can never have another one," she remembered that she didn't care about babies, and so didn't care about having another one, and that made her start crying again. She went into a back room and got into bed. But people were constantly coming in to talk. After a time, she returned to the front room. She sat with her head bent, without looking up, and nobody bothered her.

The funeral service at the gravesite was attended mainly by family. The Reverend Isaac Stratton, known as "The Little Shepherd of the Hills" for his ability to inspire the faithful to organize more than a dozen new congregations throughout the county, came all the way from Banner to preach. Burial followed immediately on the hillside. Elmer had to return to the war. The last thing he said, before good-bye, was that he knew money was tight but that he'd send more as soon as he got paid.

The letters Elmer wrote home afterward were different from anything he had written before. They were sentimental. "I hope to be with you soon, dear. I love you," he wrote in one. In another, he worried about the children. "Honey, is Judith learning anything in school? Did Margaret have to stay out many days with her ears? I hate for her to lose any schooling now. She is interested and learning fast."

In a third, "Darling, try to find a house you would like to live in. Because when we stop, we are going to roost. I'm tired of moving around. I just want to feel your arms around me the rest of my life. I will see the children grow up to be nice ladies. That will be enough for me."

That would have been enough for Mary too. By the age of twenty-five, she gave up hope of a nice, predictable life. Elmer was trying to cheer her up. She wanted to believe she would one day be a happy old lady whose three children had grown up to be nice ladies. But first she had to change her life. She got a job.

CHAPTER 14

PVT. ELMER WOLVERTON 96466351
SHEPPARD FIELD, TEXAS

Hello Nurse,

So you finally went back to the hospital. It isn't a very good job and it doesn't pay much. But if you are satisfied, it is OK.

All my love, Elmer

It was clear as soon as the patient arrived at the hospital that he would not live. His name was Otis Blankenship, and he was barely older than a boy. Otis Blankenship had turned pale and waxy during transport over bumpy roads to Beaver Valley. He was unconscious, and there was quite a bit of blood to clean up before anyone could confirm with certainty its source, a gunshot wound in his head. A few minutes earlier, he had been sitting at a kitchen table in a house on Stephens Branch. Then a shot rang out, ricocheted, and hit Otis Blankenship. The nurses suspected a poker game gone sour.

A second shooting victim arrived at the same time. His prognosis was better.

"Get a litter," Claude Allen said. "Take him now!"

The second patient was Lloyd Click, who was wounded because he had had the misfortune to sit next to Otis Blankenship at the wrong moment. He was still conscious as the orderlies rushed him up three flights of stairs to surgery.

Just before the anesthesia put him out, Lloyd Click said, "My uncle done it."

Soon after the surgeon concluded there was no bullet in Lloyd Click's body—a single shot had ricocheted to wound both men—Otis Blankenship was dead. In the operating room, Lloyd Click got sutures before being carried downstairs to recuperate.

My uncle done it. The accusation made the nurses uncomfortable. They talked about it later, after things calmed down, after the funeral home collected Blankenship's body, after the bloodied sheets went to the laundry. Blankenship had been barely old enough to have a wife. Certainly he'd been too young to suffer a senseless death. But a murder like Blankenship's was considered a private tragedy rather than a public crime. Absurd shootings were a time-tested solution to end meaningless quarrels in isolated communities. Stephens Branch consisted of an enclave of houses on the Right Beaver fork, a couple of miles past Alphoretta, and had a history of family hostilities that stretched back generations. On Stephens Branch, the earliest documented grudge against a relative dated to the Civil War. Family patriarch Samuel Stephens, who raised sixteen children on land on which he'd settled forty years earlier, disowned his son Alexander after the boy joined the Union Army (to fight not only against the Confederacy but also against two of his older brothers). Alexander Stephens survived the war only to be banished from home. He moved west, was cut out of his father's will, and was never again mentioned. On Stephens Branch, a family crime was no surprise; filed under "bad blood," most remained unsolved, at least officially.

It was impossible, however, to overlook this murder after Lloyd Click publicly fingered the killer. None of the hospital staff in the operating room took credit for reporting the accusation, but gossip carried in the hospital stairwell. Eventually the story reached the ears of the police. An officer came to Beaver Valley to interview a recuperating Click in his hospital bed. By then, Click's memory had gone hazy. He said he had no recollection of who had fired the shot. He wished he could be more help, but all he remembered was four men sitting around a table in a small room. Or maybe Lloyd had been standing. Now that Lloyd thought about it, maybe Lloyd's uncle Ray had been standing too, facing him across the table. Otis Blankenship definitely had been sitting. The lights went out. A single gunshot cracked. Lloyd felt a burning pain. The lights came on. A small rifle was on a shelf. Otis Blankenship was bleeding. That's all Lloyd Click knew. He had no idea who fired the shot. He had not known, until this very moment, that a bullet had struck him first before careening through the room to hit Otis in the head. He knew of no motive. Why would someone shoot? "For not a thing in the world," Lloyd Click said. He said it was a mystery.

A mystery was the one thing that Mary had not yet experienced since her return to the hospital. Assigned to work as Claude's personal nurse, her duties ranged from the banal—she used white polish on the doctor's shoes every morning—to the exciting. Once she helped deliver an impatient baby who arrived at the hospital faster than the doctor. Mary worked nights. For all practical purposes, that meant living at the hospital. On rare occasions when a doctor didn't sleep at the hospital, the duty nurses navigated emergencies by following the Standard Rules the physicians wrote out: "For chest pain or pain in the stomach or between shoulders, (1) Dilate arteries, (2) Demerol, (3) Start IV."

The mystery deepened. Two nights after Otis Blankenship died, a hearse from Hall's arrived unexpectedly. Mary checked the log, but no patient had died that day. The vehicle idled alongside the building. Claude went outside to greet the driver and returned a few minutes later with a peculiar look on his face.

"Stretcher," Claude called, but this time he directed the orderlies to head for the basement with their load. Two police officers and a representative from the funeral home trailed the litter, on which lay Otis Blankenship dressed neatly in his burial clothes.

The deceased had returned to give evidence. It was only after he had been embalmed, only after the mortician had applied gooey makeup to his face and combed his hair a final time, that the police had remembered the bullet. It was the most valuable clue in the case, the only physical proof that Otis Blankenship had been shot. The evidence was lodged somewhere in Otis Blankenship's brain. The mortician said there was no way he was going to go in to try to find it. That wasn't his

job. And so ownership of the hospital had conferred that particular responsibility—emergency bullet removal—upon Doc Claude.

"Find Dr. Sirkle," Claude told a nurse. "Tell him to meet me downstairs."

It was a curious entourage that headed to the hospital's cellar, a
stretcher followed by two policemen, the hearse driver, and Claude. It
didn't matter much to this patient if he got jostled or if he lay on a cold
metal table in the X-ray room. Otis Blankenship was beyond caring
about the grim tableau that greeted him downstairs, where old-
fashioned metal sinks were beaded with condensation from the cold.
Nearby hung a big, thick lead apron on a hook. Plenty among the hospital staff avoided going to the basement at all costs. Raymon Childers,
the X-ray technician, was the only one comfortable among the knocking overhead pipes. He sat on a stool beside neat rows of glass slides and
pipettes, patiently washing and sterilizing the equipment at the end of
every shift.

Raymon Childers looked up, baffled, as Otis Blankenship invaded
his domain.

"We'll need to take an X-ray of his head," Claude said. "To find the
bullet."

To Raymon's credit, his hands didn't shake as he positioned the machine. Raymon was used to dealing with the rare as well as the regular
when it came to tragedy. One time he was in Room 48 doing blood
work on a patient with a bad bullet wound when the shooter herself—
the patient's wife—burst through the door. The doctors had told her
they couldn't get to the bullet and that the victim was likely to die. She
begged her husband, "Would you forgive me?" From his deathbed, the
patient said, "No," and Raymon heard that conversation without chang-
ing expression. Things like that happened the whole time he was at the
hospital, and he worked there seventeen years.

Claude was reading the film by the time Dr. Robert Sirkle arrived
on the scene. The two physicians, who had bought the hospital from
Annie Stumbo, were a peculiar pair to be partners in a business venture
as ambitious as Beaver Valley Hospital. Dr. Sirkle was as formal as
Claude was casual. Sirkle wore dark suits and looked like Benny Good-
man. He maintained a distance. One time after Jack mashed his hand

while working at the Standard Oil, Dr. Sirkle examined it, saw the wound was infected, and without comment or local anesthesia lanced it. Before Jack could even think about fainting to escape the pain, Dr. Sirkle squeezed the wound with both hands. Sixty years later, Jack could still feel his bones rolling beneath the doctor's cold, strong fingers. Dr. Sirkle would never earn an affectionate moniker like Doc Sirkle. Not that he cared. Unlike Claude, who was acquainted on average with three generations of nearly every patient's family, Dr. Sirkle was a foreigner from Oklahoma. When Claude asked him once why he came to such a backwoods place as Kentucky, Dr. Sirkle answered that when you have to live the first half of your life in a root cellar, worried about tornadoes, even Floyd County was an improvement. Dr. Sirkle considered eastern Kentucky a mere stopover. He was a savvy entrepreneur whose goal was to take his share of the profits and build his own clinic in Lexington, where he could live among more sophisticated people. There he wouldn't have to procure his fashionable suits via mail order.

If the two physicians had very different styles, so did their nurses. Mary followed Claude's cues; she joked and laughed with patients. Theda Pennington, who was loyal to Dr. Sirkle, thought the majority of the patients were trying to get away with something. She kept track of who owed payment for a house call, and collected it on Dr. Sirkle's behalf at the first possible opportunity. She also kept track of every penny she earned. If there was a serious coal mine accident, she volunteered to ride to the site with the ambulance driver. If a miner had gotten his leg cut off, she was as able as anybody to stabilize him with shots and a tourniquet; ambulance duty paid three times as much as regular duty.

Theda and Mary arrived in the X-ray room in time to see Raymon lay out instruments on a tray. The doctors pulled on rubber gloves. When Mary noticed that neither had bothered to scrub in preparation for the procedure that lay ahead, she got a funny twinge in her stomach.

The doctors didn't need to be sterile for a dead man. But they did need assistance. Theda, who was barely old enough to be a nurse, looked at Otis Blankenship's face—the harsh light was not flattering to his makeup—and turned to Mary.

"I will clean your doctor's office and give all your shots for you for the rest of your life if you do this for me," she whispered urgently.

Mary said fine.

"It won't bother me a bit," Mary said. She washed her hands because, in her opinion, a patient didn't stop being a patient just because he had died. He was entitled to the same care she had given him when he was breathing.

Mary pulled on a pair of gloves. She went to stand at the table, closer to Claude than to Sirkle. Under the lights, Mary saw how carefully Otis Blankenship's hair had been combed. The mortician had found his natural part; the hair lay across his forehead. The funny thing about hair was it never looked dead. Otis's hands were folded and his eyes were closed.

Using the X-ray for guidance, Claude cut without hesitation into Otis Blankenship's scalp. He sliced through skin as if it were butter. Mary was trying to pretend she was in the operating room, working on a live patient. But it was a difficult trick to carry off. Here there was no urgency, no need to rush in with a clamp to stop blood from spurting. Deliberately, she used a hemostat to clamp the area, and leaned in with gauze. She tried not to dwell on how differently dead tissue reacted from live, or on the lack of blood, or on the matter-of-fact way Dr. Sirkle had begun to root around inside the incision for the bullet.

It hurt to watch. She reminded herself that there was no need to be gentle, no need to avoid disturbing brain tissue. From Sirkle's point of view, this was probably a rare opportunity: How often did he get to rummage around inside someone's brain without having to be careful? Still, she couldn't help thinking that Sirkle was a cold fish.

"Got it," Dr. Sirkle said, and he held up a dull-colored slug. It looked so benign, like a squashed bug. One of the policemen held out a bowl, and Dr. Sirkle dropped in the bullet. It barely made a sound.

Sirkle went to the sink to wash up.

"Are you all right?" Claude asked Mary as he hastily sutured the incision.

"Fine," she said. It was a lie. She watched as Otis Blankenship's stretcher disappeared through the door, headed back to Hall's for fresh makeup.

"I'll clean up," Theda told Mary. "You go."

After everyone else left, Theda and Raymon threw away all those rubber gloves—expressly against orders—instead of boiling them and drying them and powdering them and autoclaving them like usual. They never told anyone they did it.

It was only much later, after she heard that a jury convicted Lloyd Click's uncle Ray of murdering Otis Blankenship, that Mary felt she could truthfully tell Elmer that yes, she was satisfied with the job at the hospital. But Elmer had other things on his mind by then, such as the permanent loss of his trigger finger.

PVT. ELMER WOLVERTON 36466357
REGIONAL HOSPITAL WARD 1476
SHEPPARD FIELD, TEXAS

Hi Baby,

    The guy you married is doing OK. A new doctor came into the hospital and he knows his business. I went to see him yesterday and he told me my right leg would eventually be alright. He said he knew I had pain in it and it wasn't a laughing matter, but for me to keep my chin up and not worry about it. The nerves that were severed would have to grow back. Then it would be OK. He made me feel a lot better for I was afraid the leg would have to be taken off.

                                         Yours, Elmer

A bazooka grenade exploded during basic training. In addition to blowing off Elmer's finger, it sent shards of shrapnel and sharp bits of rock and gravel into his legs, into his arms, into his face. He remembered it as one hell of a day of training maneuvers at Fort Ord, California. He hadn't imagined such a possibility a few weeks earlier, when they'd checked him in, assigned him to a bunk in a two-story barracks on the sprawling, 20,000-acre camp, and pointed out the mess hall. He'd been aware, upon becoming one of the 25,000 soldiers and civilians at the camp, that the German POWs on the grounds were responsible for maintenance and upkeep. As U.S. Army Private No. 36466357, Elmer's job description had been to prepare for overseas duty. But there had been no mention of the possibility of a training accident serious enough to make him fear he might never walk again.

He'd been raised to expect the worst. So it was no surprise when it happened. He didn't take it personally. That's the way the world worked. But afterward he had plenty of time, while he lay in a hospital bed in Texas, to relive the incident. Why the grenade chose that particular moment to detonate, after it had been lying dormant in a field for who knows how long, Elmer never would understand. He liked machines because they behaved logically. But the grenade had not. He knew the facts, all right, just not the why. He'd been sitting on a rock next to a few other men from his outfit, resting after the day's training maneuvers, when some antsy kid had walked over to join the group. Elmer wasn't paying much attention to the talk. He was thinking ahead to supper. He was wondering if there would be mail from Mary. He was puzzling over Northern California, which had the damnedest climate— dry air and an ocean. It was the first time he'd seen the Pacific. Here fog rose in the morning, just like back home, but the humidity index didn't. He sweated a lot less. Somewhere in the middle of these idle thoughts, he heard pecking.

It wasn't much of a sound. It certainly was not a threatening noise, not loud, not even the sort of noise he would have noticed in another situation. But out there in the middle of a military base's training field, the metallic clang got Elmer's attention. He looked toward the source and saw the kid pecking at a grenade with a rock.

Elmer opened his mouth to yell, "Stop! Stop!"—he remembered that much, never forgot that it had been his intent to forestall disaster— just as the grenade went off. He awoke sometime later with shrapnel in his belly and his forehead, which qualified him as one of the fortunate ones. Half a dozen other men died, hurled into the air and flung back down as bits and pieces of their former selves. He felt just fine, aside from the missing index finger on his right hand, the unbearable pain in his leg, and the bandages that mummified him. The army sent him to a regional hospital in Texas, where he was declared unfit for overseas duty and consigned to a bed. The recovery was slow and painful, but he tried his best to be cheerful when he wrote home: "Hi Baby, I just came back from chow. I made it without crutches too. The old knee hurt a little but I think it will be OK."

In his letters home, Elmer concentrated on cheery topics. "Dearest,

Elmer in
uniform in 1944

Mary and Elmer's daughters—Judy,
Margaret, and Jo—around 1944

I'm glad Judith got over her sore throat and that the rest of you are OK," he wrote. Another time he confided his hope to be assigned to a military police unit in the Cincinnati Armory: "I have been disqualified from overseas duty but I haven't heard from the captain yet. I sure hope he sends for me." He assured Mary he was keeping busy. "Hi Baby, I have been working in the carpentry shop here in the convalescent training. Made me a nice pipe stand and now I am making a smoking stand."

For the first time, Elmer felt homesick. By the time he got off his crutches and was discharged three months later, he had only one goal. If the war ever ended, he wrote to Mary, he would come home to her and stay. The craziest thing he'd observed in the hospital had been another patient in the ward who had exhibited no desire to get a pass when his wife came to visit. "Now wouldn't you say he was nuts?" Elmer wrote. "Darling, you would never have to worry about a thing like that." Elmer wrote that he no longer had any desire to roam, to ever see another new town, or to stay anywhere but with his family. With one exception. He swore that he would never spend another night at Hesta's house. A man had his limits.

PVT. ELMER WOLVERTON 36466357
REGIONAL HOSPITAL WARD 1476
SHEPPARD FIELD, TEXAS

Hello Nurse,

Honey, does the sun still shine into the hall there at the hospital? You know, that is where I picked you out. So you better be careful about wearing thin uniforms. I forgot, though, you are working nights. Don't you dare change shifts just to try that out. Of course, if I was working on the water cooler, it would be alright.

All my love, Elmer

Mary took a shortcut to work. On bright summer days like this one, she walked along the railroad tracks, taking note of the stubborn wildflowers that poked through the gaps between rail and gravel, flouting danger. Without fail, each year the taller stalks would be decapitated, their blossoms sheared off by a passing freight train at the height of bloom. But the flowers were too mulish to move away; they reseeded. Mary picked a posy to save the flowers the trouble of committing suicide.

At the trestle that crossed the creek, she ignored the KEEP OFF THE BRIDGE sign, but glanced down to gauge the mood of the world by the state of the water below. Brown and muddy was her conclusion. The town faced no threat today from that trickle. If she'd been barefoot, she would have skipped the rest of the way. But she was in a nurse's uniform, starched so stiffly that in a pinch the fabric would have made a plausible substitute for wallboard. She threw her shoulders back and pretended for the sake of nostalgia, on this sunny day, that she was back in Mrs. Wurm Allen's posture class and balancing a book on her head.

Work was Mary's escape. With Elmer away, Mary and her girls moved in with Hesta and Fred—who currently lived on Main Street across from the high school—and Mary expected to remain there for the duration of the war. Hesta welcomed all of her children home for as long as they needed, whenever they needed. It was tight quarters, and a lot of worry, with Hesta's fretting about her sons overseas and her granddaughters underfoot. Hesta watched the girls while Mary was at work, favoring some children over others, bestowing fur muffs on her coddled favorites while consigning the unluckier to long stints of exile. Hesta was the sort of grandmother who said, "Go outside," and locked the door until supper. She was a whim-driven dictator, and even Mary, too old to be locked out, was happy to evade her dominion. If Mary felt a twinge of guilt about leaving her children to serve her mother's whims (Hesta was most likely to interact with the girls when she needed them to run an errand like walking to the hospital with a note asking Mary for a "loan" from her upcoming paycheck), she suppressed it by telling herself that with Elmer in the army, somebody had to earn a living.

The hospital was an empire ruled by the benevolence of Claude Allen. Claude was agreeable and he was fair; he liked people. He flirted with his nurses. The ones who were flattered, like my grandmother, stayed loyal. Those who got sick of it left. Hilma, a nurse who worked her way up from scrubbing the floors with lye, tore up his office and threw his papers everywhere before she departed in a rage. Opal, a nurse who left her job when she was expecting a baby, was grateful when word reached Claude of her long and difficult labor at another hospital. He sent an ambulance to bring her to Beaver Valley, where he delivered the baby.

Some nurses served their doctors with the dedication of highly trained personal assistants. They shined their shoes, answered their mail, and emptied their spittoons. Oma, Dr. Sirkle's nurse, quit and moved to Lexington to work there for Sirkle after he built his clinic. Penny, who worked for young Doc Slick, ended up marrying him. Other nurses, like Faye Boyd Dingus, were more loyal to one another than to their bosses. Boyd, as she was always called at work, covered for Mary if one of Mary's daughters got sick. Boyd made no concessions to fashion. Away from work, Boyd dressed country, in feed-sack housedresses that Hesta would have clucked to see. From chain-smoking, her fingers were stained as yellow as raw chicken. She lit one cigarette off another all day long unless she was in surgery or asleep.

Belonging to the hospital staff was more like being in a family than like being an employee. During slow times, the nurses and doctors played croquet on the lawn. On every holiday, there was a staff party. At Thanksgiving, they shared turkey. On Christmas, they decorated a tree and swapped grab bag gifts.

Clutching her flowers, Mary scrambled down the embankment—damn white shoes, scuffed green in too many places—and crossed the street.

"Mary Mynhier, you're high-stepping today," a voice called from the porch of the hospital. Mary shaded her eyes and saw Claude standing outside. He was talking to Dolly Mayo, who lived up the Old Hite Road but who came regularly to town to shop and catch up on gossip.

"Mary Wolverton," she corrected him.

"You look like you're sixteen," he said.

"Aw hell, I feel like it," she said. And suddenly she did. Aided by humidity, curly wisps of hair had escaped her cap. Her stockings itched, and the urge to scratch was just strong enough to make her feel like a girl playing dress-up.

"You brought me flowers," Claude said and reached over to sniff.

"I brought Boyd flowers," she corrected him.

PVT. E. WOLVERTON 36466357
REGIONAL HOSPITAL WARD 1476
SHEPPARD FIELD, TEXAS

Dear Wife,

I guess you think I have forgotten you, I haven't though. I just haven't felt like writing. My legs are giving me a fit again. I don't know what in the hell I am going to do. I tried hard to get in shape to go back to duty but my legs get so sore I can't stay on them.

Your husband, Elmer

M*iraculously, all the men in my family survived World War* II. My grandfather, who had recovered sufficiently from his injuries to walk without crutches, was reassigned to MP duty in Cincinnati in the final months of the war. Walter returned from Europe in October 1945 with two Purple Hearts—having been shot in the leg on two separate occasions in France—and a firm bias against ever again leaving Martin. Over the subsequent six decades, his stance has not changed. But the most remarkable story, as usual, belonged to Red.

After the decimation of his Ranger unit in Italy, Red joined the 1st Special Services Force at a time when the light infantry unit was on the verge of earning the nickname "The Devil's Brigade" in recognition of its fierce and relentless record in battle. Red, a gunner trained to transport and assemble heavy artillery in the field, was a welcome recruit. Red's unit was the first to reach Rome in June 1944 and two months later led the invasion of southern France. The 1st Special Services Force landed in rubber boats on the rocky Îles d'Hyères, prompting a swift surrender by the Germans, and then marched along the Riviera, securing the shoreline and providing Red with firsthand knowledge of places whose names he never would feel comfortable pronouncing: Grasse, Villeneuve-Loubet, Vence, Drap, L'Escarène, La Turbie, Menton. After three months on the French-Italian border, the unit was disbanded; Red spent the remaining months of the war assigned to the 474th Infantry Regiment before his discharge in the autumn of 1945.

Afterward, Red never talked about the three years, nine months, and five days he spent in the war. How he survived was his secret. A few brief facts, typed on his discharge papers, were the only clues his family had to the ordeals he'd endured. "Military occupational specialty: Mortar Gunner, Heavy" was all they knew of his job description and a terse list of campaigns ("Sicilian, Naples-Foggia, Rome-Arno, Southern France, Rhineland, Central Europe") the only information that described the battles in which he'd participated. He came home with a fistful of citations and decorations—six Bronze Stars, a Bronze Arrowhead, and a good-conduct medal—and a powerful desire to put the war behind him. He and Faye Chaffin were married in November. Later he would tell his children Faye chased him for eleven years before he caught her. As Christmas approached, Red settled into his old life with relief. He went to the five-and-dime to spend some of the $186.10 he had received as mustering-out pay. After the shopping spree, a pile of identical packages for all the children in the family appeared under the tree. Beneath the clumsily taped wrapping paper were boxes of big, fat crayons, the kind Red preferred because they were the only ones that didn't snap in half the first time he wrapped his fingers around them. He loved bright colors and he loved Christmas and he signed all the cards, "Love, Red."

12/7/45
CPL. ELMER WOLVERTON 36466357
FREEMAN ARMORY
CINCINNATI, OHIO

Hello Dear,

If they don't give me a discharge, maybe they will let me come home for Christmas. Honey, I will try to get those toys for the girls on Monday. Dammit, I wish I was home. I hope to be with you soon. Are you preparing a nice Christmas?

I love you.

Elmer

By the time Elmer arrived, a few days before Christmas, the tree was decorated. It looked bare. This was Elmer's first thought upon walking through the door of Hesta's house, and it was an unusual perception for two reasons, the first being that he rarely took note of a room's contents beyond observing which empty chair looked most comfortable, and the second being that it was covered in ornaments.

One look at its exuberance—popcorn strings, red glass balls, a thousand glittery gold stars clipped to the tips of branches—was all anybody needed to know that something good had happened this year. The war was over and Hesta's sons were home, and on the very top branch of the tree floated an angel in a white dress, with flowing golden hair and a beatific expression. The tree was a big fir, tall and full and well balanced; a poorly proportioned tree would have tipped over long ago. Fortunately a tree doesn't have to breathe like a human. Otherwise the fir would have been gasping for oxygen beneath its impossible load of tinsel, glass balls, and garland.

"No lights?" Elmer asked.

"No lights," Mary confirmed, coming in the door behind him.

It was just like Elmer to see what was missing. Anybody else might have walked into the house and seen a miraculous accomplishment, because somehow the family had upheld the tree-trimming tradition for one more year. It had been achievement enough just to get everybody back on the same continent this year, not to mention in the same room long enough to hang a glass ball or two, hard enough to pick a time when Jack was not working at the service station or Mary was not at the hospital or Fred was not at the depot or Walter and Red were not out in town, trying to forget the war with whiskey. All over town, survivors were celebrating, from Grover Stephens—who no longer dreaded the daily arrival of the Hite Road mailbag at the train stop beside his grocery store—to Dick Osborn. Dick had somehow managed to publish a novel called *Hike Jule*, a fictionalized account of his youth as a traveling salesman. The general opinion was that the hero was based on Dick's favorite mule of the same name. This year, anybody but Elmer might have looked at that fir and seen triumph in the glitter-covered "Merry Christmas" balls. Elmer saw darkness.

"Who needs lights, anyway?" Mary asked. She threw off her coat, kicked off shoes, and sank into a chair. She didn't mention that she'd spent the better part of last night unsuccessfully trying to fashion a makeshift set of tree lights, using bulbs from old sets, hunting for a string whose sockets weren't frayed and whose cord was not brittle. In the end she'd given up and stuffed the whole tangled mess back into the red and green box with the picture of Santa on the cover and the jaunty promise of a "Decorative Lighting Outfit for All Celebrations." During the war, replacement lights couldn't be bought. It had been a long time since American factories had dedicated production lines to the manufacture of anything as fanciful as a string of colored electric lights. Airplane parts and bullets had been coming off assembly lines instead.

Elmer set down an armload of presents—toys he'd bought in Ashland, where the stores were better stocked—and said there must be some place in town where he could get some lights.

"Not from Grigsby," Mary said.

Not even the town's most industrious retailer could sell something that didn't exist. But E. P. Grigsby had come close a few times, he was that good a salesman. The E.P. stood for Elhanan Peter, a formality universally disregarded in town, where no one ever called him anything but Pete. Pete Grigsby had proved himself to be one of Martin's savviest businessmen in the eleven years since he'd moved to the hometown of his wife, Marena. Perhaps living with his in-laws (Mr. and Mrs. Bulldog Hayes) had proved a powerful incentive to Pete to make it on his own. In less than a decade he'd gone from selling merchandise door-to-door to owning a chain of the biggest stores in town. The Federated Department Store he'd built on the site of an old chicken house. He also lived in the biggest house, a proud two-story frame box that was large enough for his family of eight children and also conveniently situated within walking distance of all his stores. If you wanted something done in town—something built, something paved, something improved—Pete Grigsby was the one to see. He'd been instrumental in persuading the telephone company to install Martin's first exchange. He'd pushed hard for the modern water-purification system. Pete had an endless amount of energy for civic improvement. It was no coincidence, when he decided to run for mayor along with some like-minded candidates for city council, that he called his slate the Bee Hive Party. Pete thought of himself as being as busy as a bee when it came to bringing progress to Martin. In addition to the Federated (which sold the prettiest hats in town), Grigsby owned the Martin Furniture Store (which sold the nicest sofas), and Martin Wholesale. The flagship of his empire was the variety store that bore his name, the E. P. Grigsby Store. It was a five-and-dime where you could buy everything from the world's biggest rainbow-swirl lollipop to bobby pins to match any hair color. Most years. But after four years of war, four years of deprivation, four years of factories' output being sent overseas to fuel the military effort, the shelves at E. P. Grigsby's store were nearly empty. In 1945, even Pete Grigsby had no colored lights.

"Tree needs colored lights," Elmer said. He left the house.

Mary was sick of making do. But that didn't stop her from feeling annoyed at Elmer. It was a waste of effort to complain about things he couldn't change. Besides, there would be lights on the tree—on Christmas Eve, if only for about thirty seconds—in the form of old-fashioned candles. The previous year, somebody had located a box of battered metal candleholders and slim white candles. Hesta had been strongly opposed to them—too dangerous!—but had given in to the opposition. With the candles clipped on to the very, very tips of the longest branches and with the children seated in a semicircle at the base of the tree, and with the front door flung open to the cold, just in case the whole family had to flee an inferno, the adults had lighted each candle. For a few seconds, just long enough for the kids to imprint a lifelong memory, flames had licked air. Hesta immediately ordered them snuffed and declared it was the last time anybody would light candles on a tree in her house. The tree ablaze was the prettiest sight anyone had ever seen.

Mary had presents to wrap. At least Elmer had brought gifts to supplement the meager pile of packages under the tree. Mary took the girls' toys—a doll for each, a doll swing to share, a little fur muff for Jo—into the back room to search for ribbon. No ribbon was on the dime-store shelves, either.

She heard clanking from the front room.

Elmer looked like a grim version of Santa, dragging an oil-stained bag into the room.

He stopped in front of the tree. He reached into the bag and pulled out a headlight. It was well-used and had recently adorned an old jalopy.

He reached in again. He pulled out a brake light—red—and another headlight. Next, he pulled out a bulb covered by a green lens. He unpacked a six-volt car battery and wire.

"Help me rig this up," he said.

Mary could not help but laugh. The living room looked like the mechanic's bay at a service station, strewn with spare parts, pliers, and tangled lengths of cord.

"Will we need this?" Mary held up a greasy gray rag.

"We may before we're done," he said.

Elmer had gone to a garage—every service station owner in town knew him and any one of them would have given him what he needed—and looted the back room for old parts. He'd built a car from scratch when he was sixteen years old; configuring a provisional string of Christmas lights was barely a challenge. The result might not come from a nice cardboard box with a printed picture and a line of type that said, "Trim the Safe and Bright Way." But there was no question about whether the outcome of Elmer's effort would light up the house.

Mary sorted the treasures, laying out taillights and little twists of copper wire in rows as neat as if they were surgical instruments. Elmer squatted beside her, patiently fashioning homemade sockets for each light. He used insulated wire connectors. He stripped about a half inch of each wire before crimping it to the connector. It would have been easier to just tape wire to the bulbs, but he was too good of a mechanic to risk a short, especially on something as flammable as a Christmas tree. Elmer's fingers were callused and cracked, but he shaped the thin wire as delicately as his mother crocheted lace.

He connected the lights to a master on-off toggle and to the battery. As soon as he flipped the switch, all the lights would get juice. Tomorrow, he could unhook the battery and recharge it before nightfall. For the first time since he'd walked through Hesta's door, Elmer looked content.

In less than an hour, Elmer and Mary had covered the tree in lights. Mary turned off the living room lamp—and the tree came to life. Green lights winked from the top branches. A yellow marker light, formerly used to light the side of a truck, was balanced to great effect at the base of a low branch, and in its new capacity as a Christmas decoration, cast a golden glow on a nearby glass ball.

With lights, the tree's symmetry was obvious. On the hillside, Jack had spent the better part of an afternoon passing up scrawnier pines and punier firs, stamping his feet in the cold and jamming his hands into his pockets to keep warm. He'd risked frostbite to find a tree whose angles were pure geometry. On a mountain that was home to the best specimens of hardwood on earth, this was the tree most worthy of a brake light.

A cluster of lights threw red shadows against the wall. Up near Hesta's angel, a clear bulb winked on and off, like a distant star. Elmer said it was a loose connection.

"Leave it," Mary said.

CHAPTER 16

*T*he weather dropped hints that a flood was coming and that it would be bad. Clues included unseasonable rain and balminess after Christmas. But Martin's citizenry paid no heed to the signs. Other people in other places might have taken the rising rivers to heart, might have reacted to rivulets that ran like sweat down the rocky, water-darkened mountains by drawing up an evacuation plan. Not here. Why bother? Nobody had the power to reroute the creek or to change a capricious climate. Prepare for a flood? That would only egg it on.

On the first Monday in January, in Prestonsburg Judge E. P. Hill opened the year's circuit court session as scheduled. He ignored a downpour and reports that distant Right Beaver towns already were drowning. He'd been waiting since Election Day, when the voters had promoted him from country judge to circuit judge, to move downstairs to a high-ceilinged courtroom, with a bigger bench and better-quality furnishings. He saw no reason for further delay. As rain pounded the roof, he took the oath of office and delivered his instructions to various jurors who'd managed to make it to the courthouse. They sat damply on the wooden spectators' benches.

"As grand jurors," Judge Hill said, "your work is most important. Your action puts in motion the machinery of the county. We cannot try cases until you have made your—"

He paused to listen to a whispered message from a clerk, who had ascertained that so many prospective grand jurors were absent that there were too few to empanel. Judge Hill inspected the jurors who had made it to the courthouse despite the weather. They looked like farmers who made their real living by serving on any jury they could. The work paid a nice per diem rate that they couldn't afford to forfeit on account of a minor obstacle like having the road washed away. In weather this bad, they had an added incentive to answer a summons because there was a chance they'd be quartered in a hotel until the water receded. This was tantamount to a vacation with pay, the first—and last—that most would take.

Behind the jurors sat the usual bystanders. Judge Hill pointed to four lucky ones.

"You're jurors now, so come on up and take the oath," he said.

The clerk whispered again: also missing, stranded on the road somewhere, was the commonwealth attorney. The judge conceded, "Him we'll wait for."

Outside the courthouse, things weren't improving. A bus left the downtown station, rounded the corner, and passed the courthouse skimming the slick surface of the street, bound for the far reaches of the county. Headed to Wayland via Martin, it was a blue bus, as big as anything Greyhound operated but with SPARKS BROS. painted in white on its flank to reassure potential passengers that yes, either Ken or Jack Sparks, probably Jack, was the driver. The brothers shared a family resemblance—both were blond, although Ken was heavier and shorter—with the main difference being that Jack Sparks was much friendlier. Both were known for their dedication to staying on schedule; passengers who changed at Prestonsburg for points distant never missed connections. The Sparks brothers rarely let a condition like impassable roads slow them. This morning the bus driver didn't know how bad things had gotten, hadn't heard the latest reports, and was unaware that water was running through the McDowell gym near Drift. Wouldn't have cared if he had heard, either. He had a schedule to keep. Probably would keep it, too, since he knew how to maneuver a bus through rising water. He knew every inch of the road well enough to gauge how deep the water was at any point along the way. The Sparks driver had started his run from Wayland early that morning (carrying a full load of damp passengers bound for work and grimly ignoring the view of the angry creek through the bus windows). The timetable for the return trip didn't allow for a marooned vehicle.

An hour later, Fred Mynhier saw the bus sail into Martin. From his doorway, where he'd been standing since sunup to watch the water rise on Main Street, the railroad man couldn't help but note that the bus was slightly behind schedule. But his bigger concern was the rain. The previous day, he'd cut a V-shaped gouge in a sharp stick and had slid down the slippery creek bank to plant the pointed end into the soft black muck. His stick kept company with his neighbors', notched at various heights, along the shoreline. The whittling had been redundant. A single stick would have been sufficient to warn the town of how quickly the water was rising. But superstition required every family to plant its own, as if a crooked row of skinny poles among the matted clots of last fall's leaves would turn back disaster.

Unfortunately, the poles had not transformed themselves into a floodwall overnight. In the gray morning light, Fred watched his stick gradually disappear under the swirling current, watched the water rise to his notch, watched his cut disappear, watched the whole length of it get swallowed. Now the view from the front porch was even less reassuring. Main Street was underwater.

The Sparks Bros. bus was unconcerned. As the vehicle approached the Mynhier house, majestically parting the sea with its nose, Fred calculated that the depth on Main Street was nearly three feet, deep enough to swamp the two lowest steps on the bus but not high enough to prevent the door from opening to discharge passengers. The engine didn't sputter. It was a hopeful sight. Already water covered the front yard, had crept toward the house and submerged the better part of the porch steps, but maybe, just maybe, the rain would stop.

It didn't. Behind Fred, the rest of the family waited for him to decide. During the past hour, they'd stacked the furniture high on the maple-veneer kitchen table, with mattresses on the bottom to provide a solid foundation for the upholstered pieces, the bedspreads, a box of books. The pile reached to the ceiling and looked precarious. But it wouldn't topple. The Mynhiers were experienced at stacking furniture. They had balanced it as carefully as fruit on Carmen Miranda's head.

Fat raindrops bombed the bus windshield. The vehicle sliced the water, sending a languid ripple toward the house as if the bus had a message to deliver. As the waves traversed the submerged yard, Jack was mesmerized. For a moment, it seemed as if the porch would repel the invasion, would send the flow back toward the road. But the wave hesitated at the very edge of the floorboards, and then—almost politely—climbed the last step to flow across the threshold. The water crossed the porch as quickly as a Sunday visitor late for dinner, didn't bother to knock, then poured over the doorjamb and into the house. Jack watched it run across the wood floor before it petered out at the toe of Fred's boot.

"Oh hell," said Fred, who was never one to fight what he couldn't change. "Let's go."

The men took off their boots, tied the laces around their necks, and put on their oldest pairs of shoes. They rolled up their pants legs as if it would do any good. Jack hoisted one of Mary's girls onto his back, Fred carried a granddaughter and a basket of food, sandwiches, and coffee for adults and pop for the kids. Hesta and Mary and Betty lifted bundles of dry clothing wrapped in blankets over their heads.

Red had already carried Faye to the school. The step off the porch and into the water was too icy to believe, the second shockingly cold, the third not something to notice, because legs went numb that fast. Beneath his feet, the sucking muck was unfamiliar, its squishiness failing to ring a bell in the part of his memory that had filed away the sensation of walking on land. Now he waded toward Main Street, two children clinging to the straps of his overalls as he navigated the new world. Walter's new wife, Marie—they'd married a month ago—held on to his arm. Brown water swirled around his waist, bubbling as if it were about to come to a boil. Red was sure-footed and steady, as if he walked through air. The rest followed him.

They were headed to the high school. The gym sat to the north of the brick edifice, removed enough to signal its separate and equal importance. The gym's functions were many: it hosted Saturday night dances, Friday night basketball games, state funerals, and flood evacuations with the same ease. From the Mynhiers' house, the distance to cross Main Street to reach the gym was only a few hundred feet. At this moment, the distance was unimaginable. To everybody but Red, who'd so recently waded ashore at Sicily under worse conditions (here he faced no enemy fire), crossing Main Street seemed an impossible task. The water made them dangerously buoyant, as off-balance as if they were drunk. Everybody tried to hold on to everybody else. Ahead lay obstacles that broke the surface—big rocks, the tips of heavy branches, broken glass bottles bobbing in the wake. Nobody wanted to think about the possibility of falling, of getting cut, of infection, of typhoid fever.

On Red's back, Jo and Ann clung like raccoons in a tree. Jo at four was excited by the storm and looked over his shoulder, daring a peep at the creek she remembered from the previous summer, when it had been a meandering stream that she had been warned away from mainly because of sinkholes. There are drop-offs, Hesta had said, never mentioning that in other seasons it also had the magical ability to transform itself into a lake in which floated milk cartons, garbage, logs. Ahead, Jo saw a big cat swimming toward high ground.

"Here kitty, kitty, kitty, come here kitty," she called as it struggled ashore. Then she saw its tail, long and smooth and icepick sharp.

"Hush, honey, that's a rat," Red said.

Soon the whole world would be underwater. As the Mynhiers forded Main Street, the debris-filled current became curiously still. The surface stopped rippling. Backwater from the Big Sandy had arrived, colliding with the flow from the creek to halt its progress. The instant passed and suddenly, as if someone had turned on a faucet, water started to rise above the men's waists and to caress the women's shoulders. Jo's legs were so cold.

"Run," Fred said.

If he could have run for them, he would have. But he could barely will himself to walk, struggling in wet clothes with a child's death grip threatening to crush his windpipe. The water rose. The family bobbed along, heavy in wet clothes, too cold to know they were cold, too cold to care anymore if they made it. For the last few yards, they moved forward from instinct rather than intent.

They stumbled ashore. From the top of the gym steps, they looked back even as they scrambled forward. The rest of the town was becalmed. Across Main Street, the Mynhiers' house was slowly disappearing. The water was above the parlor windowsills. In the distance, Jack could still (barely) make out the receding outline of a blue bus. On the side it said SPARKS BROS. It had outrun the backwater. It rounded a bend and disappeared.

The gym was dry. They had forgotten, until they walked through a doorway into heat and light, that being dry was a possibility. During their first wonderful seconds inside the building, as the rain pounded the metal roof, the Mynhiers marveled at the existence of warmth. They certainly didn't feel any, with feet and legs red and numb and shriveled. But it was enough, for the moment, to believe it was possible to feel one's feet. Dry socks and pants were a first step although they had to look down to confirm that the wet clothes were off and dry shoes were on.

The next thing they noticed in the gym was nearly everybody they knew. Mrs. Straub, a schoolteacher, had been evacuated from her house across from the depot. So had Jack Blackburn, a conductor for the C&O, and Aaron Justice and his family, who lived in the house where Railroad Street started; the Justice house was always the first to flood. Inside the gym the scene looked like a land grab, with neighbors laying claim to territory by spreading blankets along the walls, or down the centerline of the floor, or under the banner that said GO PURPLE FLASH. The residents of Martin were busy erecting a temporary town. Even with the original in the process of being destroyed, its essence was being reconstituted in miniature on the hardwood floor. Lots were marked off. Families arranged themselves and their possessions to create crude roadways through the new community. In some ways, this version of Martin, which smelled of wet wool and coffee, seemed more logical than the previous. Here friends congregated with friends, avoiding the difficult neighbors next door who—no longer forced to live next door, not until the water receded—were just as happy to spread their blankets far away, in the shade of the bleachers.

Nobody was in charge. For once, it didn't matter how many generations of your family had lived here. The social order was temporarily suspended, replaced by a heady, egalitarian atmosphere that made relative newcomers like the Mynhiers giddy. My family may have lived in Martin a mere fourteen years, but they arrived in the gym with the same claim as the valley's earliest inhabitants. Their bundles of sandwiches and soda pop were no less worthy than the provisions carried by William Dingus, a farmer from Virginia who had arrived by horseback in 1850 to buy thousands of acres, fortified by a money bag pinned inside his shirt collar and a meager supply of meal in a saddlebag. Dingus's trip to Kentucky had been motivated not only by having twelve children—too many among whom to divide his one hundred acres of exhausted farmland—but also by a suspicion, based on his wife's alarming tendency to look up from stirring the beans to ask if he liked the name "Dulcena Isabel," that another baby was on the way. Dingus made a $1,000 cash down payment on the land at the forks of Beaver Creek, and as he rode back to Virginia to get the rest of the money, the fellow who owned the property turned to his daughter and said, "That old man will never be able to raise the balance. I just got another down payment to the good." He was wrong. Within ten years, Dingus's children owned nearly all the land in and around Martin, from vast tracts they farmed— dubbed Alphoretta, Dinwood, and Hite—to the Beaver Creek sawmill that was the heart of the community. Two of William Dingus's boys married Flanery sisters, and two others married Halberts who were cousins. His daughter Phoebe Louise married an Osborn. Now their descendants huddled together under the high-roofed beams of the gym or next door in the typing classrooms. If the Dingii looked less comfortable than their neighbors, it could be because the usual hierarchy, under which everyone in town acknowledged their primacy, had been suspended. Under flood conditions, leading citizens like Annie Stumbo (who had been an Elliott before she married Walk, whose mother had been a Salisbury) and even Dick Osborn (Phoebe Louise Dingus Osborn's son) might jostle for space along with everyone else under the basketball nets or in the school library's "Fiction" section. Children enjoyed the novelty of it. They wanted to play basketball in the gym, but there wasn't room. Jack grabbed a paperback he'd thought to bring and headed off to find a place to read on the bleachers. Red Cross volunteers brought in food and hot thermoses.

Nearly sixty years later the high school, with broken windows and a locked door, sat behind a ragged chain-link fence. The gym burned a long time ago, in a fire whose origins nobody remembers. The ruins were home to an alternative high school that managed to operate with some windows boarded; from time to time, the local police were called to break up fights.

It became a very different place from the school my mother (class of 1958) attended. A few months before the Army Corps of Engineers began to knock down Martin's buildings, my mother traveled across the country for a final visit. The first place she wanted to go was the building in which she had conjugated verbs, learned to type ninety words a minute, and flirted with a boy named Billy Cleo Hale.

My mother's cousin Rebob, a police officer, suggested a day when the school was vacant. He gave my mother the heavy brass key.

We went up the saggy, oiled-wood stairwell to the principal's office on the second floor. The door was off the hinges and a wooden desk sat scarred and sad. The chair was gone. A wooden file cabinet was in the corner, half its drawers missing, and the other half full of forgotten report cards from earlier decades. My mother pointed to a hole in the crumbling plaster where the intercom system used to be.

Nobody remembered how the microphone accidentally got flipped to the "on" position on the day, so many years ago, when my grandmother came to school to appeal a detention my mother had earned for possession of a forbidden stick of gum. My grandmother, who had known Principal J. W. Salisbury since she was a girl, had arrived home from work to learn that her daughter had ruined a new dress by kneeling beneath the bleachers to scrape gum from the risers. The oiled gym floor stained the skirt beyond saving. Worse, a second day of detention loomed. Mary never would have guessed that J.W., whose mother had been a thrifty Halbert, would have condoned the ruin of clothing. Mary went to talk to the principal about it, and by the time she had marched across Main Street, into the school, and up the stairs to Salisbury's office, her composure was gone. She did not knock.

"Hello, Mary," he said mildly, his parent-handling skills honed by nearly twenty years of teaching in and running schools all over the county.

Without preamble, she blurted, "If you make her scrape gum again, J.W., I'll kick a mud hole in your ass and stomp it dry."

Her bluster was broadcast, via the intercom, to every classroom in the building.

For a principal, J.W. had an unusually sophisticated sense of humor and a fine appreciation for the absurd. One year when he had taught history to a classroom of seniors, he assigned unusual homework. He asked for a four-generation family tree from each student. The next day the class compared notes on distant cousins, concluding that every student but one had at least one relative in the room. J.W. said he hoped that painted a clearer picture of local history.

The punishments J.W. handed out were often as clever as they were diabolical. One time, he received disturbing reports of the varsity basketball team's behavior during a practice at which the coach had arrived late. Unsupervised, the Purple Flash players had been rowdy enough to disturb a church service across the street. The preacher came over to try to hush the boys, but the noise continued. The next morning, the preacher reported the team. The principal called the boys to his office and imposed a sentence that required each boy to attend three religious services at the church or churches of his choice. Salisbury asked for a note, signed by a local minister, as evidence of attendance, which he accepted as proof of penance.

J. W. Salisbury was not a principal who could be bullied. Not even the terrifying specter of my grandmother, red-faced and ready to spit flames in defense of her daughter's limited wardrobe, could shake his composure.

"You've changed, Mary," J.W.'s calm voice wafted from the speaker in every classroom. As teachers and students alike sat riveted by the drama, he added, "I hear they call you Cussing Mary down at the hospital, too."

The situation deteriorated from there. Salisbury refused to soften the terms of the punishment. My grandmother threatened to pull her girls from school. And by the time she marched out of the office, the whole school had heard enough to take sides.

To settle the issue required the intervention of the county schools superintendent (with whom my grandmother had gone to school), who negotiated a settlement that appealed to Principal Salisbury's sense of irony: a five-hundred-word essay on the evils of gum.

As we walked around the old typing classroom, my mother and I heard a noise on the stairwell. Up poked the head of Rebob, in uniform and with his walkie-talkie crackling on his belt.

"I got a call there were prowlers in town," he said.

"Arrest me," my mother said. "I was just about to break into the trophy case."

In the hallway, the smeared glass doors on the trophy case were unlocked, the shelves full of reminders of what the school once meant to the life of the town: one year, the Purple Flash made it all the way to the state's semifinals. Varsity forwards once dreamed of attending the University of Kentucky on a basketball scholarship.

"It's a shame," Rebob said.

"What? That the ceiling's about to fall in on us?" my mother asked.

"That the government is going to bulldoze the whole damn town," Rebob said. "Of course, the best part of it's been gone for about fifty years."

My mother, the baby who should not have lived, has never been sentimental. She shook her head and said that she never much cared about buildings. "The hills," she said. "That's what Martin meant to me."

Standing in the crumbling hallway—where it was impossible to suppress Chicken Little glances at the fragile ceiling—she had a point. The mountains would outlast everyone. And what else was worth saving? Certainly not the high school, which never should have been built on such swampy, unsuitable ground in the first place.

The irony was that it didn't have to be. After the population outgrew a wooden schoolhouse built in the 1920s on land donated by the civic-minded, the county school board had wanted to relocate the student body to a flatter, drier parcel at the southern end of town. The proposed site was big enough for ball fields and high enough to escape floodwater. The acreage belonged to a widowed Dingus named Mandy. Ever since her husband, Thomas Jefferson Dingus (a first cousin of Dick Osborn), had been killed years earlier—shot at a dance in Maytown—she had carried on as best she could, raising six children and hiring help to harvest corn and cut hay. But she was frugal, and to cut costs she always ended up in the fields in a bonnet, carrying armloads to make haystacks and urging the hired help to work faster. Mandy Dingus was tired of that life and willing to sell for $4,000.

The school board had big plans for the new Martin High School to become the county's first regional high school, with students bused from other, smaller towns. Had the deal gone through, Martin's high school would have become upon its christening in 1939 the county's most progressive. But Martin's citizens fought the plan. Dr. Orris Gearheart (who had considered swampy ground downtown to be just fine when he chose a site for his Martin General Hospital) and a consortium of Main Street restaurant owners (who feared losing the lucrative after-school trade in fountain sodas and french fries) filed suit to block the move. Dick Osborn was opposed, too. The original school had been in the heart of the town he'd dreamed up back in 1923, and he saw no reason for change. "I was here before Martin and I'm still for Martin," he said.

While the fight raged, the old school was so overcrowded that Jack had attended fourth grade in a rented room on River Street. When Walter reported for fifth grade, the first thing he learned was that all the classrooms already had been claimed by other grades. Principal Monroe Wicker, a pickle barrel of a person who had a square forehead, blunt eyes, and a fighter's bulbous nose, pointed the fifth graders toward the library, where the first lesson they mastered was furniture arrangement. They pushed aside bookshelves to make room for desks. That semester, high school students had to fend for themselves during study hall.

The residents prevailed in court. Amanda Dingus (who, as people pointed out, wasn't really a Dingus anyway, her father having been a Salisbury and her mother a Justice) kept her land. The school board built a new $40,000 school on the same site as the old, shoehorned onto a small downtown parcel between a restaurant and a gas station. The day the building was christened, the PTA board members served refreshments—punch and covered dishes—and complimented one another on the modernity of their new building; not only was it heated with gas, but it also had running water and the novelty of indoor toilets.

The impact of the town's fight against dry ground wouldn't become clear until decades later, when the school board embraced countywide consolidation. By then, Martin's high school was too small and too old and too flood-damaged to become a regional school. Instead of a hub, Martin High School became a memory, its students bused elsewhere. Six decades later, those who lived through the fight over where to build the school no longer remembered details. After her visit to the school, my mother said she didn't think she'd be back. As Rebob locked the front door, she saw above the doorway, chiseled in stone, the date "1939"—how proud they must have been, to authorize the added expense.

The Sparks Bros. bus made it to Wayland during the flood of 1946. But overnight, more rain pummeled Floyd County. By the next morning, water was three feet deep in the Greyhound station in Prestonsburg, causing the bus to cancel its run. A four-mile stretch of railroad tracks was covered in mud and silt between Orkney and Drift; service was suspended. Little towns upriver were as hard-hit as Martin; more than a dozen families in Lackey, Garrett, Maytown, and Punkin Center saw their homes and possessions wash away.

In Martin, Main Street was a memory. The Grigsbys' store was underwater, hundreds—or maybe thousands—of dollars' worth of merchandise ruined. But E. P. Grigsby didn't despair; he had managed in ten years to turn a fifty-dollar bank loan into a retail empire, and despondency was not in his vocabulary. When his children asked if they were ruined, he reminded them that the flood of 1940 had been far worse, as far as the family had been concerned. Remember how we lived in the wooden frame house on Main Street next to the dime store, he reminded Pete Junior, and you woke up in the middle of the night and your mattress was literally floating on floodwater? Remember how we had to climb on the banister and out onto the roof of the front porch, and over to safety at the Keathleys' house?

In 1946, the gym stayed dry. The first night wasn't too uncomfortable. The second day, though, felt like being in jail—a jail without baths, hot food, or bunks. Suddenly, late Tuesday night, the rain stopped. Fred was awake to hear the silence. At dawn, he ventured outside to investigate. By noon, the water was going down as quickly as it had risen. It was less than a foot deep on Main Street and contracting to puddles everywhere else. The Mynhiers' porch steps were visible. The house wore a belt of mud. Below the high-water mark, the exterior walls looked filthy.

"Oh hell, let's go," Fred said.

They waded cautiously, approaching with the peculiar combination of dread and relief that nobody ever felt except after a flood. Relief, because they could see the water hadn't gotten high enough to ruin most of the furniture. But dread, terrible, bone-wearying dread, because of the cleanup ahead.

Hesta marshaled her forces. Jack hooked up a hose. The rest of the family braved the porch—it was so slick with mud that they practically slid across—and went inside to survey the damage. Water had seeped in under the closed door and through cracks around the windows and through cracks in the floors that nobody could even see. Inside was mud, a deep slick two inches thick on the floors, a heavy coat on the walls to a height of about two and a half feet, and deepest where the floor met the walls.

Shovel first, then hose, then broom. Even the littlest kids could shovel. Meanwhile, Jack hosed the porch and the walls, knowing that if he waited the mud would dry into a rock-hard coating that they'd have to chip off. They worked all the rest of the day and into the night, and when they felt too tired to stand, they made up beds and set up a table where they could eat. Jack was so exhausted he could have slept standing up or hanging on a nail.

It took three days to clean up. The linoleum in the kitchen they picked up—luckily, they'd known better than to glue it down—and threw away. They'd order more from Sears and Roebuck as soon as they could locate a dry mail-order catalog.

Next they sanitized. The county health department, vigilant about the typhoid risk, warned Martin's residents to pump their wells, to wash their walls with a strong chlorine solution, and, as a further precaution, to boil drinking water until further notice. Fifty-eight families applied for Red Cross aid. County nurses arrived in town to dispense typhoid shots.

The house would smell musty for weeks.

The town would smell musty for weeks.

The county would smell musty for weeks.

The only sane response was to ignore the smell.

Life went on. On Wednesday, the Sparks Bros. Wayland-Prestonsburg bus resumed its route. On Friday, Lawrence Keathley opened the theater to show, as scheduled, *Born for Trouble*, a jailhouse saga starring Van Johnson in the big house. Keathley hired boys to shovel the mud out the side doors and to wash the walls with disinfectant where necessary. The rear of the building was on higher ground; most of the seats had stayed dry. Those that weren't, he roped off. (They'd be dry by next week, in time for *Paris Underground*, starring Constance Bennett as an American married to a Frenchman during the war.) The Slade sisters, who owned the Twin Modernistic Beauty Salon, started packing in preparation for their February winter vacation in Florida. That weekend, 109 students attended Sunday school at the Church of Christ. Floyd Skaggs and his son-in-law Ott Frazier went ahead with plans to open a grocery store. A few days later, Pete Grigsby announced his intent to buy Kiser's five-and-ten to add the square footage to his own recently sanitized store.

In conversation, the flood got no respect. Everybody remembered one that had been worse. This year had been nothing compared to, say, the flood of 1939, when the counters in Parker's Drug Store had been underwater and refugees in the Maytown schoolhouse scurried to the second floor to avoid drowning. During the flood of 1935, more than two thousand county residents declared themselves homeless and the health commissioner had predicted of most of the rest, "Tonight they will lie on wet beds." Now, those were floods.

By the middle of February, the weather was cold again. The ground froze. The news, according to the local newspaper, was good: "The war is really over. Various grocery stores in town will now deliver."

CHAPTER 17

All her life my grandmother saved the pale blue sheets of tissue-thin paper on which Elmer wrote home while serving in the army. At first, she may have hoped they accurately predicted his postwar future. Later, she may have saved them out of nostalgia for a husband who had never existed except on paper. Elmer quickly reverted to his prewar restlessness. He wanted to escape to, well, he couldn't say where exactly. But he knew that he had to leave. When home, he worked at a garage in town. But when he wasn't home, he could be anywhere—in Chicago, sleeping on the couch at his brother James's house or in Detroit, where his mother had moved and where he might sleep for weeks on another couch, or in Virginia, to sleep beside his cycle on the dirt in some farmer's field. At home, the quarrels became worse after Mary heard rumors that he had a girlfriend. He and Mary fought over his disappearances, over her mother, over the long hours she worked at the hospital. The strain took such a toll on Mary that one day she looked in the mirror and was surprised to see someone who was not yet thirty years old. A decade of marriage felt like a century.

Nothing was right anymore. Bodies were coming home from Europe in baggage cars. In the noon sun, caskets sat on the platform, draped in American flags while they waited for the ambulance to carry them the last few miles up narrow roads along the branches of Beaver Creek. Other bodies never would come home. Smalley Crisp's great-grandson Herbert, a gunner in a B-24 bomber, was shot down in the South Pacific in 1943 and all his family ever heard was "Missing in Action." The high school yearbook listed what the town lost, all the boys who would never graduate: Warren Vaughn, Wiley Elliott, Sandy Martin, Sherridan Martin, Charles Hunter, Robert Marshall, Edward Wright, Lester Long, and James McGlothen, who died on a Pacific island with a copy of the school newspaper in the pocket of his uniform. James McGlothen's mother reported that among the personal items mailed back from the Philippines was a note she'd written: "Please be careful, Love Mom and Family." Her son had been drafted his junior year. With boys like James McGlothen in the ground instead of playing varsity basketball, with coffins at the depot, with reports of Elmer boldly riding down Main Street with another woman on the back of his bike—was there anything left that was too absurd to be real?

The person most qualified to answer that question was John Henry Osborn. The son of Dick Osborn's first cousin, John Henry was the town's most creative inventor, a mad scientist who specialized in big ideas that would change the world. His calling was refrigeration. He and at least four of his brothers operated a repair business that serviced commercial refrigerators throughout the valley. John Henry was president of the company. He had been the first person in Martin to believe in air-conditioning. He installed a refrigeration unit on a 1937 Buick to create the town's first air-conditioned auto, whose only glitch was that it froze from the inside like a refrigerator. As John Henry and his brothers drove down the street in the summer, they used ice scrapers on the inside of the window glass. Another time John Henry got an idea for a coal-cutting machine he dubbed the Termite. He built a prototype in the middle of the street, exciting enough interest to attract investors. Unfortunately he never could perfect the Termite enough to make a penny, and just about everybody in town lost money on the venture.

John Henry, who became Martin's first mayor, had a falling out one day with George Ryan, a local undertaker who served a stint as the town's police judge. Later no one remembered the details of the dispute, but it was well known that Ryan was unpopular with local officials because of his views on incarceration. George Ryan was an upstanding citizen who as a young navy reservist had learned the burial business from a Norfolk, Virginia, undertaker from whom he'd rented a room. Thirty years later, Ryan was an exacting mortician. But he was a lenient judge, which others considered unfortunate. The mayor, the police chief, and many merchants believed that all sorts of lawbreakers—drunks, scoundrels, those who fell behind on their monthly credit payments— should be locked up. But Judge Ryan's inclination was to turn everybody loose. He didn't like to jail his neighbors for minor infractions. One day when John Henry and Lawrence Keathley and some of their buddies were standing in front of Gardez Dingus's Beaver Hardware, bemoaning the menace of miscreants on Main Street, the subject turned to Ryan. The newspaper had carried a circumspect announcement about Ryan's intention to run for county coroner. John Henry expressed disbelief that the same fellow who advertised "Day and Night Ambulance Service, Flowers for Every Occasion" was seeking the Democratic nomination. If Ryan could be coroner, who couldn't?

John Henry's big ideas often started with a rhetorical question. As he was pondering the answer, the honey wagon pulled around the corner, emitting a telltale odor that announced the arrival of Judge Bush. "Judge" was his first name, not an honorific. Judge Bush, a simple man who made a living by cleaning out other people's outhouses, waved as he passed the gaggle of gossipers. He was on his way to dump a load of excavated human waste into, well, come to think of it, nobody really knew how he got rid of it. Nobody asked. Maybe old Judge Bush was smarter than he looked.

The casual comment was all it took.

"Judge Bush," John Henry Osborn said. "Judge."

With a name like Judge, voters might mistake Bush for an actual justice. On a countywide ballot, a candidate with a name like Judge Bush would look like someone with solid legal experience. After all, outside of Martin nobody knew who he was.

By the end of the week, John Henry Osborn had officially launched Judge Bush's campaign for coroner. Judge Bush went along with it. He had nothing to lose. Half a dozen merchants kicked in contributions. A discreet notice in the next issue of the *Times* read simply, "We are authorized to announce JUDGE BUSH of Martin, Ky., as a candidate for CORONER subject to the action of the Democratic Party primary." Then John Henry and his brothers went around the county, telling everybody what a fine judge Bush was.

Judge Bush won the primary, flabbergasting George Ryan. Ryan had long suspected he wasn't the most popular citizen in town. (After arriving in Martin in the late 1920s, Ryan had gotten into such a row with Doc Walk over the necessity of embalming that when the hotel where the Ryan family lived subsequently burned, Stumbo was considered the likely arsonist. The case never went to trial; later Stumbo and Ryan became friends. Ryan was always happy to bury the hatchet—and a former enemy. He oversaw every detail of Doc Walk's funeral, from the slow procession down Main Street, to the big tombstone erected in the cemetery at Eastern, to the line of nurses who walked behind the hearse carrying tasteful bouquets.) But even Ryan couldn't conceive of a county Democratic Party silly enough to put Judge Bush's name on a ballot instead of his. Three years later, he closed his funeral home and retreated to his property on the hill above Beaver Valley. There he had two cows, a horse, and a lot less nonsense to face every day.

Judge Bush, meanwhile, won the election in November. Everybody in town was in on the joke by then, and even the voters who knew him voted for him. A scrawny little character no more than five feet tall who had never held a job that paid better than four dollars a day (when Keathley had hired him to help build his new theater), and who'd been raised by foster parents who could no longer remember why they'd nicknamed him Judge, become coroner of Floyd County. Nobody could die officially without his say-so. He took the job seriously, and upon examination of a corpse would pronounce, "Yep, he sure is dead."

Transforming Judge Bush into county coroner was John Henry Osborn's greatest invention. His success as an alchemist emboldened him to dabble in the black arts of marital therapy. Well versed about the cause of Elmer's problems from observing my grandparents ever since their courtship days (when they often double-dated with John Henry's brother Junior), John Henry prescribed a cure: extravagance. He recommended that Elmer buy an expensive gift for Mary to prove that he loved her more than his girlfriend.

Elmer bought an entire set of bedroom furniture. It was a reckless expense—a bed frame, a dresser, a mirror, a cedar trunk—and it was a novel way for him to say he was sorry. The furniture was solid cedar. It was by far the nicest Mary had ever owned. The dresser drawers slid as smoothly as skates across fresh ice. There was nothing rickety about the bed. And the mirror was better than her old, wavy one. It was the sort of furniture Mary would have greatly enjoyed owning if she didn't know that it was a bribe.

Mary was not acquisitive. She had one really good dress and one pair of jewelry-store earrings (opals, her birthstone) and that was enough. But a little voice in the back of her head told her she deserved something nice for once. All her neighbors on Front Street were embracing postwar upgrades that made their lives more comfortable. Telephones were becoming common in private houses. So was indoor plumbing. The Griffiths had a bathroom. The Rices converted a lean-to off the back of the house to install a flush toilet. The Grigsbys had the nicest bathroom, though; kids played in the yard in hopes of gaining permission to enter that palace of hot and cold running water. Mary had never believed it prudent to waste time aspiring to expensive luxuries like telephones or toilets—or new bedroom furniture. But the little voice wondered if a new mattress would feel like sleeping on a cloud? Mary told Elmer thank you.

Next, Elmer asked Mary if she wanted to go to the movies.

Maybe she'd heard wrong. Or perhaps she was too distracted by the unusual largesse to concentrate on conversation. When Elmer suggested a movie, Mary had just finished making up the bed. The new spread was pink satin, the shiniest and smoothest fabric that anyone in Martin had ever owned. The linen set came with two matching pillow shams, and when it was all made up, the room looked as crisp and elegant as a page from a catalog.

"What's playing?" she asked.

As if it mattered. How many times in his life had Elmer asked her if she wanted to see a movie? Once? Never? He might as well have suggested a weekend in Rome. The invitation was beyond novelty and beyond refusal. She would have seen *King Kong* for the fortieth time, if necessary, simply to experience the rare sensation of strolling in public with her husband.

She ran her hand over the bedspread. The fabric was smooth and her skin was rough. She spent too much time washing surgical instruments in scalding water.

On her way out the door, Mary issued to her daughters a set of unconditional orders not to be disobeyed upon threat of terrible punishment. She warned them not to run in and out while she was gone, not to go into the kitchen, not to tromp through the place with a pack of friends, not to trample Miss Rice's hydrangeas, not to wander too far— it would be dark soon—and not to bother Hesta, who lived next door (having recently rented a house on Front Street).

The children listened carefully. From the yard, they had an unobstructed view of the ticket booth. After Mary and Elmer disappeared inside the lobby, they started running in and out to get important items (a teaspoon to dig for treasure, a colander to sift dirt). On the way in, they slammed the door. On the way out, they threw it open hard enough to make the hinges creak. After tracking a sufficient trail of mud from the living room to the cookie jar, they got bored and decided to go up on the hillside, way beyond the depot, to play in the cemetery. Ghosts might come out at dusk. If lucky, they could see spooks.

They left the front door ajar.

This was careless but not dangerous. Nobody in Martin locked a door. Hardly anybody even had a key. The only home invaders who disturbed the peace with regularity were mosquitoes and flies. No one would enter someone's house without knocking and hearing in response, "Door's open." No visitor went unnoticed. Anybody who walked down Front Street toward Mary's had to pass the open doors of the Methodist church. Next came Annie Stumbo's house, with Annie likely to be on the porch. Then came the Childers house. The Childers girl was the best sentry there was. She played under crawl spaces, behind stoops, beneath bushes. Mata Hari could learn surveillance techniques from her. Next came Miz Norris's house. Then came Hesta.

The only way to escape Hesta's detection was to be too short for her to see with a casual glance through the window. The Grigsbys' dog was the right height. He was a bulldog, part pit, and a familiar sight patrolling the neighborhood. He was a house pet, handpicked from one of Bulldog Hayes's litters upon determination that the pup was gentle enough to live peacefully with children. He strolled down Main Street to sprawl on the sidewalk in front of Pete Grigsby's store, not caring who might trip over him while he napped. He barked at anybody with the audacity to walk past his yard, day or night. He menaced cats. He peed on roses. When visiting, he never bothered to knock.

Tonight the bulldog sauntered past Hesta's house, hindquarters swaying as sassy as a cheerleader's, and without hesitation walked up the path to Mary's porch. He pushed open the door with his snout.

Afterward, no one could say what attracted the dog to the bedroom. Maybe it was the scent of new cedar. Maybe the smell of freshly starched linens is just as irresistible to a canine as to a human. The bulldog evidently believed that a throne had been prepared for his pleasure. He jumped onto the bed—claws catching in satin—and spun around and around, sniffing his tail a few times, wadding the spread to make himself a nice nest in which to sleep.

The dog snored. As Mary came through the open door, she heard someone asleep in her bedroom. From the deep, throaty sounds, she could tell the intruder was no Goldilocks. A tramp was possible but unlikely. Her first reaction was not fear. It was curiosity. Her second was outrage. She got the broom.

Mary strode into the bedroom, flipped on the light, and—

She screamed.

Next door, Hesta heard her. Elmer heard her from the road, where he was tinkering with the car by streetlight. It was a muggy night, and bugs circled his head as he poked under the hood, checking for loose wires, caps, or screws. Going to the pictures had been a fine way to pass an hour or two, but this was real entertainment. He had been about to check the level on the oil dipstick when the yelling started.

Was Mary being murdered? Elmer slammed the hood—protecting an engine was reflex—and took the porch steps two at a time. The screams continued.

He burst into the bedroom to find his wife in a standoff with a four-legged Grigsby. Mary stood at the foot of the bed, brandishing a broom. The dog, backed into a corner, was growling at the handle. Mary yelled, "Get out of here, get out," at the dog, even as she pushed him farther against the wall.

"Move aside," Elmer said, as he took Mary by the arm and tried to back her up enough to give the dog breathing space. But she shook him off. She was in a rage. She pointed the broom and cursed the dog.

This seemed like an overreaction until Elmer glanced at the bed. There—on his side!—was the cause of her distress: a big, wet puddle.

Elmer cursed the dog.

Mary cursed the puddle. The pink bedspread was ruined. Into her bedroom had come a dog that belonged to the family she most resented, the richest family, the family that never had to scrimp. The Grigsbys had things other people didn't, like a telephone number (2980), fancy kitchen appliances, and an upstairs. The Grigsbys were so rich they even risked carpet.

"Shoo," Elmer said to the dog. Instead the dog backed into the corner.

"Come on, git," Elmer said, taking a step toward the dog and waving.

The dog made his second serious mistake of the evening. Instead of skittering out of danger, he got tough. He bared his teeth and growled. He snapped at Elmer's hand.

"Damn you," Elmer said. He pulled a pistol. He might forget his wallet, he might forget his chewing tobacco, but he always had a loaded gun.

Mary moved aside, fast.

"No, Elmer," she said.

The dog growled and edged toward Elmer.

Elmer aimed.

Mary covered her ears with her hands. She covered her eyes. Then her ears again. She needed four hands.

She ran. She ran from the room toward the street, calling in the saddest voice that anyone had ever heard, "Don't shoot, Elmer, don't shoot."

Next door, Hesta arrived at the window in time to see Mary emerge.

Elmer pulled the trigger. The shot rang out. Mary stumbled on a loose step and fell off the porch. Hesta ran into the street, waving her arms: "Elmer shot Mary! Fred, wake up, Elmer shot Mary!"

Mary sprawled in the grass. She'd tripped on the step. Elmer appeared and offered a hand to help her up.

Hesta, hysterical, started patting Mary all over her arms and legs to find the bullet hole. Fred came running in time to see Mary shaking off Hesta.

"Where's his gun?" Hesta yelled, as if she feared the next bullet was meant for her. "Where's his gun?"

"Mom, hush, he shot a dog," Mary said. "Go to sleep."

"A dog?" Hesta said.

"The Grigsbys' dog."

Normally information of this magnitude would have been Hesta's cue to create a scene. She enjoyed nothing more. She could walk into a quiet room and without speaking a word prompt an uproar with her presence. But one look at Elmer's face persuaded her it was time to return to bed. As Fred steered her back into the house, she looked at Elmer and muttered, "Damn dog."

Mary sat on the steps for a long time as Elmer rolled the dead dog in the dead bedspread and carried the evidence to the car. She sat long enough to reflect. Some problems, like a lack of Christmas lights, Elmer could fix better than anybody. But the business of day-to-day living he messed up. Mary sat on the porch with the suspicion that the dog had died simply because Elmer had a powerful urge to shoot someone. He'd exhibited similar tendencies at a recent Saturday night dance. Mary had attended with friends from work, off-duty nurses mostly, and with Claude Allen. When Elmer had walked in unexpectedly—nobody even knew he was in town—Mary had been dancing with Claude, and laughing because nearly everything Claude said made her happy. Elmer had grabbed her sleeve. She had gone with him to the car. His jealousy had surprised her, especially when he pulled a pistol and said she was crazy if she thought she could leave him for Claude. If Elmer hadn't looked so wild, she would have tried to reason with him, would have told him Claude would never leave his family. Claude might work twenty-four hours a day for seven days a week for seven years, as his wife had once accused him when in a dramatic protest she dressed up the children, took them to the hospital, and pointed out Claude as if he were a zoo specimen: "Children, this is your father." But though physically distant, he was always connected to his family. The day his daughter Liz's dog got hit by a car, the vet wanted to amputate. Instead, Liz carried Baby to her father, who took the mutt into the operating room to stitch the leg. "Now get her out of here before the inspector sees a dog in delivery," Claude had said. Claude may have wished some things had turned out differently—he got a wistful look whenever he heard a train whistle, and confided to one nurse that he'd wanted to be an engineer, not a doctor—but his family wasn't one of them. The Allens of May-town stood for something fine, and had ever since Claude's father, Dr. J. H. Allen (whose mother was a Stephens), had returned from medical school in 1910 to begin his practice and, soon after, a family (Claude's mother, Bertha, was a May). Doctor J.H. had always wanted a son in the medical profession. George was a year older than Claude and the natural candidate. But at medical school, George had to catch his own cat for anatomy class and that was it for him. He became a plumber. Claude carried on the family tradition. His patients appreciated the gesture. If Claude drank too much, if he took sudden fishing trips, if he flirted with nurses, people looked the other way. His easy competence, his patience with patients, and his sense of humor outweighed the rest. To distract a screaming child, he would stride into an exam room and exclaim, "That mean nurse. Did she give you a shot?" He'd pretend to pinch Mary on the arm and everyone would laugh. Would Claude Allen relinquish the adulation? Never. But Mary couldn't convey this to Elmer while sitting in the car with a pistol pointed at her. Elmer, who came as he pleased, who had never cared about being liked, could not comprehend people who felt differently.

The bulldog disappeared that night. And soon afterward, so did Elmer. Mary suspected the bulldog ended up in the creek and Elmer left town with a woman. By the time word got back that he had gone to Illinois with his girlfriend and that the two were living with his younger brother's family, she said she was glad to hear he had no plans to return to Martin.

CHAPTER 18

One day Jack answered the door to find the C&O's call boy on the step, his bicycle leaning against the Mynhiers' porch.

"E and BV shifter at four o'clock," the boy said.

"I'll be there," Jack said.

The boy nodded, and biked away to fetch another crew member.

Jack's father had gotten him a part-time job working for the railroad. My great-grandfather Fred, unhappy to hear that Mary was getting a divorce, had turned his attention to the offspring whose lives he could still shape. So as he neared his sixtieth birthday, Fred wangled railroad jobs for all his sons. The Mynhier boys knew they were lucky to have them.

Working for the C&O required delicate navigation—not so much of the trains, which ran straight ahead on well-laid track, but of the most cantankerous of the men who operated them. No one wanted to work with Flat-Wheel Weiss, an engineer who earned his nickname by ignoring the *Book of Rules*. The rules stated that in bad weather it might be necessary to travel slower than the posted speed limit. Instead, Weiss held the throttle open. In wet weather his train practically flew, spinning the wheels on slick tracks. He didn't care if the wheels had to be replaced. He had no regard for safety. Weiss was heavyset, with a permanent grimace that announced his attitude: *Get out of my way.* Life had conspired to stand between him and the one thing he enjoyed, playing cards in the bunkhouse. The faster he drove the train, the faster he'd be off it and dealing a hand of pinochle. The engineer was boss. If Weiss wanted to speed toward the yard faster than anybody else, if he wanted to push the limit in restricted zones, if he forced his brakemen to jump off cars traveling twice as fast as was safe, nobody complained.

Jack was still in high school, so to work he cut class. Principal Salisbury, who saw the big picture, looked the other way. Jack would have graduated two years earlier if he hadn't dropped out as a sophomore, restless to join the war. Hesta had persuaded Jack not to enlist, but to instead enroll at the new Mayo State Vocational College in Paintsville to study business skills. Jack had been a whiz; after he completed the course, the college hired him to fill in for a sick teacher. There he had been, seventeen years old and lecturing to a classroom of older students about business accounting, business English, shorthand, and typing. But after the war, he couldn't get a decent job without a high school diploma. J. W. Salisbury had seen plenty of less motivated students in the years he'd been at schools in Wayland, Garrett, and Auxier. He had welcomed him back to high school. As long as Jack passed tests, Salisbury let him skip the rest.

At the yard office, Jack punched in. Right away he saw Weiss striding toward the engine. A few weeks earlier they had worked together on a yard job on a hot day. All afternoon Weiss had ignored hand signals, refusing to couple cars gently. He had slammed into them hard enough to knock Jack off a couple. The clanging could be heard three blocks away. Jack had ended the day with coal dust down his collar and a neck rubbed raw from grit. As the train approached a long cut of cars in the dark, Jack had held his lantern straight up to signal "Take it easy." Weiss had ignored the signal, as usual. Jack, fed up, had for a moment stopped caring about seniority or rules or whether he'd lose the job. He had dropped off the car and swung his light in a circle to encourage Weiss to speed up. For the first time that day, Weiss had heeded a signal. The train had slammed into the line of cars. Six derailed. This created an instant traffic jam, blocking the yard's three busiest tracks. Weiss had climbed out of the engine, walked back to investigate and had said angrily, "Why'd you give me a flying kick signal?"

"I thought I'd give one you'd like," Jack had replied.

Now as Jack climbed onto the engine to take his post as front-end brakeman on the Right Beaver shifter run, Weiss ignored him. Jack said, "Good evening, Mr. Weiss." It was more a challenge than a greeting and earned a grunt.

Weiss pumped air, released the brakes, and pulled back the throttle. Slowly the train left the yard, the reluctant engine moving as stiffly as an old man climbing out of bed. Behind the engine trailed 120 cars, a mile and a half of train to pull. The list man and the conductor waited by the track, then jumped aboard the caboose as it passed.

As the train picked up speed, Jack enjoyed the rattle and jolt. He loved the power of the engine, the way the front drivers made a distinctive clicking noise as they crossed the switch points on the tracks. He loved being part of a crew that could get the job done, even with Weiss in charge.

The first mine's tipple came into sight, a big, black skeleton with a conveyor to dump coal into the cars. As the shifter slowed, the conductor, Jack Blackburn, sorted through his paperwork, checking the sequence of the cars' waybills to make sure everything was in order. Within minutes, the shifter smoothly dropped empties from the front of the train, and then backed up to couple a string of full coal cars.

Then they were off to nearly a dozen other mines with names like Dinwood and Glogora. At each stop, mine workers loosened the brakes on the full coal cars to allow them to gently roll down to the load track, where the shifter would pick them up. Jack jumped down, signaled Weiss to back up, and then jumped back on. Blackburn collected the waybills and off the shifter went.

The repetition was soothing. After the last mine below Lackey, Jack watched the final car couple onto the train. Wayland, the next stop, was the end of the line. Jack checked his watch reflexively; the shifter was on time. His next responsibility would be to jump off the engine to throw the switch to send the train onto a side track, out of the way of the Wayland-to-Martin passenger train scheduled to pull away from the station in a few minutes.

But something felt wrong. The train wasn't slowing. Six or eight miles per hour was a comfortable speed for jumping off. Instead, the shifter was picking up speed. At the door, Jack hesitated. He looked at Weiss. The engineer was opening the throttle. Weiss saw him poised to jump and said, "Where the hell you going?"

Jack was confused. "Aren't we going to get in the clear?"

By now they were traveling at fifteen miles an hour—too fast to jump off safely—and accelerating with every second.

"We've got plenty of time to do that once we reach Wayland," Weiss said. "Mind your own business."

But this was the brakeman's business. If the switch didn't get thrown, the shifter would stay on the main track and collide with the passenger train.

Had he heard wrong? One look at the stubborn set of Weiss's profile was all it took to answer the question. He had heard right.

Flat-Wheel Weiss had decided to race the passenger train.

The shifter was traveling at the posted speed—thirty miles an hour—and hurtling along with the invincible momentum of a mile-long train. Weiss was betting he could make it to the Wayland station before the passenger train pulled out onto the main track. If right, Weiss would have time to pull past the depot, where the train could be switched out of the way before the other engineer started to move.

But Jack the accounting whiz knew Weiss's calculations were wrong. The passenger train was scheduled to depart in three minutes. Two miles of track lay between the shifter and the Wayland station, and at a speed of thirty miles per hour, it would take four minutes to reach the station. Alongside the tracks, the trees and rocks and creek and hills rushed by in a blur. In the cab, Jack felt sick with anxiety.

"Mr. Weiss?" he asked.

No answer.

Jack glanced at the fireman in the cab, hoping to enlist him in the cause of sanity, but was unable to catch his eye. Firemen knew better than to question Weiss. The engineer was notorious for making trouble, reporting them for insubordination or inadequate steam pressure or whatever else had irked him on a particular day. Although the trainmaster tended to ignore Weiss, no fireman wanted to risk a report's getting into a permanent file to delay a promotion. So instead of yelling, "Weiss, you'll kill us all," the fireman concentrated on the water gauge, as if his life depended upon keeping the steam pressure up.

Weiss *was* going to kill them all. And for what? Because he wanted to get back to the bunkhouse a half hour sooner.

Jack could picture the E&BV passenger train as it prepared to depart Wayland. In his mind, he could see the passengers climb aboard. They settled into gray mohair seats, with an armrest on the aisle and the window side. He could imagine the brakeman, ready to open the switch to the main line. The fireman stoked the furnace. The engineer prepared to release the brakes. Jack could imagine the conductor, walking the aisles, taking tickets, marking destinations, handing back stubs. The conductor wore a navy blue uniform with gold buttons. The conductor greeted every passenger courteously and the ones he knew warmly. The conductor was Jack's father.

Fred loved railroading more than anybody alive. In the early days of the century, when he got his first job as a brakeman for the Kanawha and Michigan Railway Co., the world was a bigger place. People saw less of it. They lived where they'd been born. Fred's natural destiny was to spend his life stuck in one spot, working on his father's farm or in a local sawmill. He defied that fate. First he joined the army, and later he found the only other job he could envision taking him to new and strange places every day. There was a kind of magic in those days to starting the day in one town, traveling to another by lunch, and returning home by dark. To cover so many miles—a lifetime of miles for some people—during a single shift was nothing short of miraculous. From a train, the country looked exotic. Trains went places people didn't. Trains cut through underbrush, followed the meandering curves of a creek, explored narrow passes that nobody had thought to traverse. Fred could feel the hills press in on both sides, threatening to suffocate the tracks between steep, green walls. Then round a curve, and suddenly a strange town came rushing to meet the engine.

One time—and one time only—Jack could remember taking a trip alone with Fred. When Jack was twelve, they had traveled by train to Indianapolis to retrieve Walter from a Civilian Military Training Corps program. Fred and Jack had set off early one morning, Jack in an itchy three-piece suit Hesta had insisted on buying for the occasion. They took the passenger train to Allen, where they had changed for Ashland, and again for Cincinnati. At every stop, Fred pulled out his Hamilton pocket watch—with its handsome black letters and sweep second hand—to check the time against the schedule he carried in his pocket because even as a passenger, he maintained a healthy interest in adhering to the timetable. The watch, whose accuracy had been approved by the railroad, ran accurately at temperatures ranging from freezing to August and was precise to within thirty seconds a week. At every stop, Jack pulled out his own pocket watch, a cheaper imitation purchased with proceeds from his newspaper route. Upon arriving at Cincinnati's Union Terminal, Fred and Jack spent the better part of the day in the majestic rotunda waiting room. The domed ceiling soared a hundred feet over their heads. Outside the concourse, ninety-four miles of track could accommodate more than two hundred trains a day. Fred and Jack wandered through the station as if it were a museum, marveling over the twelve-foot-high mosaic murals, each section of the wall glorifying a different mode of transportation or industry that had made America great: pioneers' wagons, steamships, and airplanes. They lingered longest in front of railroads and, when they were too tired to stand anymore, sank into the plush red leather settees that made the station feel like the lobby of a grand hotel. That day Jack learned from his father how it felt to be rich.

Fred offered the same legacy to all his sons. Although Red preferred to eke out a living working for no one but himself, Billy would also join the C&O as a car whack, working maintenance in the yard. And for Walter, who returned from the war with his faith in life shaken to a degree no one could have predicted, a steady job as a brakeman would prove the closest thing to salvation he would ever know. Fred got Walter the job within weeks of his discharge from the army, and for years—no, decades—afterward, the steady demand of the railroad was the only discipline to which Walter would acquiesce. Along with the things Walter had gained overseas—two Purple Hearts, a Bronze Star, a good conduct ribbon, an Army of Occupation ribbon, and the combat infantryman's badge, which had a blue field with a rifle on it—he'd lost something he couldn't describe. He tried to explain to Fred once, when he asked his father to go to the movies. They sat in scratchy red mohair seats and watched *Battleground,* a Van Johnson war picture in which the 101st Airborne's predicament reminded Walter of his own in Alsace-

Lorraine. Marching across France, the 42nd Rainbow Division had gotten caught in an artillery barrage that forced them to dig in behind a four-foot-high stone wall. Walter could not see through the fog to what was on the other side. By the time they had dug holes in the frozen ground and lay in them, it was night. Spotters had seen them; the Germans bombed the nearby fields. Bright explosions lit the night. Walter realized that on the other side of the wall was a graveyard. Caskets flew open and bodies flew into the air, six feet high, eight feet high, bodies dead a hundred years and bodies dead a hundred days. Walter returned from Europe with a keen sense of smell. He was the first in town to know if something was on fire. He could smell a cemetery before he saw it. One time, he smelled a rabbit in the graveyard. He shot it and took it home. By the time the stew was ready, he didn't feel like eating it after all.

Walter had seen *Battleground* about a dozen times. Fred hadn't seen a movie since *King Kong*. And life had not prepared him to know what to say about war to a son who'd served in the modern army. During Fred's own service in the 5th Infantry Division at the turn of the century, soldiers had been on horseback and far less efficient about killing one another. Fred had served in the Mexican uprising in Texas, he'd seen men die, but nothing onscreen bore any resemblance to his own experiences prior to discharge in 1912.

After the movie, Walter had wanted to tell Fred about all the smells he suddenly couldn't bear anymore. Wild game, for instance, any kind of game. He couldn't walk into the hospital, either, not even if he wasn't sick, because the smell of the disinfectant in the waiting room would make him deadly ill within ten minutes. He could smell the ether from the street. As they had walked out of the theater Walter talked about the movie. He said the only thing missing from it was the smell of war. Fred couldn't imagine that odor.

Fred understood the known world. At work, dangerous things happened all around him—cars derailed, engines flipped over, men who misjudged the distance to jump onto a moving caboose missed the stirrup and lost a leg—but they never happened to him. He was careful and diligent. Most days he stood unperturbed in the yard, smoothly signaling to the brakemen his plans for moving hundreds of coal cars around on the tracks during an eight-hour shift. It was as complicated as doing a jigsaw puzzle to figure out how to couple the cars in the right order, to make sure that the Inland Steel Company in Wheelwright got its daily supply of 115 empties and that the Elkhorn Coal Corp. mines got their 90 and that the empties moved out of the yard within hours. Fred fit the pieces together as if he had, in his mind, an aerial view of the complete train, ready to pull out.

Fred wished he could fit the pieces of his children's lives together as easily. He worried not only about Walter, who drank and "swarped" with the ladies, but also about Mary. Divorce was her idea, and Fred agreed she was better off without Elmer. But life without him did not agree with her. As months passed with no word from Elmer, she went on a few dates. She dressed up, she wore perfume, and her girls thought she was the prettiest woman alive. But Fred noticed a change in her. She became quiet. She stopped joking. A few times she went to a speakeasy with Jack, where she nursed a single drink for an entire evening and sneaked peeks at her watch. Her girls she left to Hesta to manage while she worked long shifts at the hospital, and putting Hesta in charge of children made neither generation happy.

Fred had other worries he didn't discuss. He didn't feel well. Sometimes he got big, painful carbuncles on the side of his neck that made it impossible to turn his head. Sometimes those sores lasted for months. They always went away, but something about their tenacity suggested their absences were temporary.

Lives didn't run according to a timetable. Luckily the C&O did. In Wayland, Fred stood on the platform and checked his watch. As the engineer blew the all-aboard whistle, he noted with satisfaction that the passenger train was on schedule.

Aboard the shifter, Jack heard the faraway whistle. He checked his watch, a wristwatch, bought to replace the pocket watch he'd smashed while jumping on and off engines. The new watch was nice-looking, a Hamilton like Fred's, and he knew it kept good time because the railroad required quarterly inspections by a representative from Polan's Jewelers in Ashland. Usually it gave Jack pleasure to take note of its unbreakable crystal and red jewels to mark the hours of 9, 12, 3, and 6. But now he saw that in less than two minutes the passenger train was due to depart. He saw time running out.

Jack didn't scare easily. As a rookie, he was used to drawing the most dangerous jobs, assignments no one else wanted, like riding on the front of a coal car as it was being pushed onto the tracks at a mine, the engine half a mile behind him. At night, he sat atop a drawbay with a lantern, a lonely firefly blinking in the blackness and waiting for hazards to loom ahead. One night, he saw a horse on the tracks. By the time it had come into view, it was too late for Jack to do much about it. The horse was tethered, and panicked when it saw the light on the approaching train. Instead of moving off the tracks, it reared. Although Jack knew the horse was doomed, he had dumped the air to the brakes to stop the train. The horse whinnied and pawed the train and, in the same instant, flew thirty feet through the air. Jack didn't consciously hear the thud as coal car hit horse. All he thought about was bailing off the other side into the high weeds. As Jack rolled down the embankment, the train stopped. By the time the conductor walked up to investigate, Jack was dusting off his pants and a farmer had emerged from the underbrush to retrieve his rope. To the conductor, the farmer said, on cue, "You killed my animal. I'll sue." The conductor nodded. It was standard procedure. Two or three times a month, there was a dead livestock report to fill out. Certain cows, horses, and hogs were worth more dead than alive, because the C&O would pay as much as a few hundred dollars to settle a claim out of court. Hogs were the worst. They were so short and squat that they got caught under the wheels and usually derailed a car.

Now Jack wished for a livestock casualty. A collision would stop the train. But the tracks were clear. He checked his watch again. At this speed, a shifter this long would need nearly two miles of open track ahead to come to a complete halt. It would do no good to stop the train.

It was not in Jack's nature to mutiny. He was Fred's son, after all, and my great-grandfather had faithfully followed the railroad's rules for more than thirty years. To Jack's knowledge, Fred's only lapse had occurred nearly twenty years earlier, when he'd been caught smoking a forbidden cigarette on a caboose. But that incident, which had led to a reprimand and a transfer to a new city, was hardly inspiration for a situation like this. If it were Fred instead of Jack in the engine alongside Weiss, what would his father do?

Fred would follow the rules. The rules required the shifter to be diverted to a spur track to avoid collision. It was too late for Jack to throw the switch. But another brakeman at Wayland station still might have time.

The whistle.

Only the engineer was allowed to sound an alert. Jack glanced at the cord. It dangled near Weiss's right hand, which was otherwise occupied with the throttle. Jack had never blown a whistle except to get someone's attention a couple of times from a train that was sitting still. He had never imagined blowing it when a train was moving.

Jack reached for the cord and pulled hard. A high-pitched warning pierced the air. Jack winced. The sound was shrill enough to hurt his ears and loud enough to carry two miles.

Weiss, whose eyes had been on the track, was so startled that he nearly lost control of the throttle.

"Get your damned hand off of that whistle!" Weiss yelled. Instead, Jack pulled harder on the dirty-white cord.

"Get away!" Weiss yelled. But he couldn't take his own hand off the throttle.

As Jack held on, the volume increased. He could picture the brass whistle on the cab, shrieking and shrieking as the air rushed through.

"I'm going to report you as soon as we lay up!" Weiss yelled.

Seconds to go.

The train hurtled past the last bend and ahead lay a sudden picture-postcard view of Wayland nestled at the base of the mountains. On the left side of the tracks sat a neat row of two-story white frame houses. To the right were coal tipples and mine tracks. Above the station lay the schoolhouse, the gym, a bank, and shops. Instead of congregating at a post office, the citizenry waited at the depot for the arrival of catalog orders and packages. A crowd stood on the concrete platform beside the spur track.

The long, sustained blast of the whistle puzzled the throng. They were used to a short toot from any engineer who might want to announce to his girlfriend that he was almost home. But this whistle signaled trouble.

Ott Frazier, the passenger train brakeman, was conditioned to listen for trouble. He got the message.

Frazier sprinted toward the switch. The lever was about two feet long, with a twenty-pound weight at the end. Jack prayed the lever wouldn't stick. Frazier ran fast. He reached the pedal, stepped on it to release the switch, and, with seconds to spare, the shifter veered from its collision course and onto the mine track alongside the passenger train.

Jack kept blowing the whistle as the shifter hurtled past. It never occurred to him to stop. As the engine passed the depot, Weiss didn't look up. But Jack caught a glimpse of the surprised look on the other engineer's face. He saw passengers looking quizzically out the windows at the freight with the shrieking whistle as it slowed to ten miles per hour—the posted speed at the depot—and sedately continued on to the mine tracks. Out the window, Jack saw the last passenger car pass and on the rear platform was Fred. His father was holding up his watch and shaking a fist.

CHAPTER 19

F*red was not a wealthy man. He had no estate to divide among* his sons. So he passed along to them the one thing that had made him feel affluent all his life. The railroad was their inheritance, and it was a good thing he gave it to them when he could.

There were no professional consequences of either Flat-Wheel Weiss's recklessness or Jack's insubordination, but soon after the day the shifter barreled into Wayland, Fred's aches and pains got worse than ever. This time they didn't go away. Within a few months, he was forced to retire. Not long after that, his world narrowed. The foot of his bed became his horizon.

So much about impending death came as a surprise. The first shock was the diagnosis. In the eleventh month of his sixty-second year, Fred learned he had terminal cancer. He struggled to make sense of the bad news as he lay in an unfamiliar bed at the C&O Hospital in Clifton Forge, Virginia, where he'd gone because his employee health plan covered the cost of treatment. The sheets were scratchy. He called home to inform Hesta, hearing her voice across the vast, whispering emptiness of an open long-distance connection. Everything about the experience of illness was strange to Fred, who in his life had rarely consorted with physicians, much less been probed intimately by them. From the flimsy hospital gown he wore on the men's ward to the sharp, hot pains in his abdomen whenever he tried to shift to a more comfortable position— stitches were to blame—the episode was unreal.

The C&O Hospital was state-of-the-art. The operating room had a high ceiling from which was suspended an enormous, gleaming metal cone that focused hot, probing lights onto a patient's shrinking skin. A rolling anesthesia cart was stocked with a half dozen canisters of gas. Attached to a black rubber mask, a long tube hung ready to administer oxygen. The surgical team wore white coats, white hats, white masks, and white shoes. The room was bright enough to make teeth ache. But that sterile intensity wasn't enough to prevail against cancer. Soon after the surgeon made the first incision, he knew. Fred was riddled with disease. There was no point in trying to remove the tumor, not in a case like this where the malignancy already had invaded a number of organs. Upon inspecting Fred's insides under the pitiless light, the surgeon decided the most humane treatment would be to sew up the patient and send him home to die.

As a token, the doctors suggested radiation therapy. Fred had no alternative with which to counter. As he lay looking out the hospital window and into the deep, green mystery of the high branches of a tree—a scene of such breathtaking normalcy that it hurt him worse than the cancer they said he had—he felt he had only himself to blame. Had he ignored the pain for just a little longer, maybe it would have cured itself. It had long been Fred's philosophy to combat threats to the status quo with patience and optimism. His strategy was to outlast change. Fred survived plenty of upsets merely by refusing to acknowledge them. He had survived such menaces as the Depression, two world wars, and nearly four decades of Hesta's moods. The successes had prompted him to take the same approach toward the first symptoms of physical change—fatigue, aches, puffiness around his eyes, an odd weight gain that made him feel bloated—that had signaled serious illness. But his plan to ignore the aches until the day he woke up feeling fine had failed.

Men in Fred's family were not used to long, drawn-out death sentences. Fred descended from generations of healthy, hard workers who toiled until their bodies wore out. Then they dropped dead. Fred's father, a woodcutter with rosy cheeks and a snowy Rip Van Winkle beard, had still been cutting timber for cross ties when he was nearly eighty years old. From a distance, the strong thwack of John Mynhier's ax had sounded like a steady heartbeat, and Fred had no doubt that his father might still be swinging that same ax today, at the age of one hundred, if not for an unfortunate accident that occurred by the side of a river. One wet winter day at about eight in the morning, John Mynhier had rowed his boat across the Lincoln River to work and had never come back. That night his sons found him where he'd slipped on a rock, fallen on a stump, and ripped open his belly. In the space of an instant, he'd lost his footing, dropped his tools, rolled down the hill, and injured important organs. Twenty-four hours later, Fred's father succumbed to internal bleeding. It was a tidy, no-fuss death that required little effort, beyond the requisite grieving, from his loved ones. Fred, who had never taken a sick day from work, had expected to one day extend the same courtesy to his family.

Instead, here he was home in his bed, dying. And now he was suddenly unable to load his own pipe. He was propped on pillows in the living room where the bed had been moved to make it easier to care for him.

As Jack walked in, he saw his father reach for his curved, short-stem briar, which hung with two others on a rack that sat on a round table near the bed. The pipe, one that Fred had smoked for years, was an old friend.

"How are you feeling, Dad?" Jack asked.

Fred didn't answer. Jack saw recognition in his eyes, but some days Fred couldn't speak. Today he was too doped to try. He got a shot every few hours. Most days he recognized not only his children, but also their spouses and offspring. Jack had recently married Viola Baldridge, who was called Pete and had been since she was a baby, the nickname's origin traceable to the day her father had tossed her in the air while chirping, "Pete, pete, pete." The baby laughed, the name stuck, and when, twenty years later, Jack had brought his own newborn daughter to introduce to his father, Fred had stared a long time before he reached out to brush the baby's smooth arm. "She looks like Pete spent the whole day polishing her," he had said. Other days, Fred thrashed restlessly, and at the Methodist church across the street they turned on the loudspeaker to play his favorite hymn at full volume. Ann and Margaret sat beside him and sang along: "Beyond the sunset, O glad reunion with our dear loved ones who've gone before."

There was a brighter world beyond the sunset, Fred knew, because he remembered living in it. There, men enjoyed their evening pipes.

Determined to join them, Fred managed to unhook the pipe from the rack that hung off the side of his humidor. He closed his shaking hand around its familiar stem of smooth, polished wood. But that was as far as he could get on his own. He looked astonished that all he could do with the pipe was fumble.

Jack watched his father pick up the matchbox. Fred forced open the lid. With shaking fingers, he isolated a single slender matchstick and trapped it between the pincers of his thumb and forefinger. It took all his concentration, and it took a long time. Slowly he conveyed the match from the box to freedom. He examined it closely to identify the tip. Then he used the last bit of his strength to will the matchbox to hold steady in one hand while with the other he struck the flint.

The match flared.

Fred watched the burning match fall onto the bed. He looked at Jack. He smiled, as if he were somehow ironically amused that he couldn't do anything for himself anymore.

Jack grabbed the match. He held it to Fred's pipe and lit the tobacco for him. He handed the pipe to Fred. It was the last one Fred would smoke.

Fred already had been robbed of so many things. For his family, the day he had returned from the Clifton Forge Hospital was the worst they could remember. He had looked as pale as saliva, wasted from the surgery and radiation. Fred said the ordinary days that followed were far more terrible, because they measured the slow, gradual collapse of a life he had loved well. He missed shined shoes and starched shirts in the mornings. He missed walking home at suppertime as his grandchildren ran down the road pell-mell to meet him and claim the right to carry his empty rolled-top metal lunch box. The first thing he lost was his work. He retired from the railroad after thirty-seven years of service. Papers were mailed to the Railroad Retirement Board in Chicago to request an annuity. Next, he lost his garden. No matter where he lived or how often he and Hesta moved, Fred had always planted vegetables. It didn't matter to him that the soil was so poor that, as he said, "any rabbit who visits better bring his own lunch." He missed the twilights he had greeted with sleeves rolled up and his hoe sending clots of dirt into the air.

—

Hesta fought death in her own way. She bought a business—a restaurant—and operated it on Main Street. The building had an apartment unit in the back and there she moved with Fred, setting up the bed in the front room. The Hob Nob Café was a risky proposition from the start, an underdog whose competitors were established restaurants like the Big Eat (where the secret of the chili was rumored to be three kinds of beans, including a particularly small strain of white northerns shipped in from a distance) and Verl's (where the specialty was an open roast beef sandwich). Although Hesta was suspiciously bony for a restaurant owner and her entrepreneurial experience was limited to brief stints as a dress saleswoman at the Federated Store and a part-time waitress at Miz Hunter's restaurant, she had hopes.

The Hob Nob looked modest from the outside. It was a white frame building on Main Street, with wide windows flanking the door and its name painted on the glass. Inside was better. There was a pinball machine and a long soda counter along one wall. The Hob Nob had a few tables, a few booths, and no pretensions. Hesta haggled with the truck drivers who delivered produce. She made supply runs to Prestonsburg to load up on ginger ale at wholesale. She kept track of the railroad employees who paid for lunch with C&O meal books, and she redeemed their coupons for cash. To cook, Hesta hired Alafair Flannery, one of Tavis Flannery's fifty-seven first cousins on his father's side. The air smelled of grease, fried meat, and the lard that made Alafair's pie crusts flakier than average. This was a good smell in a county where some of the poorest hill folks still relied on a recipe for "Starvation Bread," which in place of flour called for sawdust from a log (beech and birch were tastiest). After eight hours of boiling the sawdust, eight hours of cooling, and more boiling, a jellylike substance emerged for baking; at mealtime the hungry persuaded themselves it tasted like cornmeal. Compared to Starvation Bread, Alafair Flannery's custard pies tasted like art.

But music was the Hob Nob's main draw. Hesta had a jukebox. The first time a customer came in, he might not even notice the old gilded-wood machine near the door; it looked like every other jukebox in town.

It cost a nickel a song or a quarter for six to hear selections like the latest from the humorous duo Homer & Jethro, who lampooned popular country songs like Hank Snow's "I'm Movin' On" with their own corny versions ("The old hound dog was feelin' fine / till he fell in a barrel of turpentine"). Whenever somebody dropped in a coin, the jukebox accepted it with a gnashing of gears, a rumble of thanks, and what sounded like a sharp intake of breath. Then it released a song. As a record started to play, the machine lit up like a preening peacock, sending bursts of red and blue and green light through the room. Customers got more than music, they got a rainbow, and as the sound and the light wafted together out onto Main Street, the combination proved irresistible to casual passersby.

Hesta, who noticed this right away, capitalized on it. Each afternoon as she heard the dismissal bell ring across the street at the high school, Hesta dropped in a quarter. Within seconds, the voice of Hank Williams would fill the air, belting a chorus of "Poor old Kaw-liga, he never got a kiss / Poor old Kaw-liga, he don't know what he missed." Within seconds, the first students would drift in to order a scoop of sherbet and a bottle of pop. By the time Hesta's next nickel unleashed the melancholy strains of "My daddy's only a picture that hangs in a frame on the wall," the restaurant was full of teenagers ready to dance.

Live music was the next logical step. The Hob Nob was the only restaurant in town with a dance floor. On Saturday nights, Hesta moved aside the tables for square dancing and hired Buddy Ratliff from Bucks Branch to bring his bluegrass band. Everybody in Hesta's family danced. Ann taught Mary's girls to jitterbug. Billy loved Homer & Jethro's spoof of Hank Williams's "Jambalaya" so much that he must have spent a hundred dollars playing "Jam-bowl-liar," feeding coins into the jukebox and earning himself the nickname Billy Gumbo. The dancing drew crowds, and the police came for a walk-through, but there was no serious trouble.

But the clapping and hooting and a general air of gaiety felt desperate. It was impossible to forget for long that Fred was getting sicker in an apartment behind the café. Walter's wife, Marie, was with Fred most nights, trying to coax him to eat with bites of oatmeal, which he had always liked. Other favorites, like pork tenderloin and cured ham, he had

given up forever. Marie patiently offered substitutions—stewed toma-
toes, buttered white bread sprinkled with a little sugar—but he rarely
took a bite. Mary, who worked the overnight shift at the hospital, came
home in the mornings and at lunchtime to give Fred morphine injec-
tions. As the dosage and frequency increased, Mary taught Marie to
give Fred the shots.

The Hob Nob's health failed along with Fred's. In a county suddenly full of automobiles, fewer rail passengers arrived in town looking
for lunch. The C&O switched to diesel trains. Fewer men were necessary to run them, so part-timers like Jack left town to work in Prestonsburg. Hesta, not good at managing a budget, never knew where the
money went each month. Maybe it was because the restaurant fed her
family along with the customers. All she knew, one day, was that it was
time to sell the jukebox to pay debts.

Soon after, Fred died. In Mary's white frame house on the corner of
Front Street, his casket sat in the living room for three days. People
needed that long to say good-bye. Someone cut off a lock of his hair to
keep in an envelope. A spray of black-red gladiolus sat on a table by the
window, and one or another of Fred's children sat in a chair by the coffin through the night. The house was full, with Fred's brother Walter
and his sister Lilly and the rest of the extended Mynhier clan of cousins
and uncles and aunts who, upon hearing news of death, had miracu-
lously appeared en masse on the doorstep. They traveled in a pack when
they traveled, and they always traveled for funerals. There weren't
enough beds, which didn't matter because nobody cared to sleep. Grabbing an occasional catnap was enough, and then it was time to give
somebody else the bed. In the front rooms, a stream of friends and
neighbors brought flowers and food—the kitchen table threatened to
collapse under hams—and the kids were underfoot, having been kept
home from school. Hesta stayed in the bedroom. Every few hours a visitor would slip in to pay respects and to return with an account of her
condition. Hysterical, somebody said. Calm, a different neighbor reported. Napping fitfully, a cousin said. Not hungry, another said. There
were so many flowers that overflow vases stood sentinel on the porch
steps and along the path to the sidewalk. Nobody had expected the
scent of the lilies to be so overpowering.

The day of the funeral was damp and gray. Mourners carried the flowers to the Methodist church. There wasn't enough seating. The loudspeaker came in handy again, this time to broadcast the sermon. Ashes to ashes, dust to dust, and a hundred people listened outside the church, waiting in the mist for the service to end so they could accompany the pallbearers up the hill to the graveyard. Fred's children walked past the casket and squeezed their father's shoulder.

CHAPTER 20

N o one could remember, later, who proposed staging a grand Easter Pageant on the hillside. It may have been L. B. Kiser (who later landed the role of King Herod) or Z. A. Burcham (Caiaphas) or any of the twelve apostles. It became clear, during rehearsals, that the spectacle's scope would be majestic. By the time various Sunday school teachers and choir masters put in their suggestions, the script included the reenactment of more than thirty scenes from the life of Christ. Throngs would jeer at Jesus, Romans would wander the meadow in colored sheets dyed with Rit. Angels would wear wings fashioned from bent coat hangers and gold tinsel. The pageant would be an extravaganza, and if that required construction of a replica Sea of Galilee capable of holding real water, the high school Fix-It Club was up to the challenge.

Roles were assigned in March. Principal Salisbury was a shoo-in for master of ceremonies; nobody else could have coordinated the contributions of the band, the glee club, and the home ec club as seamlessly. Mayor Grigsby offered the full support of the city council. Committees were formed to handle "Wardrobe," "Scenery Construction," and "Supplies and Hauling," whose chairman was also responsible for overseeing the progress of such subcommittees as "Cardboard," "Sand," "Lumber," and "Rocks."

Jesus encountered a lot of rocks in the road, pageant director Blanche Dingus reminded her cast at rehearsals, and just as He moved them out of the way, the actors would be expected to overcome anything that stood between them and the memorization of their lines. As an English teacher, Blanche had high standards. Walk on water if that's what it takes to get the part right, she told Pete Grigsby, Jr., who was to play Jesus. Pete Junior was an obvious choice for the lead not just because he had recently brought glory to Martin by being named to the all-state high school basketball team, and not just because he happened to attend the Mormon church with Blanche, but also because he was a fine all-around athlete (he also played varsity shortstop) who could be counted on not to fall off a donkey during his triumphant arrival in Jerusalem. Other main roles were judiciously divvied among members of the town's various religious denominations—Methodist, Pentecostal, Freewill Baptist, and Church of Christ.

By Palm Sunday, with a full dress rehearsal under way, the hill had been transformed. A main stage dominated the area formerly known as the pasture. Off to one side was a manger (for the nativity scene). In the distance stood a lumpy Mount Calvary. Beyond that was the Holy Sepulchre, with a huge papier-mâché boulder blocking the doorway. At the end of a long day of dry runs, Blanche Dingus predicted success. "Nothing can stop us," she said. "Except rain."

Easter morning was cold and overcast. That didn't deter the crowds. They arrived early, traveling from all over Floyd County to get a view of the pageant that the newspaper described as "one of the most pretentious Easter observances ever staged in eastern Kentucky." Most came directly from Easter Sunday services. By noon, parking lots were full. Cars lined Main Street. They filled the spaces at the depot and behind the high school and along the highway. Estimates placed the head count at well above three thousand.

Scene One: The Annunciation. Onstage, Sallie Shannon (Mary) tried her hardest to ignore thunder in the distance. Instead she focused on the Angel who addressed her. "Behold thou shalt conceive in thy womb, and bring forth a son; and thou shalt call his name Jesus and—"

A flash of lightning split the sky.

Three thousand people studiously ignored the weather.

Scene Two: The Nativity. The audience moved downfield to gaze on an array of cows, sheep, and poultry (in a town with no shortage of barnyard performers, even the chicken had auditioned) grazing near a straw-roofed manger. Inside, Mary and Joseph fixed their eyes rapturously on the infant Jesus in his mother's arms as the Wise Men—and heavy black clouds—approached from a distance.

Scene Three: Freezing pinpoints of rain began to fall, distracting the crowd and lacerating the bare shoulders of the bedsheet-swaddled cherubs who were peeping over a stone wall. Gold tinsel on the angels' halos started to droop.

Scene Four: Hail.

Scene Five: More hail, falling harder, slammed the surface of the Sea of Galilee.

Scene Six: Torrents of rain. Chaos broke out as the crowd cowered, ran for cars, or galloped toward the dry spot inside Jesus' crypt. A donkey, waiting patiently at stage left, hung its head. In the confusion, Blanche Dingus managed to climb onstage and announce, in her loudest director's voice, a rain date. Then Blanche sprinted for cover, holding her program over her head.

Two days later, after the weather no longer mattered, the sun broke through the clouds. The day was a pretty spring miracle. On Front Street, Walter's wife, Marie, shooed the kids outside to play and warned her son Rebob, who was not yet seven, to stay away from the creek.

He assured her he would.

The creek ran right behind the house. If a boy followed a narrow footpath through the yard and down a hill through the horseweed, in no time he would find himself at the edge of a steep drop-off above a section of Beaver Creek that had been nicknamed Log Pond. From the bank, a boy could see that Log Pond was nothing more than a deep spot where the men liked to fish. Huge catfish and carp liked to lurk in the depths. What a boy couldn't see was how Log Pond had earned its name. He couldn't know that a tangle of big, underwater boughs upstream directed the current toward the center of the sinkhole. Mud and silt washed away, leaving a crater in the floor of the creek. What a boy couldn't possibly realize from personal experience, if he was six years old and did not know how to swim, was that nobody had ever touched bottom. Anybody who tried it surfaced, seconds later, at least twenty feet downstream. The undercurrents were strong.

Drop-offs were common in Beaver Creek. During a flood, the current would wash out a new sinkhole. A week after a flood, a boy might be wading along his favorite stretch of shoreline in ankle-deep water, intent on a dragonfly just out of reach, and suddenly take a step and fall face first into a deep spot. A boy better know how to swim. Log Pond was at least ten feet deep, not two steps away from the edge of the water.

From the creek bank, the surface looked placid. Rebob looked at the brown, foamy water and wondered if it was possible to wade across. Beyond the opposite bank, on a rise, was the depot where Walter was at work. Rebob thought his father would be surprised to look up and see Rebob walking toward him across the tracks.

On the bank next to Rebob stood Jimmy Wallen, who was older. On the other side of Rebob was Jimmy Wallen, who was younger. All the Wallen boys had hair cut so short you could see scalp, and all the Wallen boys were named Jimmy. Often they traveled in a pack of Jimmys.

Rebob threw a stick. That should impress Jimmy. Maybe Jimmy, too.

Rebob watched the stick disappear downstream. He grabbed another and started to fish for a piece of floating cardboard. He leaned way out.

Call it a mother's intuition. Something made Marie wonder what her son was up to. She looked out the window. She saw nothing. She walked to the back door. She saw nothing. She stepped outside.

The boys did not hear Marie call Rebob. She tried again. No answer. Kids were always slipping off somewhere to play, losing track of time. Marie wiped her hands on her apron, calculated how many minutes had passed since she'd heard the boys—five? ten?—and wondered if her son had gone next door to Pauline's to play with cousins. It seemed unlikely. Pauline didn't like the Wallens; she suspected their mother of giving them all the same name so no one would know which one to accuse if trouble broke out. Pauline wouldn't encourage the Jimmys to linger in her yard.

Marie called, "Re-bob! You answer me!"

He didn't.

The boys were missing. If Marie had wanted to investigate further, she could have walked around to the front of the house to see if Rebob was playing kick the can in the street. Or she could have popped over to Pauline's house or to Betty's or to Billy's—a large percentage of the street's inhabitants were Hesta's grown children and their families—to look for him. Or she could have gone back inside to cook supper, figuring he'd show up in another five minutes.

Instead, an uneasy instinct sent her down the back steps and toward the little old path that led to the creek. A few seconds later, she was wading through horseweed, calling Rebob. There she met one of the Jimmys, headed in the opposite direction and running hard.

"Rebob's in the creek," Jimmy said.

Marie ran. Skidding along the edge of the bank, which suddenly seemed as steep as a cliff, she peered into the water. She couldn't see much on the surface, just dirty clots of foam and, oh God, an inch or two of Rebob's dark hair. The hair was floating in the deepest part of Log Pond.

She scrambled down the hill, grabbing fistfuls of weeds and roots to steady her balance, slipping in the slick mud, panting, and screaming his name. At the shore, she didn't hesitate. Shoes on, she waded into the sticky, sucking muck, intent on reaching him. She didn't notice that the water was so cold it burned. She didn't notice how quickly her clothes soaked and turned heavy, ready to pull her down. All she noticed was that the first step into the mud immobilized her as surely as if she'd stepped into glue. Her shoe wouldn't lift. She left it behind.

She stepped off the edge of the earth. She walked right off the drop-off. It was the strangest sensation, to lose footing and suddenly be transformed from a purposeful if waterlogged mother into a flailing, unmoored bit of flotsam. She was weighty for flotsam, in a dress and a sweater and a shoe.

A thought occurred to Marie and it was this: she did not know how to swim. This was not a fact to which she had given any thought a few seconds earlier. She was Rebob's mother. It had been her job to save him. It had never dawned on her, as she had so frantically waded toward his hair, that she might find herself in need of a rescue as well.

Marie sank. She kicked. She flailed. She pumped her arms. She clawed at the water. She surfaced, nowhere near shore, but inches away from Rebob's hair. She sputtered and screamed and sank again.

How long that went on she never would be able to say, even fifty years later. When drowning, people tend to lose track of details. All she would remember was that by the second or third time she came up she was choking and spitting—and that she had her arms around some part of Rebob. She didn't know if she was holding on to an arm or a leg or a torso. But she had him. And he was heavy too.

As she broke the surface, Marie thought she was hallucinating, because she saw a crowd on the bank. She saw Betty standing on the trunk of an old willow tree that leaned way out over the water, upstream from Log Pond. She went under again.

"Marie!" Betty screamed. She was wild-eyed and panting, too, having been summoned to the scene seconds earlier by a scared Jimmy. "Marie!"

Betty leaned over the water, hand outstretched, grabbing air.

"Don't fall!" someone called from the shore. Betty teetered precariously on the slippery log. As Marie and Rebob surfaced again, she made a desperate lunge across the last few infinite inches of space and latched on to a handful of Marie's sweater. It ripped.

They were gone.

"Marie!"

As she searched the surface—looking for air bubbles, for cardigan, for black hair, for any glimpse of hope—Betty heard a splash. Pauline had dived from the tree trunk into the water. Another splash: Billy.

Hesta's children were strong swimmers. They'd learned on Arkansas Curve, where there was a nice stretch of sandy beach and a swimming hole that wasn't too deep. Every spring of their childhoods, they'd hit that wide curve in the creek soon after the ice melted. They'd known better than to challenge Log Pond. Now Pauline broke the surface with an arm hooked around Marie's neck. She treaded water to the shore.

An alarm had gone out. It looked like the whole town was gathering on the creek bank. Red Ison, who had recently bought the Pure Oil station from Charles Crum, came running with emergency equipment as soon as he heard the news. As head of a local volunteer lifesaving crew, he knew how to use the oxygen tank and pump he carried. A worker who had been doing yard work at the Grigsbys' still had his rake. He dropped it and waded into the water to help drag out Marie.

She emerged sputtering and coughing and sobbing. She emerged without Rebob. Her legs were scratched and bleeding from branches that had slashed at her underwater in the strong current. Wrapped in a blanket, she shivered on the shoreline until somebody led her up the hillside toward the Rices' house to dry off. Even after she disappeared from sight, the crowd could hear her wailing for Rebob.

People drowned in the creek. What else was there to say? It had happened before. It would happen again. The swirling currents presented a danger that everybody in town took seriously, everybody except a six-year-old boy who had been captivated by the swift downstream journey of a stick. At this time of year, after a flood, the creek was particularly undesirable, filthy and germ-ridden from runoff, thanks to the town's lack of a sewer system.

"How long has he been under?" Betty screamed at a Jimmy. "Five minutes? More?"

Pauline dived again and swam to the deepest center of Log Pond, where Billy was still diving, surfacing, diving again into the black, unseeable depths.

They'll have to put a boulder in the water to dam up the creek to find the body, someone on shore murmured.

The dragging crew is on its way from Prestonsburg, somebody else said. They'll search with grappling hooks.

An ambulance is up on the road, and Doc Claude is in it, somebody else said.

Pauline, blue-lipped and shivering, hoisted herself onto the tree trunk. Her hair was plastered to her head and her clothes dripped steadily. Betty put an arm around her. They started crying. Billy surfaced. He flipped his hair from his eyes and looked at his sisters. He grabbed a willow branch to keep from being swept downstream. What should he do? What could he do?

"It's been ten minutes, at least," Pauline said.

"One last time," he said.

Billy dived. And this time, deep in the terrible cold blackness of Log Pond, he felt something that was not a branch brush against his leg. He reached for it. He grabbed a handful of something that was not weeds or garbage. It felt like fabric. Billy pulled. Nothing happened. By now he was sure he had a handful of shirt. He pulled again. He kicked deeper. He had his hands on Rebob's suspenders. But the braces were tangled in brush.

Almost out of air, Billy gripped the boy's body with both hands, pulled harder, and with a final kick broke to the surface. Rebob was in his arms.

The crowd cheered, but halfheartedly. More than ten minutes underwater was a death sentence.

As Billy swam to the shore, Doc Claude and Mary appeared on the creek bank, their uniforms blindingly white against the backdrop of dirt and rock. They waded into the water and helped Billy pull out Rebob.

He wasn't breathing. He was blue. He felt icy to touch.

Red Ison kneeled on the soft ground to give Rebob artificial respiration. He pumped Rebob's chest, and a stream of water poured from his lungs. He breathed air back in. He pumped again. Another gallon. More air.

As Red Ison worked, Mary packed hot-water bottles and pillows— sent from the Grigsbys' store—under Rebob's body.

Minutes ticked by. Pump, breathe, pump, breathe. Finally, Red Ison sat back on his heels.

"He's breathing," Ison said.

And he was. He remained unconscious, but his chest moved. Mary lifted one of his eyelids and squirted in some antibiotic drops.

"Oxygen," Doc Claude said.

They put Red Ison's oxygen mask over the boy's face. The crowd watched his chest move up and down, up and down. Rebob was definitely breathing.

Doc Claude said they had to get him to the ambulance right away.

Somebody else said, Too bad we can't get the ambulance to him.

Red Ison picked up the limp boy and started to climb toward the road.

Doc Claude asked Marguerite Johns if G. D. Vines could back the ambulance into her yard.

"Back it through the middle of my house if you have to," Marguerite said.

As they strapped Rebob onto a stretcher, Ora Mae Allen put her hand on Mary's arm. "Is he going to make it?"

"I don't know," Mary said. Her white uniform was stained brown as high as her waist. With each step, she left a wet footprint. She climbed in beside the stretcher. The driver slammed the door.

The crowd watched in the street, curiously silent until the ambulance turned the corner. Nobody knew what to say.

Suddenly Hesta's front door flung open. She stood at the top of the steps, afraid to come down because, she said, she had a weak heart.

Hesta called, "Do you know anything about the boy who drowned?"

Nobody wanted to answer yes. Nobody wanted to say the boy was Hesta's favorite grandson.

"He didn't drown," Ora Mae said. "They took him to the hospital."

Hesta saw Pauline and Billy walking toward the street. Her children didn't look like bystanders. They looked a lot wetter than anybody else in the crowd. Hesta didn't say another word. She sank. She sat on the steps and she stayed there a long time before she felt strong enough to phone.

"Mom, what do you want?" Mary asked when she got the call.

She sounded so harsh that Hesta took it personally.

"Well, don't talk so sweet," Hesta said sarcastically. "I guess it's not like anybody's sick. Why would I be calling?"

"We're working on him," Mary said. She hung up.

Hours later, after Marie had been medicated to calm her, she awoke in a hospital bed. It took a few seconds to remember why. The last time she'd been in the hospital she'd come home with a baby. Where was the baby now?

She started to call for Rebob again. By now she was hoarse, but still loud enough to attract attention from the nurses' station. Mary came in. Her hair looked scraggly, but she wore a clean uniform. She was carrying a letter. She'd read it a hundred times since it arrived a few days ago. She tucked the envelope into her pocket.

"He's going to make it," Mary told Marie. "He's here, on another floor."

Marie didn't believe it. In her mind, Rebob was gone. All she could remember was how he'd slipped away in the water, how hard she had held on, how she'd lost him anyway. She remembered reaching down, down, down through the cold to grab his hair.

"He's here, on another floor." Mary said it again. Rebob was conscious and receiving antibiotics as a precaution against typhoid fever. He was lucky. The only reason he'd survived, Mary said, was because the water was so cold. He might as well have been packed in ice for all those minutes. The temperature had slowed his metabolism; his brain had required less oxygen.

Marie wasn't convinced. "Take me to him." She climbed out of the bed.

Marie refused to leave Rebob's room. She grabbed his arm and didn't let go. She sat by the bed clutching him until night, when they fixed her a cot to sleep in. She vowed not to leave his room again until he did.

The next day, visitors came. Rebob was awake and sitting up. He said hello. He said, fine, after Ora Mae Allen asked how he was. He nodded after she pointed out he'd been lucky. (Years later, he would not remember the visit. He would remember the water taking his breath, the cold—it felt like February in the creek—and then nothing, until days later when he woke to find Betty and Billy at the foot of his bed.)

After Ora Mae said good-bye, she saw the doctor in the hallway.

"Claude, will he be all right?" she asked.

Claude said, "Orrie, he'll be all right, but he won't be perfect."

For once, Claude was wrong. Rebob's resurrection was nothing short of a miracle. Red Ison was a hero for giving Rebob artificial respiration. Billy Mynhier was a hero for pulling the boy from the creek. Pauline was a hero for saving Marie. Marguerite Johns was a hero for sacrificing her turf to the ambulance's treads. At least one Jimmy Wallen was a hero for running for help. The story of the near drowning made the front page of the county newspaper, alongside an article about a freakish windstorm that blew down the rear wall of the Farm & Home Store in Prestonsburg. Elsewhere in the county, shattered plate glass windows plagued the Floyd Motor Company and the Fountain Korner. But in

Martin, according to news reports, "Dr. Gross of the Beaver Valley Hospital advised Wednesday that the child was 'doing fine.' He said oxygen was given upon arrival at the hospital."

Oxygen was a wonder drug. In a week, Rebob was back home and was seen playing kick the can at twilight.

A few Sundays later, when the pageant's rain date arrived, Rebob was spotted roaming Bethlehem with his friends. This time, the weather cooperated with Blanche Dingus. The action unfolded smoothly; after the ushers from the American Legion seated everyone, they slipped backstage to change into the colorful costumes of Roman soldiers in time to appear in the final scenes. Flower girls tossed blossoms and heralds spread news. From the audience, as Marie watched Mary Magdalene converse with her risen Lord in a garden, she decided she believed in miracles.

The town had never seen such a crowd. Mary's girls were cherubs, wandering the hillside in their colored sheets as they waited for cues. It was work for the older kids like Margaret, who were expected to stand at attention on a high platform behind a wall. It was confusing for the littler ones like Jo, who tripped along behind the throngs and the peasants in a pinned-up bed sheet, hoping for more specific stage directions. For years afterward, Jo would believe that her role had been to play a sheet.

Mary sat with Marie, but her attention wandered. Rebob's recovery aside, Mary no longer believed in miracles. Sometimes she was still tempted, though. The letter in her pocket teased her. It had arrived weeks ago. She'd known, from the instant she'd unlocked the post office box to see a thick, square envelope, that the letter was from Elmer. It was the first he'd mailed since leaving town, the first word from him in the two years since their divorce. "Dear Mary," he'd written, "I hardly know how to word this." The familiar handwriting was enough to make her queasy. Seeing the confident, swirled loops he put on his capital letters, especially the curly "M" in "Mary," hit her hard. For an instant, she'd heard him saying her name out loud. She might as well have been seventeen years old again, watching him ride up on a motorcycle to ask, "Want a ride, Mary?"

The pageant unfolded. On the elevated stage, the throngs jeered

Barabbas. As coins flew past her ears, Mary pulled the letter out again. "There aren't words to express how sorry I am for what I did to you," Elmer had written. Apologies didn't come easily to Elmer. She wondered what it had cost him, wondered how many drafts he'd written and crumpled before making his peace with being so publicly wrong. "Well, I just pray that you can forgive me," he'd written.

Could she forgive him? She missed him. She was the marrying kind and Elmer was the one she'd chosen. She was not a successful divorcée. Dating was a chore. Although Savage Cooley had courted her steadily for more than a year, she had been unable lately to work up much enthusiasm for nightclubs or dances or flirting. Savage had sent her a Christmas card with a jaunty, candle-covered tree on the cover. But the halos on the tree did nothing but remind her of the Christmas when Elmer had rigged up brake lights on the branches. Savage was a nice guy. But next to Elmer, Savage seemed colorless. She also declined to date Carl Woods, the blond and bashful civics teacher who had coached the basketball team before being replaced by Haskell "Ducky" Vince, who waddled.

"I wanted to call you before but was afraid you would hang up on me," Elmer had written. Along with the letter, he'd enclosed fifty dollars. "Will send more as soon as I can," he'd written, adding that he currently was operating a garage in Detroit. "If this business doesn't pick up soon, I will give it up and get a job so I can help you every week."

She'd pored over what he'd written and what he'd left unwritten. She knew, even before she got to the end of the letter the first time, that the decision about their future was hers to make. He regretted leaving. He missed his girls. He missed her. "Honey, I don't guess you care too much about reading anything from me so will stop and mail this. I love you Mary."

The pageant ended with Pete Grigsby Jr.'s triumphant ascension into heaven. Blanche Dingus immediately started planning for the next year—for fifty scenes, instead of thirty-two, for a professionally printed script book with advertisements, for expanded roles for Matthew, Mark, Luke, and John. Blanche Dingus looked into the future and saw Magdalene Branham as Mary Magdalene. She saw Urban Peters as a king. She saw Denzil Halbert as a Roman. And why not? The Floyd County

Sesquicentennial celebration, for which every man in the county had been urged to grow a beard in tribute to his pioneer ancestors, had recently featured high-wire acts, a stunt man frozen in ice, and a drawing for a $500 savings bond. And the county had merely been honoring history, not the risen Lord. As applause thundered across the hillside, Mayor Grigsby presented the key to the city to the Mormon church's Elder Leo Smith on behalf of the town's Sunday school teachers.

A few weeks later, Mary phoned Elmer and told him to come home. When Pauline heard, she confronted her sister.

"You're going to marry him again, aren't you?" she asked.

"Yes," Mary said.

"Why?"

"I can't resist him," Mary said.

"Why?"

"I guess it's because he looks so much like my first husband," Mary said.

Mary and Elmer drove to Paintsville to remarry. The Mayo Trail was as narrow and twisted as it had been in 1937, and the future as uncertain. It was a warm, sunny day, the sort that made her feel like she'd live forever. A Baptist minister named C. Hoge Hockensmith performed a simple ceremony. This time Mary didn't lie about her age.

The *bulldozers came to Martin in August 2004. They demol-*ished a pair of rickety rental houses that Dick Osborn, ever the entrepreneur, built a long time ago at the base of his property. The backhoes cleared a roadway up Dick's hillside, snaking by the spot where he used to keep a pigsty and past the tomato and onion farm he nursed through the war. Then the drilling and blasting got under way, to remove a million cubic yards of Mulberry Hill to make a plateau big enough for a new downtown.

It's a big job. These days, truckloads of rock and dirt rumble downhill, loud enough for Dick and Myrt to hear from the Ice Plant Hollow graveyard where they're buried. The trucks turn right. On Main Street flagmen wave them past Mr. Keathley's theater building and the red-brick high school and the turnoff to the wagon road where Red kept his smokehouse. Dust from truck after truck coats the First Guaranty Bank building, the Pure Oil station, and the window glass at Grigsby's Five-and-Dime. The Methodist church, where Annie Stumbo belonged to the Ladies' Aid, has been knocked down already. At the north end of town, just beyond the perimeter of the flood zone, the trucks lumber past Ora Mae Allen's house, and there's her mailbox by the front walk.

Soon my family's Martin will be a memory. So will most of the people who would have mourned it most. I still see them on Main Street, though. Officer Tavis Flannery died in 1975, after a peaceful retirement. There he is now, marching Step-'n'-a-Half toward jail as Walter Kiser bursts through the saloon doors to try to stop him. And there's Kermit Howard, racing an ambulance in a snowstorm as my grandmother clutches the door handle in terror. The smell of Hesta's chili wafts from the Hob Nob as Doc Walk, in chaps and boots, strides toward Zott Dingus's store to count the coins his slot machine collected this week.

I used to think it was a blessing that some—like Lawrence Keathley, dead for thirty-five years before the wrecking crew arrived at the theater where he ran cowboy movies on Saturdays—never knew the town's fate. But that was wrong. They know. The ones in the C&O graveyard on the hill above the depot have the best view. They see Doc Claude Allen in a flood, loading the sick into a rowboat through a hospital window. They see him signing papers to sell the place before he died in the 1980s, they see it being razed for a parking lot, and nothing left but one patient log. At the local Mormons' history center, the water-ruined ledger lists births, in ink, on paper that yellowed long ago: "August 27, 1952, Mrs. Maudie Hicks, Garrett, Ky., one male . . . August 29, Mrs. Wanda Howell, Orkney, Ky., one male . . ." The handwriting belongs to my grandmother, who is in the delivery room to witness the arrival of Dollie Mae Mollett's stillborn male (prolapsed cord), Ruby Akers's baby boy, Lula Tuttle's little girl, and nearly a thousand more.

Up here in the high wild grass, the oldest tombstones belong to fine upstanding citizens like Susan Frazier Hunter (1849–1904), Columbus Crisp (1872–1928), and Logan Dingus (1865–1939), members of the same families who still live in town. Newer stones belong to my family. Hesta (1895–1967) has a fine vantage from which to watch so many houses she once inhabited crumble into heaps of water-ruined timber. She lies near Fred and two of her sons, Billy (he died in a car wreck in 1958) and Red (1917–1961). One autumn day Red, who had moved to Bucks Branch after the war, collapsed in his yard. At a veterans' hospital two days later he died mysteriously—the death certificate blamed "liver insufficiency"—but my family suspected tainted well water. At the funeral, Hesta's sister Garnet threw herself across the coffin and had to be pried off.

From the sunny hillside, the dead see the raw earth of the government's Phase One Redevelopment site and the green mountains that ring the valley and beyond, above the trees, hints of the towns that lie along both Fur Beaver and Nigh. At night, they see the moon over Martin as the fog rises from the creek to erase, one by one, the houses below. By day, dump trucks head out of town, north toward Arkansas Curve, to turn into steep-sided Mayo Hollow, where dirt from Mulberry Hill is stockpiled against the day it will come back to town as fill. In the distance, a whistle signals the arrival of the 11:20 passenger train from Allen. Fred, natty in his uniform, glances at his Hamilton to confirm the train is on schedule. The dead see lights in the school gymnasium and they hear dance music float through open windows and they watch my grandparents fall in love.

My grandparents fell in and out of love all their lives. They moved north to Chicago, where my grandfather worked as an electrician and my grandmother as a private-duty nurse. Decades later, they divorced a second time. Eventually, Elmer moved to Florida, where he remarried yet again, and Mary moved to my aunt Margaret's house. After my grandmother died, Margaret found a greeting card in an envelope under her pillow. "Get well," it said. "Love, Elmer." Get well, he writes. Love, Elmer.

September 2005

Many of the long-ago details described—from how the flood-water looked as it oozed up through manholes to the sad fact that Walter Kiser didn't have a chance to shave before he died—would have been lost to history with the rest of Martin, if it were not for the excellent memories and tireless patience of my three great-uncles: Jack Mynhier, Walter Mynhier, and Joe Wolverton. They endured many hours of piti-less questioning and parted with the particulars of their childhoods in service to this story.

Other family members and nearly a hundred past and current resi-dents of Martin kindly agreed to interviews. My mother flew across the country with me to confront her past. Archival material, court docu-ments, and published sources provided historical context, and I was es-pecially fortunate to have access to back issues of *The Floyd County Times* and the *Quinton Times*. The books I relied on most for perspec-tive were Henry P. Scalf's *Kentucky's Last Frontier*, Lowell Thomas's *Hungry Waters*, James Altieri's *The Spearheaders*, Nora Miller's *The Girl in the Rural Family*, Ronald D. Eller's *Miners, Millhands, and Moun-taineers*, and Harry M. Caudill's *Night Comes to the Cumberlands*. Li-brarians who pointed me in the right direction were Mindy Robertson at Pikeville College, Susan Arnold at the West Virginia University Health Sciences Library, Maureen Will at the Kentucky Department for Libraries and Archives, and Katherine Johnson, an archivist at the Kornhauser Health Science Library at the University of Louisville. Susan Mollohan and Mildred Mairs at the Children's Home Society in West Virginia helped unravel a mystery that had haunted my family for decades. Renee Thornsberry was a tireless researcher and tour guide who located many sources and showed me old roads people don't use much anymore.

For suggestions and support, I want to thank Bruce Headlam, Amy Wilentz, Lisa Benenson, Ramona Egbert, Mary Ann Prater, Paul Baldridge, Ann Osborne, Tina Jennings, Ilana Friedman, Cathryn Ramin, Elizabeth Allen, Douglas Scutchfield, Daryl Luxmore, Sue Schiesser, and Robin Reisig. I am grateful to my literary agent, David McCormick, and to my editors, Lee Boudreaux and Bruce Tracy, for helping me turn an idea into a book. And how lucky I am to have married a man who is one of the most talented editors I've met. I think he can recite this book by heart.

ABOUT THE AUTHOR

MICHELLE SLATALLA, a columnist for
The New York Times's Thursday Styles section,
writes weekly about how the Internet has
changed shoppers' habits and lives. She lives in
Northern California with her husband
and three daughters.

ABOUT THE TYPE

This book was set in Caslon, a typeface first
designed in 1722 by William Caslon.
Its widespread use by most English printers in
the early eighteenth century soon supplanted
the Dutch typefaces that had formerly
prevailed. The roman is considered a
"workhorse" typeface due to its pleasant,
open appearance, while the italic is
exceedingly decorative.